PREFACE

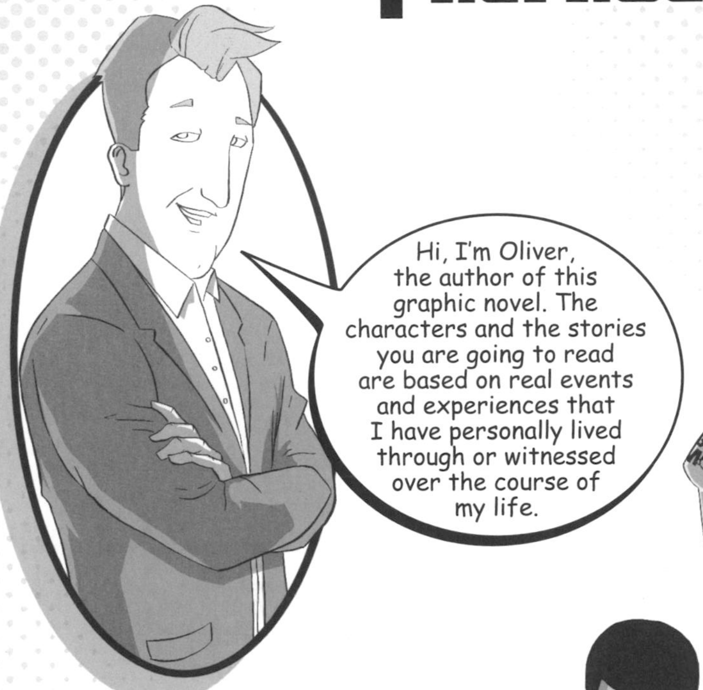
Hi, I'm Oliver, the author of this graphic novel. The characters and the stories you are going to read are based on real events and experiences that I have personally lived through or witnessed over the course of my life.

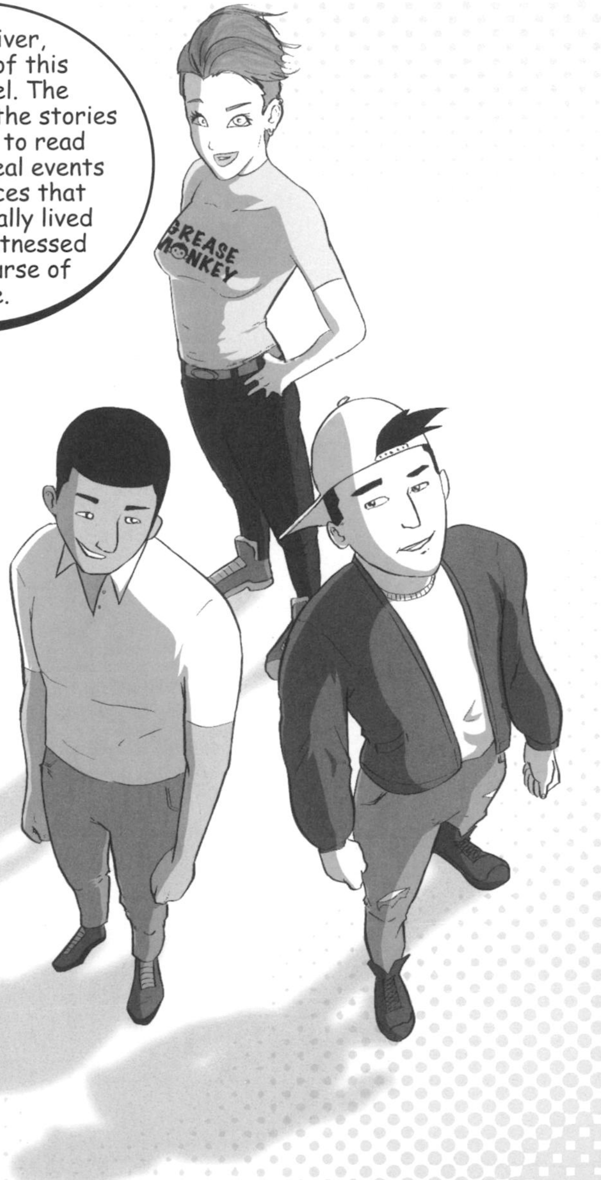
GREASE MONKEY

As a professional financial advisor who started his career nearly 30 years ago and has frequently been on CNBC, Bloomberg Television and Radio, and interviewed countless times by leading business publications like The Wall Street Journal, Dow Jones and Forbes amongst others, I am often asked "what should I invest in?" This, of course, is the wrong question, as the answer will inevitably change and will greatly depend on the person asking.

The more critical question for just about everyone is "how much should I invest, how long should I invest for, and what else should I be doing?"

I hope that this graphic novel helps answer these and other important questions in a way that will help you make smarter financial decisions.

Maybe John or Adam's story will resonate with you, or perhaps you will find Mary's experience more intriguing.

PREFACE

Most importantly, I sincerely hope that you walk away from this book having a better understanding of the likely consequences of the decisions you will have to make over the course of your life.

There are no absolute answers when it comes to finances, as everyone's unique circumstances will not only determine their needs, but also the options available to them. And as you will learn later in the book, even well into my career, when I was in my mid-thirties, I made - what ultimately turned out to be - regrettable choices. And today, as a 51 year old, having gone through a divorce and going through the challenges of a new job, I find myself looking back wishing I knew some of the things I know now when I was younger.

Before we get started with the stories I want to share with you, let's hear what some other professionals have to say about this graphic novel.

ADDITIONAL PRAISE

"As someone with her first job, I found Money Can Grow on Trees to be very instructive to myself on how I spend and save my money. It helped me in understanding the in's and out's of money management and how I can use the salary I'm making now to better myself in the future. I have learned more from Money Can Grow on Trees than I ever had from any teacher or adult in my life, money is taught in a relatable, understanding way I've never seen before."

- Josephine Barsky
15 year old student

"Author Pursche develops identifiable and credible characters to deliver timeless financial advice that Barbosa illustrates in graphic novel style. Scenes leap from the pages in easily-digestible lessons in personal finance. From credit card dos and don'ts — to tackling the dreaded "b-word" ("budget") — to avoiding debt traps like buy-now-pay-later — "Money Can Grow on Trees" offers a realistic, approachable framework to the building blocks of personal finance that compound and deliver dividends over a lifetime."

- Jared Blikre
Global Markets Reporter
Yahoo Finance

"No one adequately teaches high school students how money works, and Oliver Pursche has done a wonderful job doing just that, in a relaxed and informal graphic novel that will appeal to any high school student who is interested in finding out just how money can indeed grow on trees for them! It is a guide of important information, providing young adults with a roadmap to their economic freedom. And kids, when you're done with it, leave it out so your parents can read it, too!"

- J. Gary Caputi
(Oliver's) Retired AP Economics Teacher

"Oliver Pursche has always been one of the most fun-loving and friendly figures in finance. He also has the rare ability to communicate the abstruse dynamics of financial markets in a lucid and straightforward fashion. So the format of the graphic novel, with Mr. Pursche himself as a narrator, is perfect for this author. Imagine the approach of the great comic writer Scott McCloud applied to finance, and you will have a taste of this fun and informative book. Teaching young adults about managing finances is one of society's most urgent responsibilities, and this is a rare book that will actually achieve that goal, with sections on budgeting, saving, investing, loan management and more."

- Rob Curran
Contributor, Dow Jones Newswires
The Wall Street Journal, Dallas Morning News

ADDITIONAL PRAISE

"I wish there had been a book like this when I was a teen! An easy-to-digest and relatable guide for young AND old that hits all the important points for lifelong financial health"

- Amanda Drury
Senior Anchor
CNBC

"Oliver Pursche has created an invaluable tool for young people to get an early start on the path to financial freedom. As navigating the financial world becomes more and more perilous, this resource could not come at a more important time Today, instruction of the ideologies behind financial literacy is crucial in high school and college age students, and this book could easily serve as a mentor text that is both informative and accessible to all types of learners."

- Michael Gianfrancisco
ELA Teacher, North Providence High School
Adjunct Professor, Rhode Island College
Founder of LitX

"An accessible introduction to key financial concepts that will serve any student well. Pursche and Barbosa are truly 'paying it forward'."

- Philipp Hecker
CEO Bento Engine Inc.; Columbia University Advisor,
former Head of Wealth Planning & Advice JP Morgan Chase

"As a teacher and administrator in secondary and higher education for twenty five years, I am constantly striving for new and exciting ways to ignite that spark in students. The antiseptic, dry approach that we've used for ages does not inspire willing learners. This book is a breath of fresh air, packaging finance in an exciting, new way. Pursche and Barbosa deliver relevant content as a fun and easy to read graphic novel."

- Dr. Timothy Lance, Ph.D.,
Assistant Head of School for Academics
The Storm King School

Additional Praise

"The emphasis on graphics really meets the student audience where they are, and the real-life examples are explained in straightforward language that resonates with high school students. Teaching financial literacy early on is critical to future success and Oliver Pursche's novel is a valuable tool to do just that. Case in point, it passes muster with my 17-year old."

**- Greg McBride, CFA
Chief Financial Analyst
Bankrate.com**

"Oliver Pursche provides a delightful guide in an easily understood presentation full of important information for those of us who want to understand the "likely consequences of the decisions you will have to make over the course of your life." Reading the information provided in this book provides guidance that many people miss in their journey to financial freedom. Understanding personal finance is an important step. This book provides clear and compressive examples to assist everyone with improving their understanding of personal finance and how positive personal decisions regarding financial decisions provide productive and worthwhile outcomes. I highly recommend that everyone read this book to further their personal journey to financial freedom."

**- William C. Nantz JD, CPA, MBA
Contributing Author, Business & Accounting Textbooks
Forensic Accounting Professor at Houston Community College**

"If someone would have given me this book while I was in High School, it would have opened my eyes to many of the pitfalls that I plummeted for the past 30 years. The basic mechanics of credit, investing and saving were never broken down into a language I could easily understand. A book like this would have given me at least a foundation to build upon, which would have been much more preferable to the "long-tail-cat-in-a-dark-room-filled-with-mousetraps" financial journey I have endured throughout my adult life."

**- Jason Safran
Founder & CEO
Lost Tribe Creative**

MONEY CAN GROW ON TREES

WHEN YOU TAKE CARE OF IT.

Oliver Pursche

Writer

Brian Barbosa

Illustrator

Published by Imagine & Wonder
Irvington, New York 10533 USA
www.imagineandwonder.com

Text: © 2022 Oliver Pursche
Comics and Illustrations: © Brian Barbosa

Cataloging-in-Publication information is available from the Library of Congress.

Library of Congress Control Number: 2022931607
ISBN: 978-1637610503

First Edition
Printed by Marquis Book Printing
Montreal QC Canada

10 9 8 7 6 5 4 3 2 1

VI

DEDICATION

I dedicate this graphic novel to my mom and dad,
who have steadfastly supported me throughout my life.
Thank you both.

Oliver

EDITOR'S NOTES

When this project first began we had really great conversations about how this concept could be better taught. The 'cup of coffee' analogy has been beaten so long it no longer resonates and can we really expect anyone to give up their daily caffeine boost just because it cuts into their budget plan? The answer was a resounding 'Noooo'! All the financial advice books in the past, while created with the best of intentions, never really seemed to be speaking to an audience of new adults in a way that actually connected.

With this graphic novel Oliver found new and better ways to show you the real life situations for people who have lived through them.

During the early days of development we also kept brainstorming the pitch line for the book. One that kept coming up most often is this: "There are two things parents avoid discussing with their kids, sex and money. This book is about money." While at first blush it's a funny observation but it is essentially quite true. Most often this fear of money is created by a simple misunderstanding of how money can actually work for you. And as it is with many other misunderstood concepts, the legacy (and fear) of that misunderstanding is handed down to each generation.

Another very influential element in our conversations was on how much cultural influences and perceptions impact how we view money. The concept of credit cards and debt to Americans can be entirely different from European or Asian cultures. In American culture we are encouraged by all kinds of messaging to spend money we don't have.

It is our goal to empower the reader of this book and establish a comfort and confidence of how money can be better and successfully managed. The concept of money is not just for an 'elite few' it is something that can and does fundamentally change how well we can live our lives. The use of the tree as a metaphor is incredibly appropriate. Trees begin from a small seed and with proper care and feeding, they grow healthy leaves and provide much needed shade and shelter when they mature.

John Shableski
Publisher/Editor-in-Chief
Imagine and Wonder

TABLE OF CONTENTS

Introduction

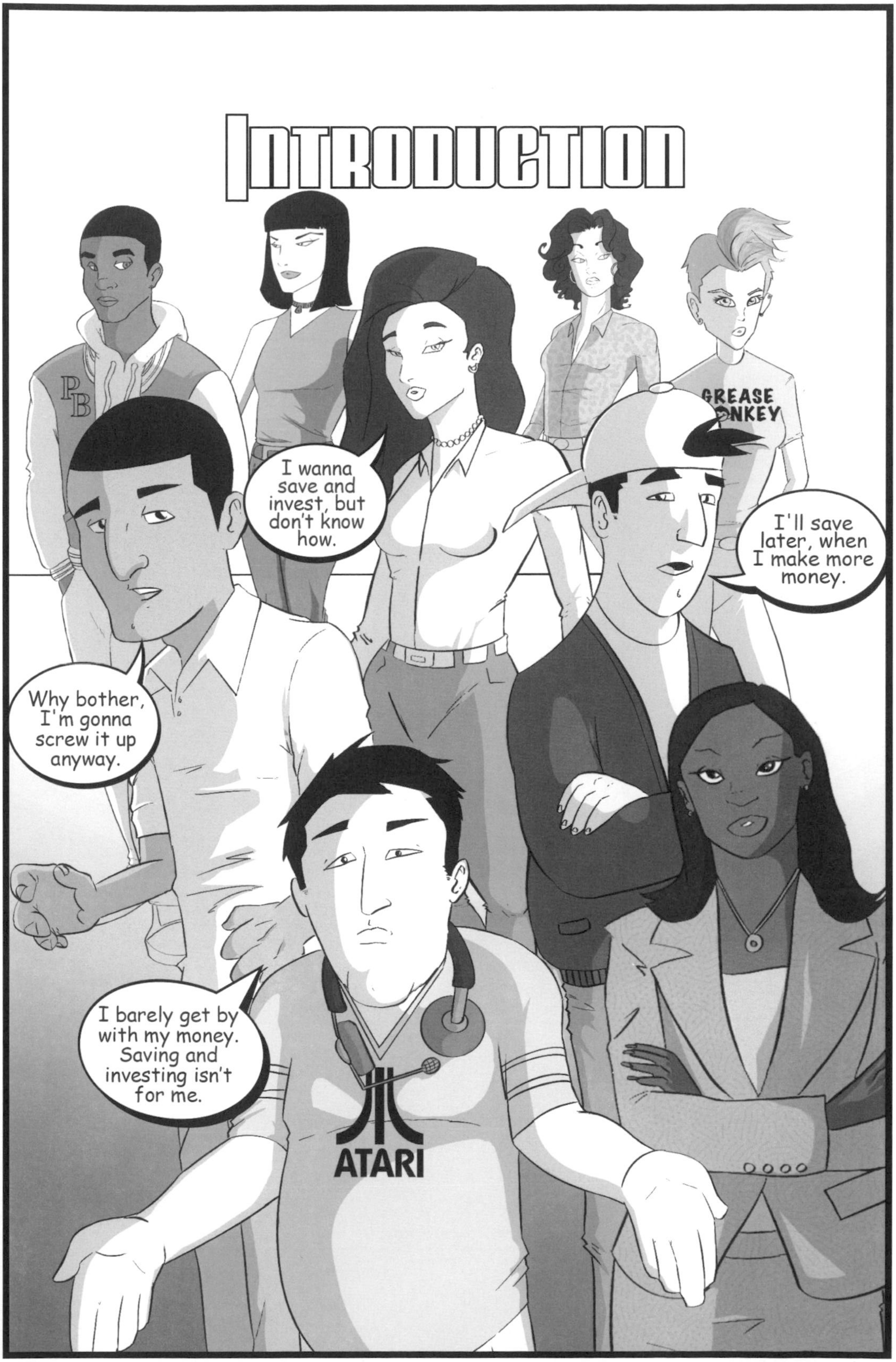

I wanna save and invest, but don't know how.
I'll save later, when I make more money.
Why bother, I'm gonna screw it up anyway.
I barely get by with my money. Saving and investing isn't for me.
ATARI

INTRODUCTION

Each chapter is going to start with Key Definitions that include common sense explanations and applications of that term. For instance, in this "Introduction", Key Definitions are

Key Definitions:
{Credit Card}
A credit card gives you the ability to buy things new and pay for that item later - typically with interest being charged on the purchase. A credit card is also an important tool to help you build credit and your credit score (which we will learn more about in chapters 2 and 8).

{Targeted Psychological Marketing}
The use of carefully crafted messaging and images to subconsciously influence someones decision making process.

{Compounding Interest}
Paying interest on interest, thereby greatly increasing the cost of whatever you bought on credit. Credit card companies and other lenders charge you interest on the entire balance you owe, including previously accumulated interest charges - not just the principal. Meaning that the amount you pay-off is much less than you think.

At the end of each chapter you will find a lesson summary as well as a QR code that you can scan to provide you with additional information.

LOOk for Resources

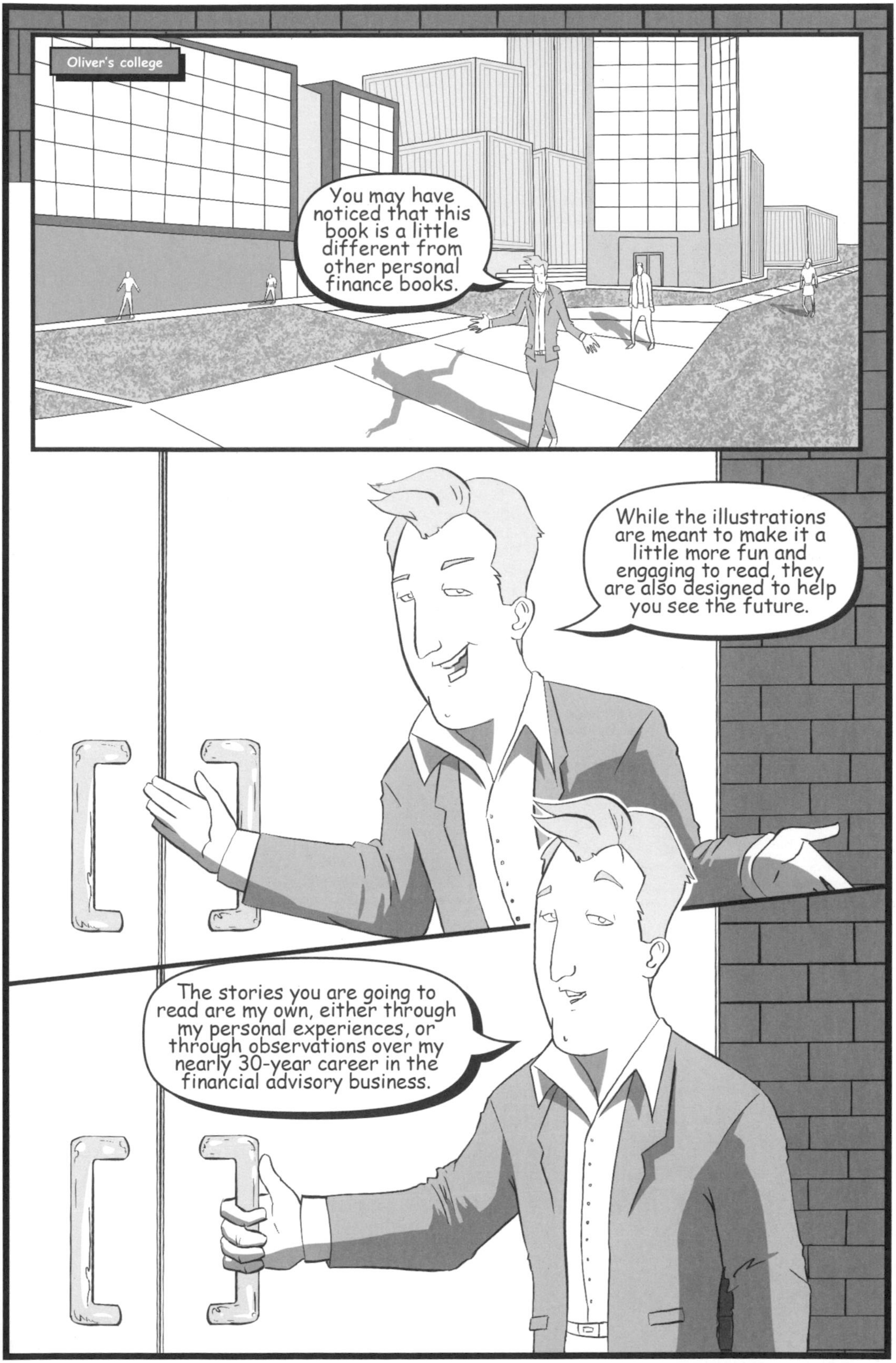
Oliver's college
You may have noticed that this book is a little different from other personal finance books.
While the illustrations are meant to make it a little more fun and engaging to read, they are also designed to help you see the future.
The stories you are going to read are my own, either through my personal experiences, or through observations over my nearly 30-year career in the financial advisory business.

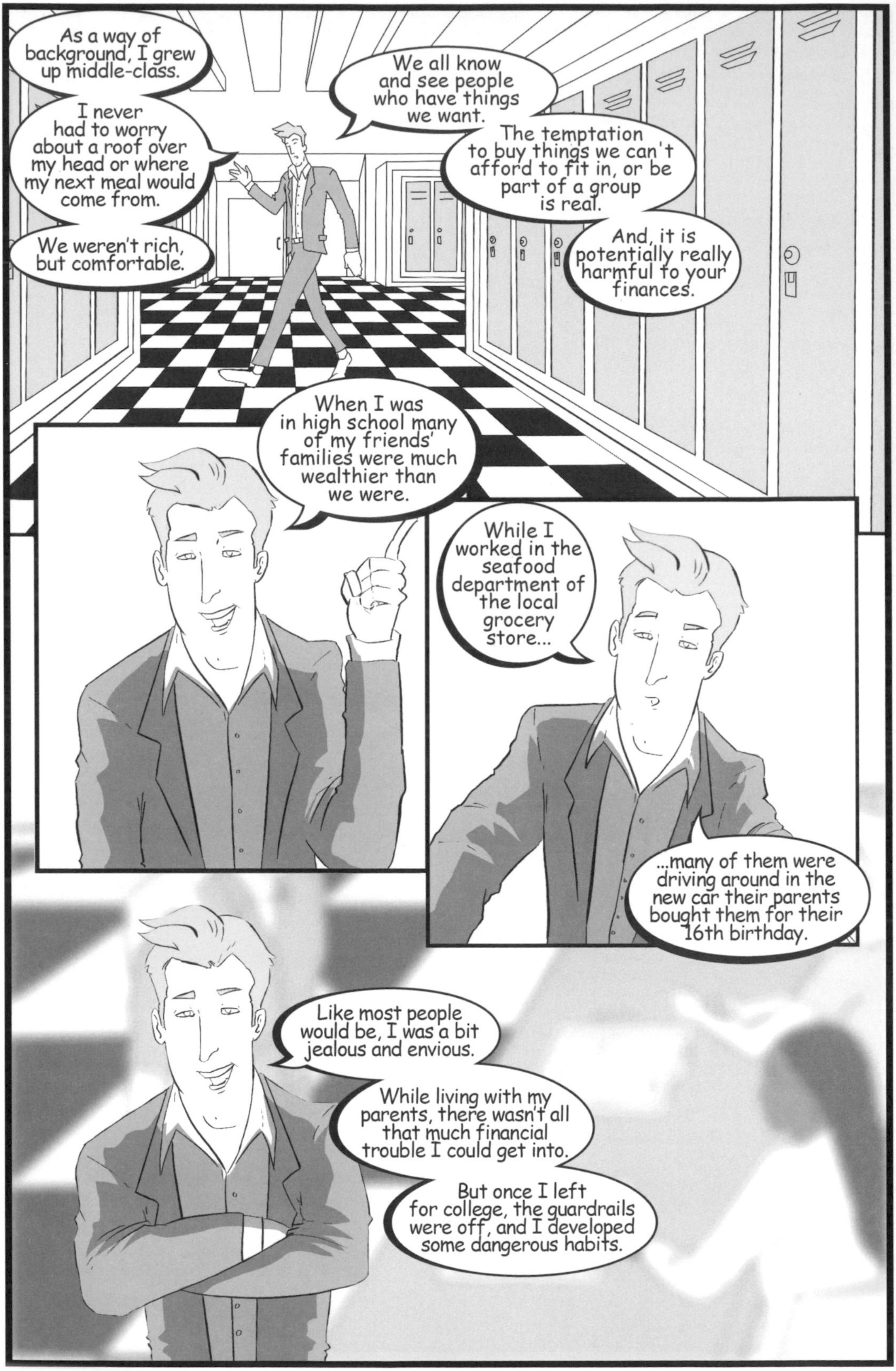
As a way of background, I grew up middle-class.
I never had to worry about a roof over my head or where my next meal would come from.
We weren't rich, but comfortable.
We all know and see people who have things we want.
The temptation to buy things we can't afford to fit in, or be part of a group is real.
And, it is potentially really harmful to your finances.
When I was in high school many of my friends' families were much wealthier than we were.
While I worked in the seafood department of the local grocery store...
...many of them were driving around in the new car their parents bought them for their 16th birthday.
Like most people would be, I was a bit jealous and envious.
While living with my parents, there wasn't all that much financial trouble I could get into.
But once I left for college, the guardrails were off, and I developed some dangerous habits.

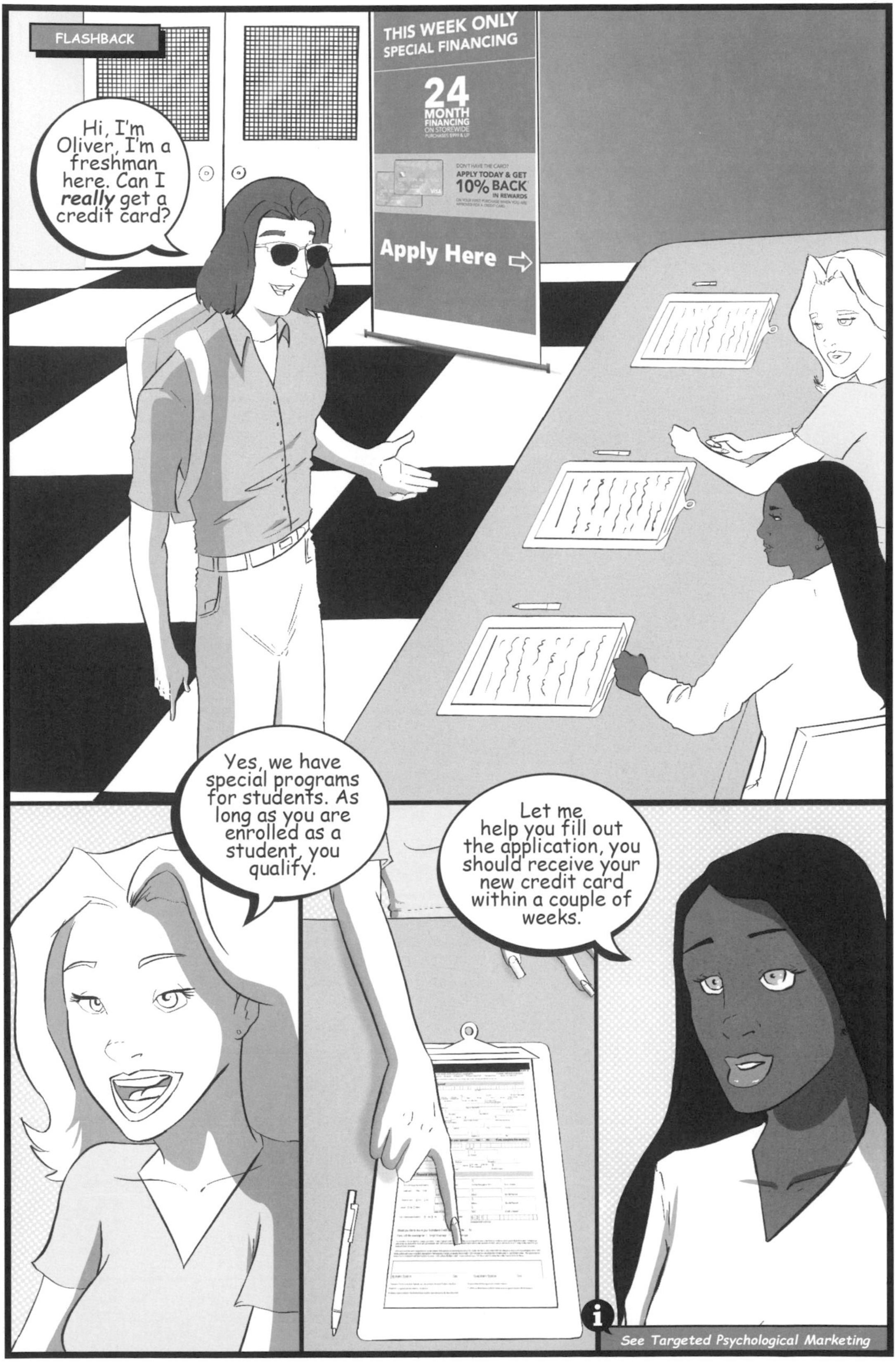
FLASHBACK
Hi, I'm Oliver, I'm a freshman here. Can I ***really*** get a credit card?
THIS WEEK ONLY SPECIAL FINANCING
24 MONTH FINANCING ON STOREWIDE
DON'T HAVE THE CARD? APPLY TODAY & GET 10% BACK IN REWARDS
Apply Here
Yes, we have special programs for students. As long as you are enrolled as a student, you qualify.
Let me help you fill out the application, you should receive your new credit card within a couple of weeks.
See Targeted Psychological Marketing

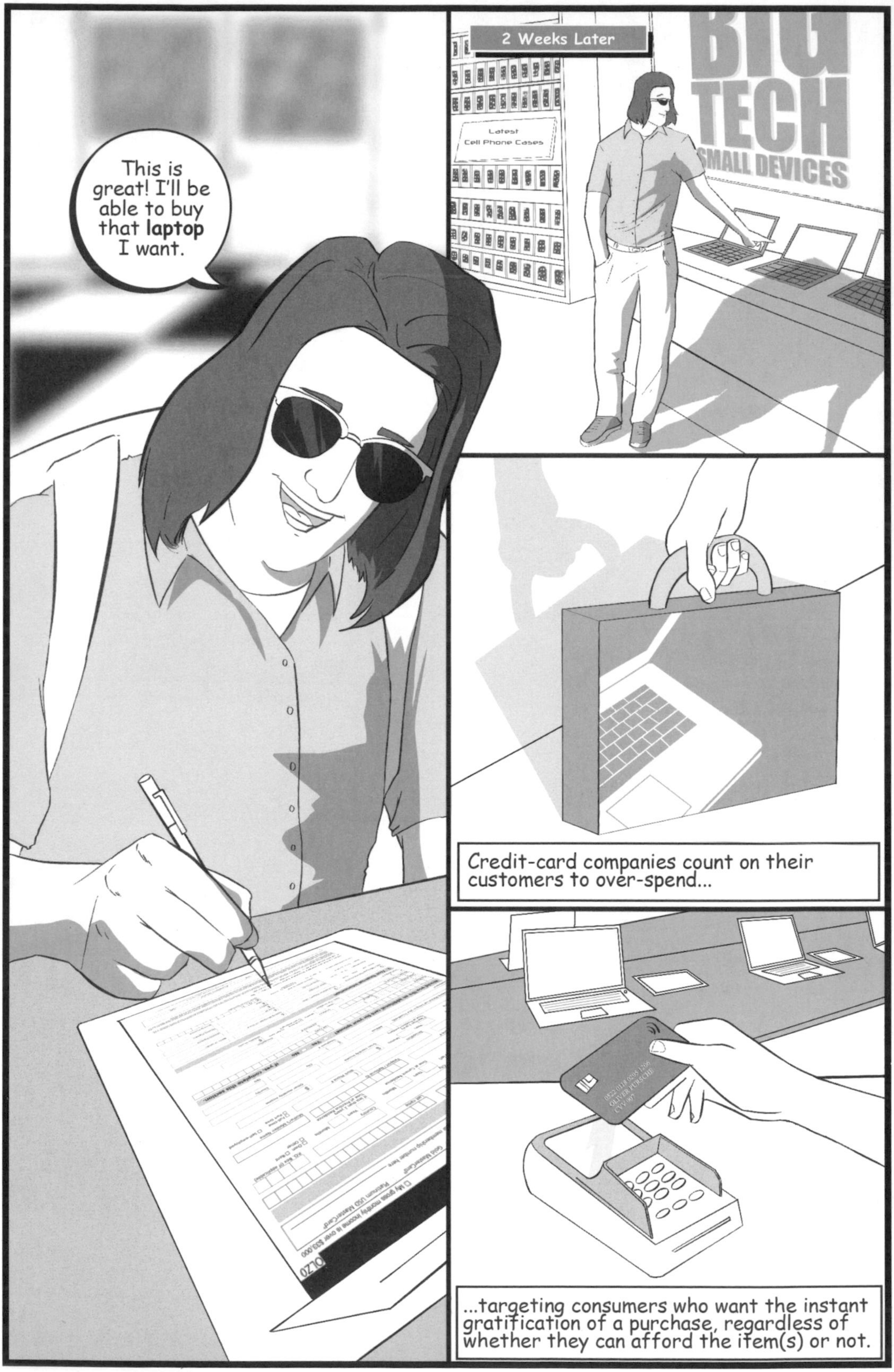
This is great! I'll be able to buy that **laptop** I want.
2 Weeks Later
Latest Cell Phone Cases
BIG TECH SMALL DEVICES
Credit-card companies count on their customers to over-spend...
...targeting consumers who want the instant gratification of a purchase, regardless of whether they can afford the item(s) or not.

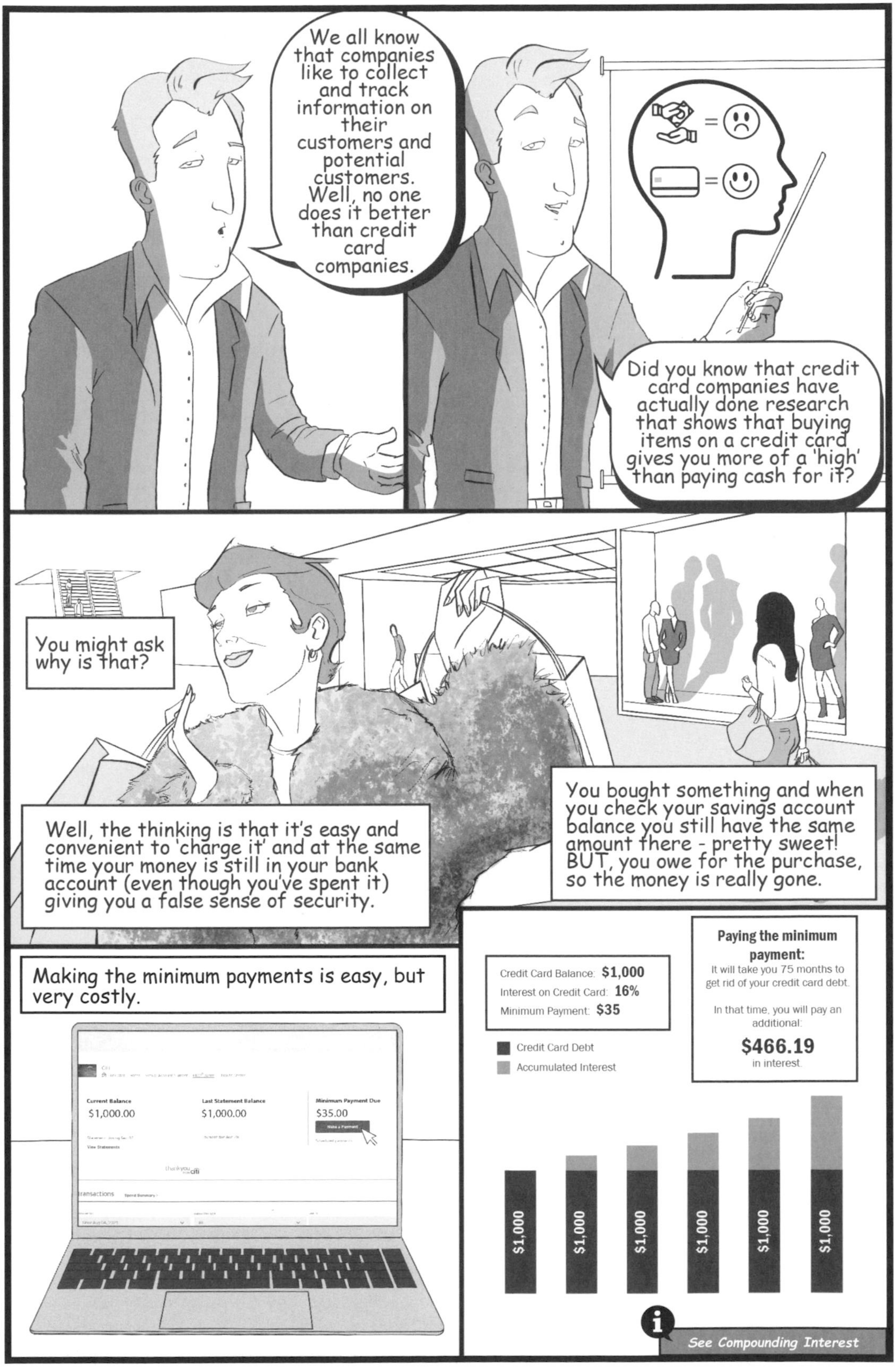

We all know that companies like to collect and track information on their customers and potential customers. Well, no one does it better than credit card companies.
Did you know that credit card companies have actually done research that shows that buying items on a credit card gives you more of a 'high' than paying cash for it?
You might ask why is that?
Well, the thinking is that it's easy and convenient to 'charge it' and at the same time your money is still in your bank account (even though you've spent it) giving you a false sense of security.
You bought something and when you check your savings account balance you still have the same amount there - pretty sweet! BUT, you owe for the purchase, so the money is really gone.
Making the minimum payments is easy, but very costly.
Current Balance
$1,000.00
Last Statement Balance
$1,000.00
Minimum Payment Due
$35.00
Credit Card Balance: $1,000
Interest on Credit Card: 16%
Minimum Payment: $35
Paying the minimum payment:
It will take you 75 months to get rid of your credit card debt.
In that time, you will pay an additional:
$466.19
in interest.
Credit Card Debt
Accumulated Interest
$1,000
$1,000
$1,000
$1,000
$1,000
$1,000
See Compounding Interest

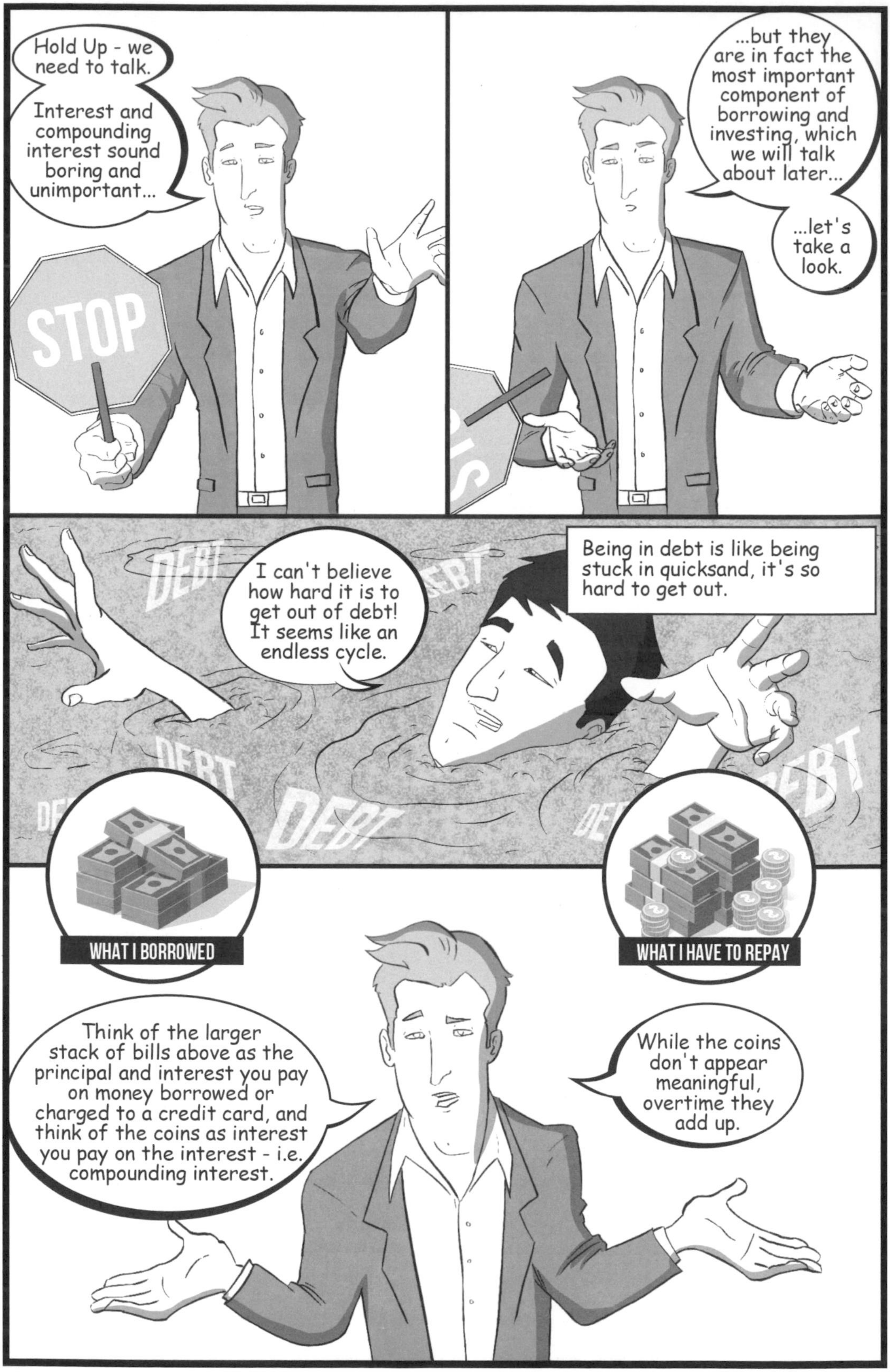
Hold Up - we need to talk.
Interest and compounding interest sound boring and unimportant...
STOP
...but they are in fact the most important component of borrowing and investing, which we will talk about later...
...let's take a look.
Being in debt is like being stuck in quicksand, it's so hard to get out.
I can't believe how hard it is to get out of debt! It seems like an endless cycle.
DEBT
WHAT I BORROWED
WHAT I HAVE TO REPAY
Think of the larger stack of bills above as the principal and interest you pay on money borrowed or charged to a credit card, and think of the coins as interest you pay on the interest - i.e. compounding interest.
While the coins don't appear meaningful, overtime they add up.

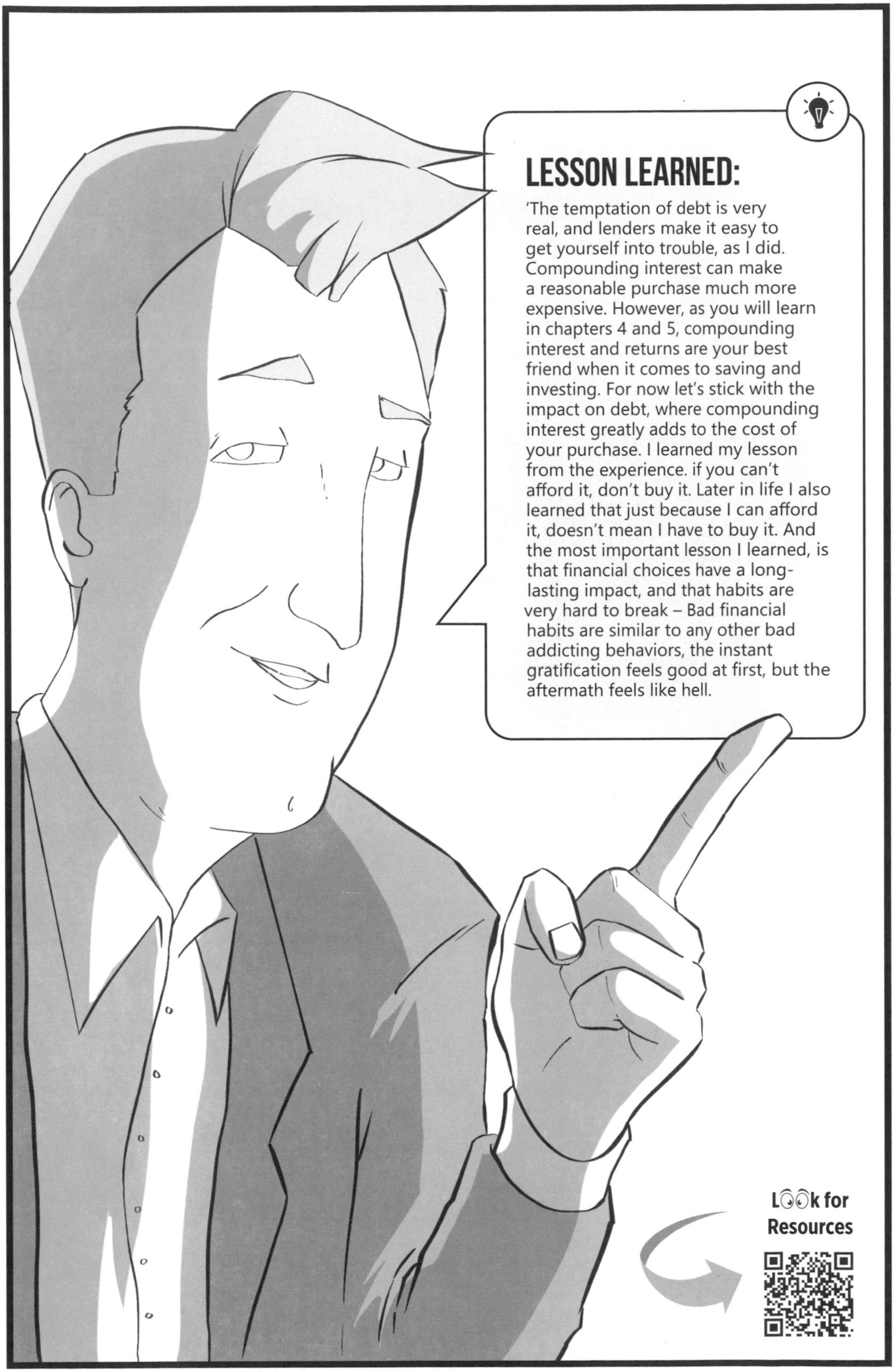
LESSON LEARNED:
'The temptation of debt is very real, and lenders make it easy to get yourself into trouble, as I did. Compounding interest can make a reasonable purchase much more expensive. However, as you will learn in chapters 4 and 5, compounding interest and returns are your best friend when it comes to saving and investing. For now let's stick with the impact on debt, where compounding interest greatly adds to the cost of your purchase. I learned my lesson from the experience. if you can't afford it, don't buy it. Later in life I also learned that just because I can afford it, doesn't mean I have to buy it. And the most important lesson I learned, is that financial choices have a long-lasting impact, and that habits are very hard to break – Bad financial habits are similar to any other bad addicting behaviors, the instant gratification feels good at first, but the aftermath feels like hell.
LOOk for Resources

Chapter 1
Financial Literacy

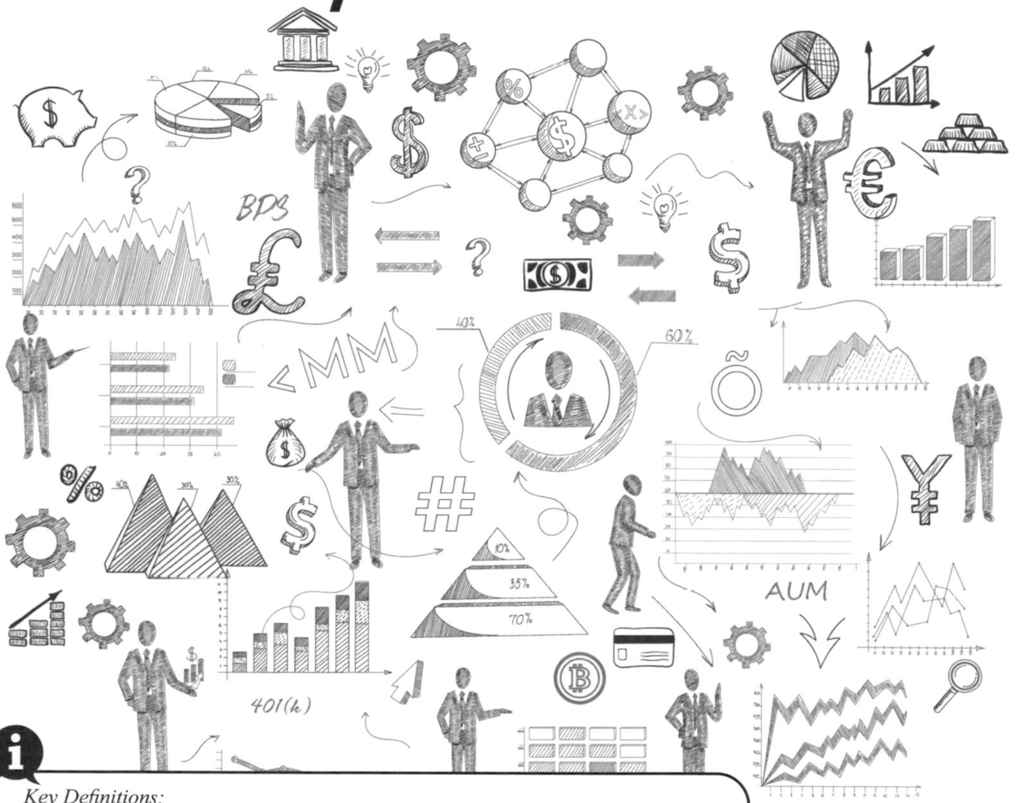
BPS
<MM
40%
60%
10%
35%
70%
AUM
401(k)

Key Definitions:

{Financial Literacy}
Being generally knowledgeable and understanding various consequences of financial decisions you make, in the short and long term.

{Budgeting}
Think of this as simply tracking your spending in order to prioritize where and what you spend your money on. For a teenager, this may mean saving money to buy a car, for a college student it may mean beginning to invest, and for young adults it likely means paying the rent or mortgage first, then perhaps the car payment, then food, etc.. as well as putting some money away in the form of saving and investing.

Also see Chapter 10 - Don't Spoil a Good Thing

{The Power of Time}
Little steps and habits add up over time. The most dangerous phrase in finance is "I'll start saving and investing when I make more money". The simple truth is that in almost all cases, that never happens - you have to start early and be disciplined.

Also see Chapter 5 - The Value of Time

{Mortgage Refinancing}
You have made significant progress in paying off the mortgage that helped you purchase your home. You now have equity in the house and decide to get a new, larger mortgage to help with some bills or extra cash in the bank. Not a bad idea, but potentially a dangerous one as it adds more debt to your balance sheet. More on ***Balance Sheets*** in Chapter 3.

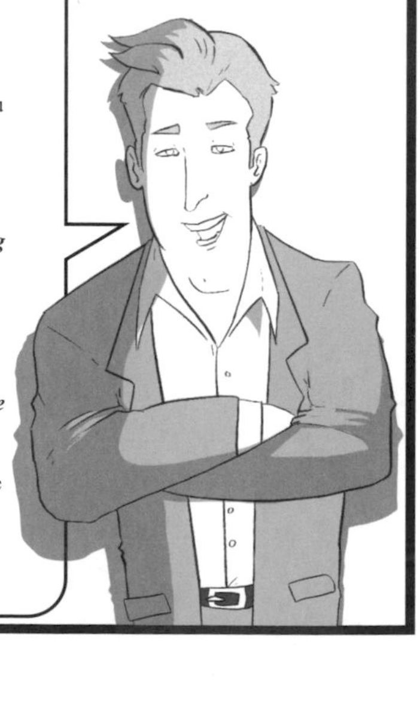

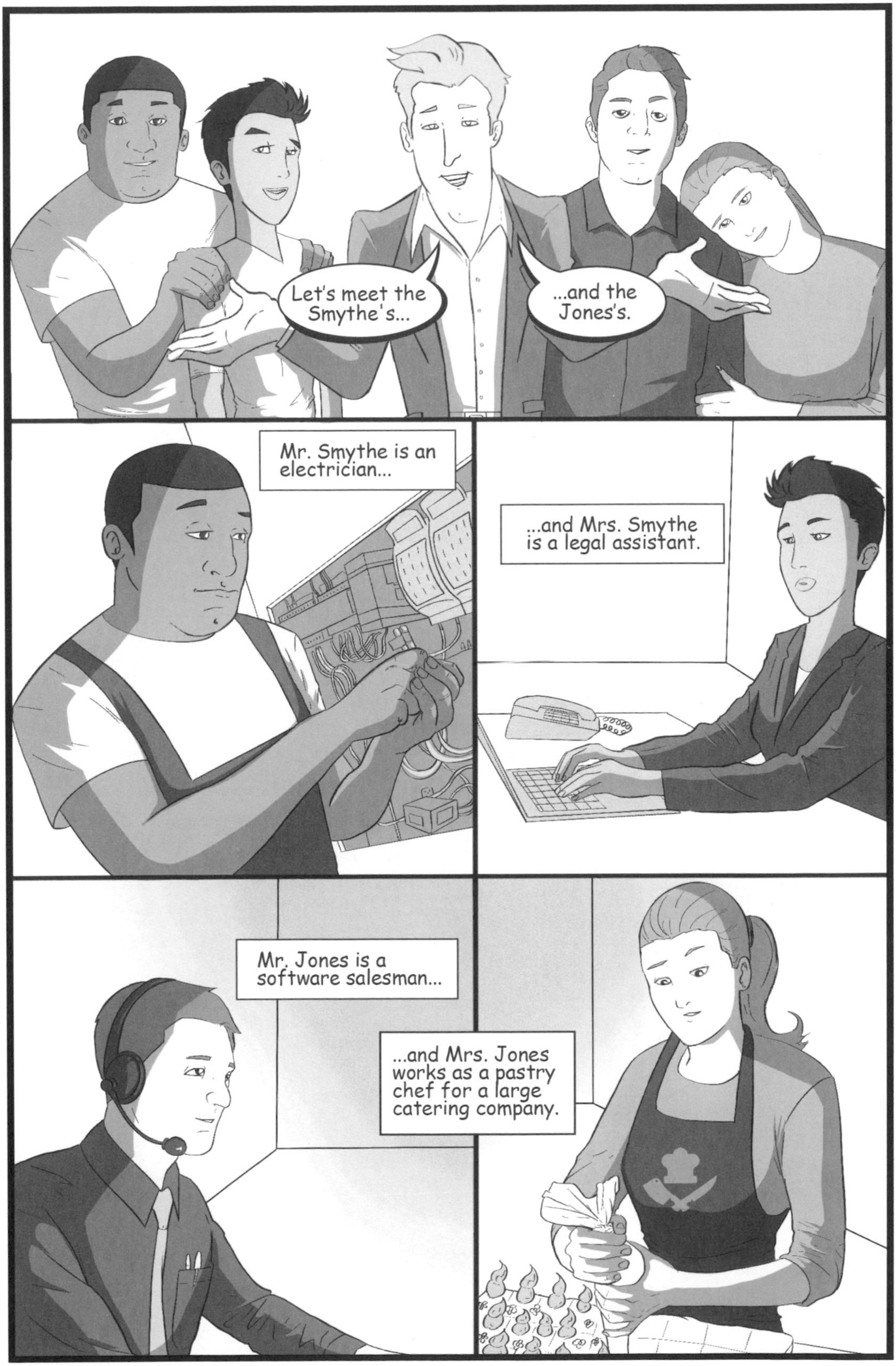
Let's meet the Smythe's...
...and the Jones's.
Mr. Smythe is an electrician...
...and Mrs. Smythe is a legal assistant.
Mr. Jones is a software salesman...
...and Mrs. Jones works as a pastry chef for a large catering company.

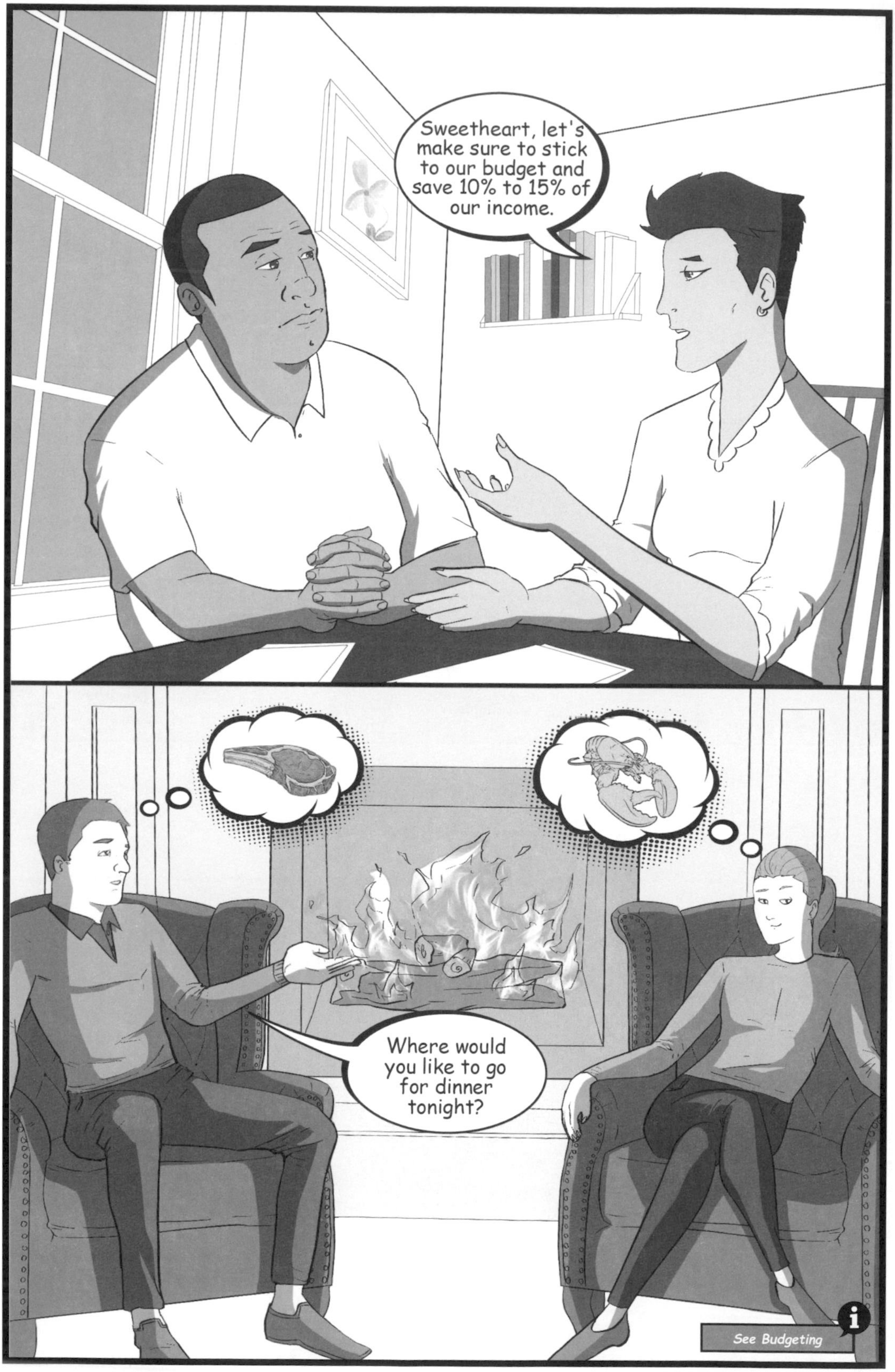
Sweetheart, let's make sure to stick to our budget and save 10% to 15% of our income.
Where would you like to go for dinner tonight?
i
See Budgeting

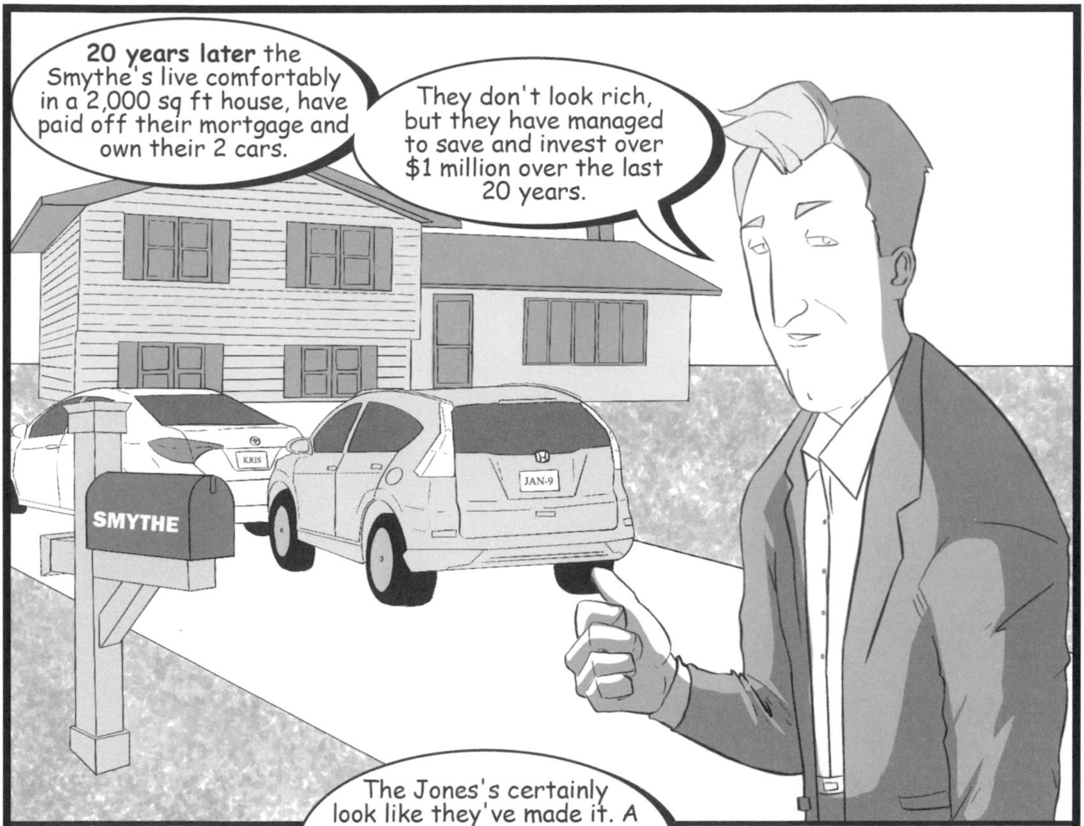
20 years later the Smythe's live comfortably in a 2,000 sq ft house, have paid off their mortgage and own their 2 cars.
They don't look rich, but they have managed to save and invest over $1 million over the last 20 years.
KRIS
JAN-9
SMYTHE

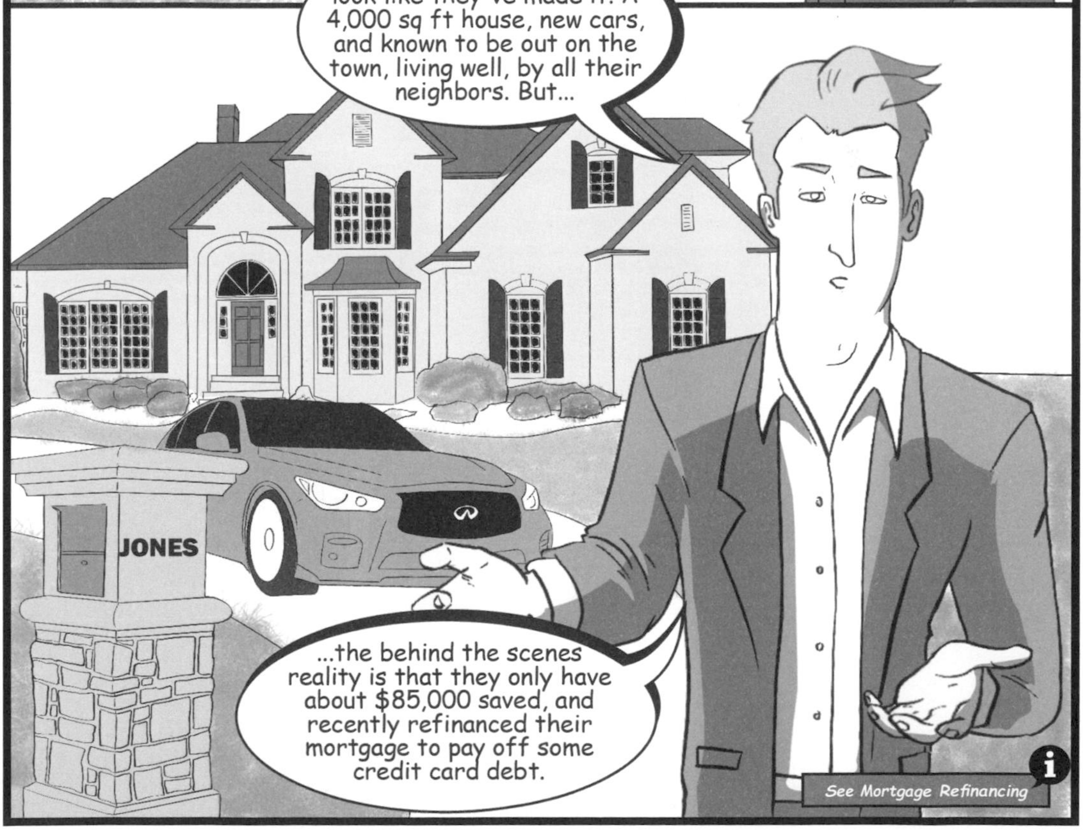
The Jones's certainly look like they've made it. A 4,000 sq ft house, new cars, and known to be out on the town, living well, by all their neighbors. But...
JONES
...the behind the scenes reality is that they only have about $85,000 saved, and recently refinanced their mortgage to pay off some credit card debt.
See Mortgage Refinancing

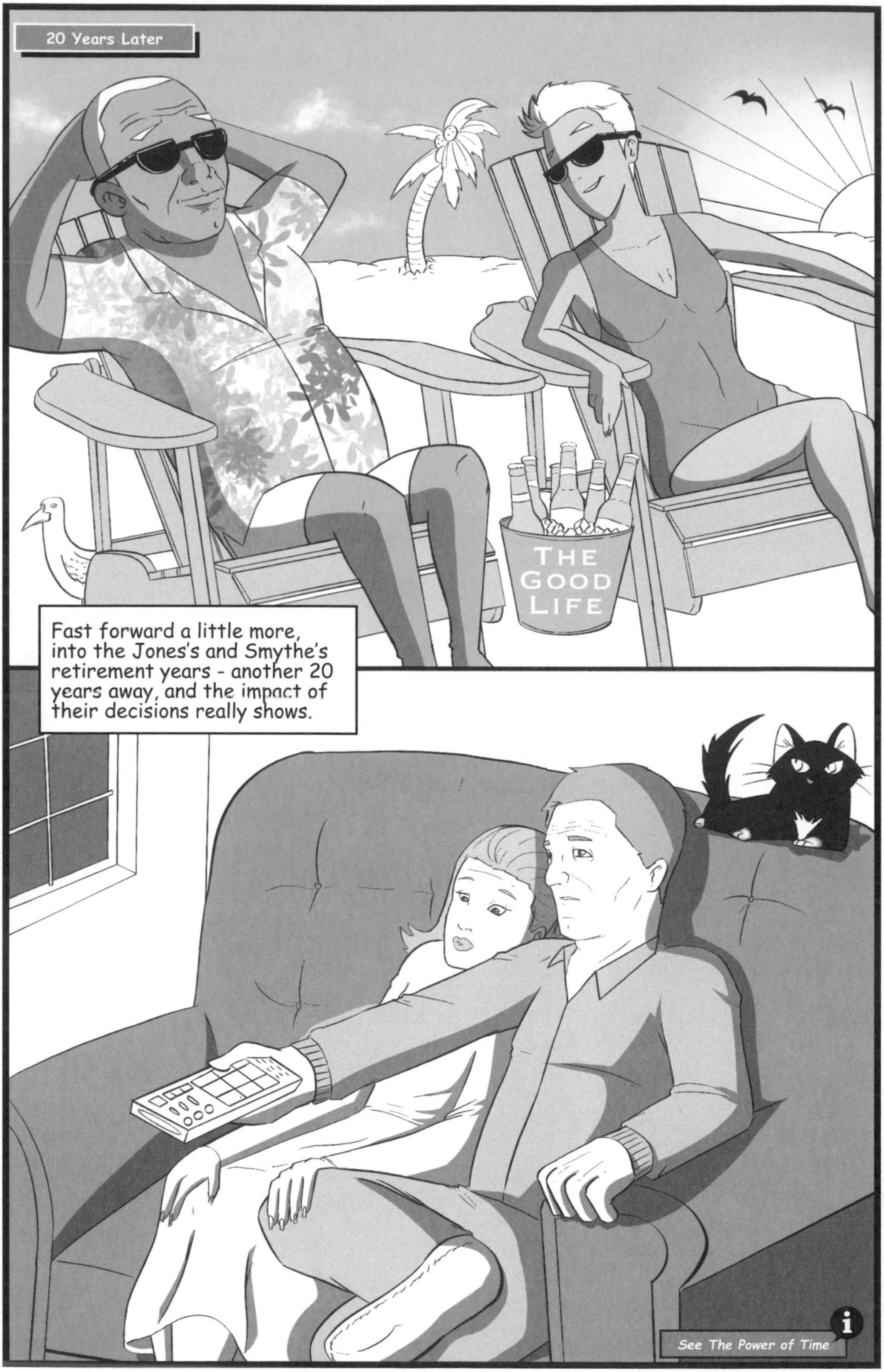
20 Years Later
THE GOOD LIFE
Fast forward a little more, into the Jones's and Smythe's retirement years - another 20 years away, and the impact of their decisions really shows.
i
See The Power of Time

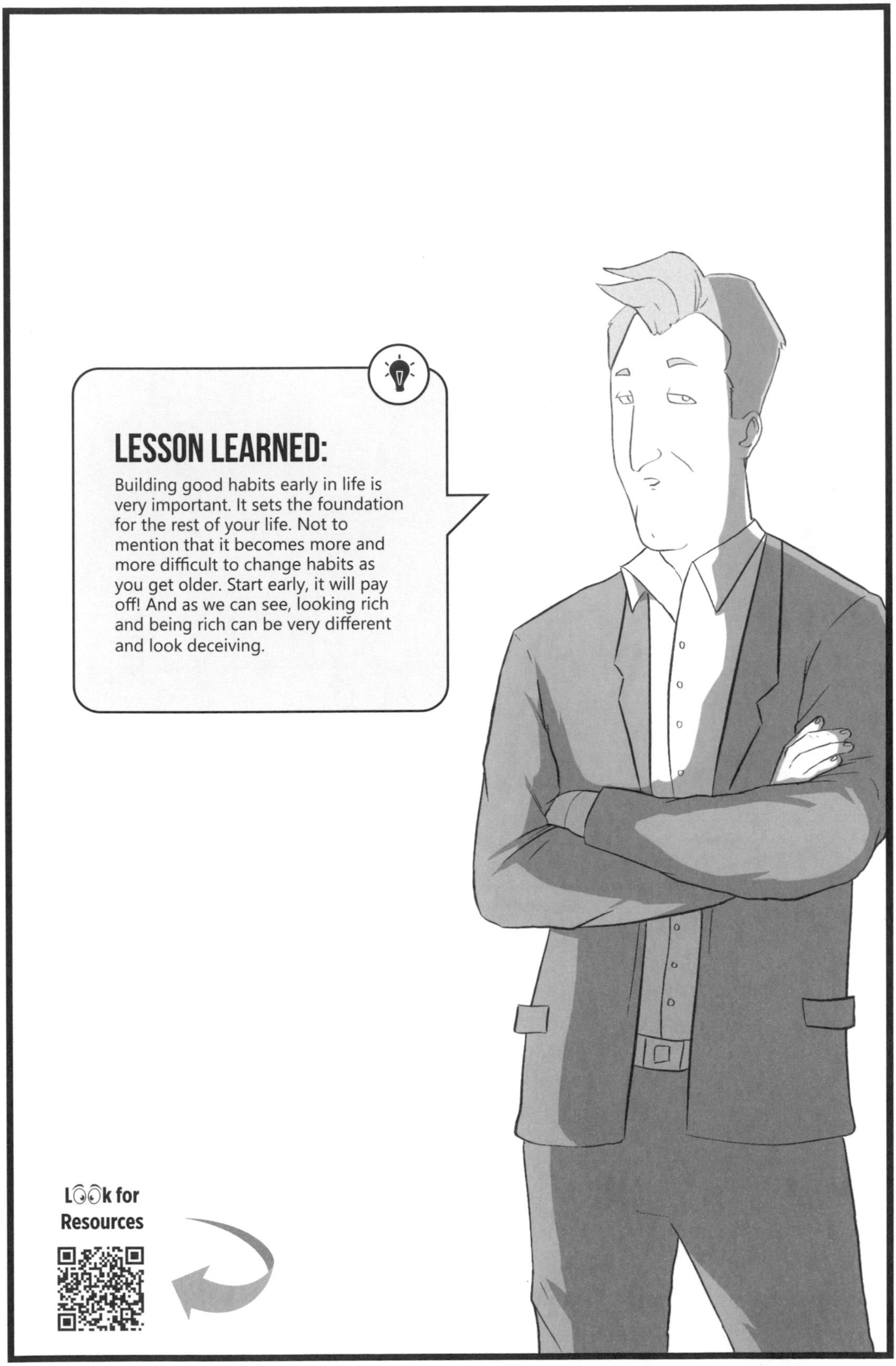
LESSON LEARNED:
Building good habits early in life is very important. It sets the foundation for the rest of your life. Not to mention that it becomes more and more difficult to change habits as you get older. Start early, it will pay off! And as we can see, looking rich and being rich can be very different and look deceiving.
Look for Resources

Chapter 2

Savings - Paying Yourself

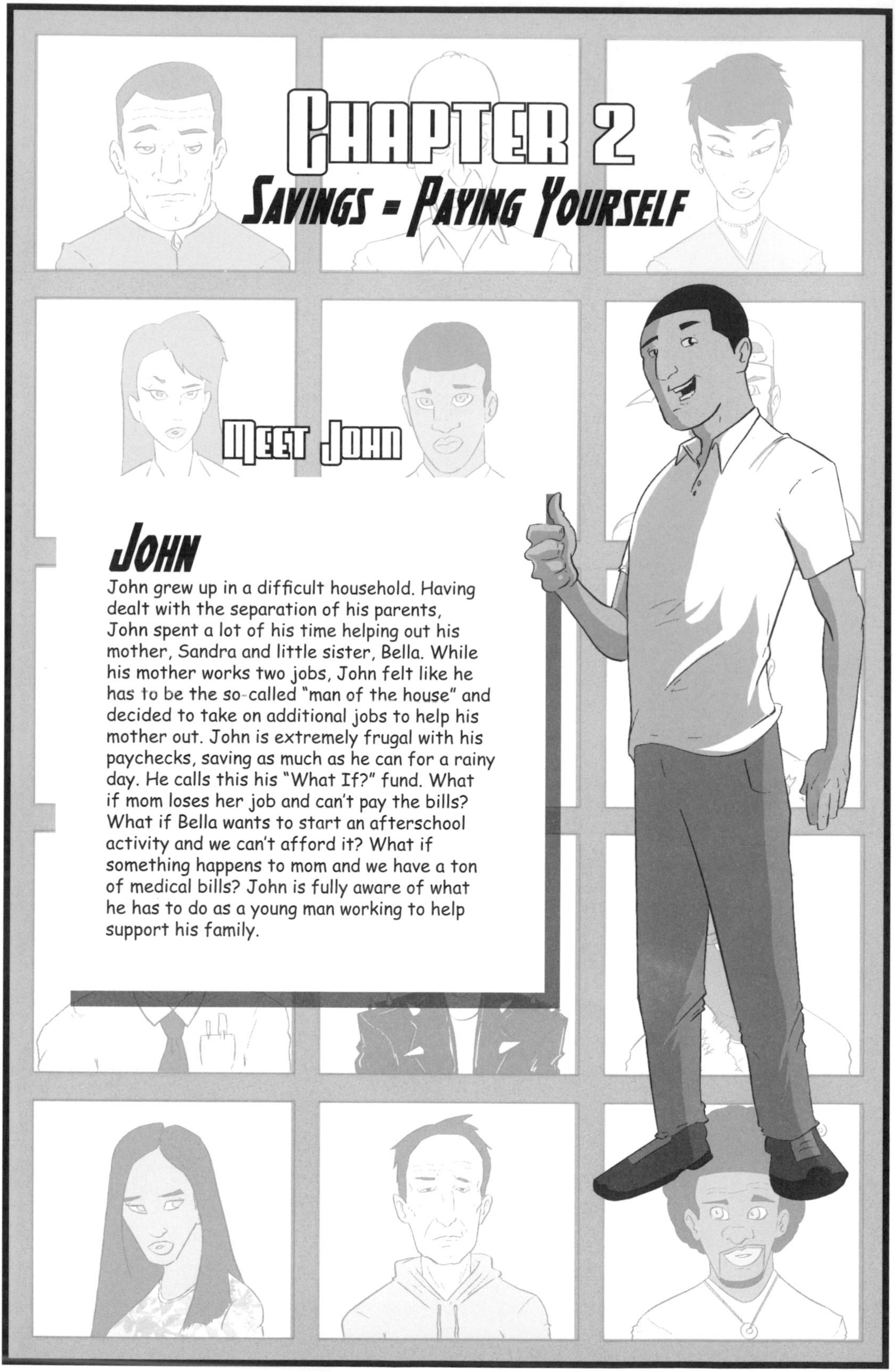

Meet John

John

John grew up in a difficult household. Having dealt with the separation of his parents, John spent a lot of his time helping out his mother, Sandra and little sister, Bella. While his mother works two jobs, John felt like he has to be the so-called "man of the house" and decided to take on additional jobs to help his mother out. John is extremely frugal with his paychecks, saving as much as he can for a rainy day. He calls this his "What If?" fund. What if mom loses her job and can't pay the bills? What if Bella wants to start an afterschool activity and we can't afford it? What if something happens to mom and we have a ton of medical bills? John is fully aware of what he has to do as a young man working to help support his family.

CHAPTER 2

SAVINGS = PAYING YOURSELF

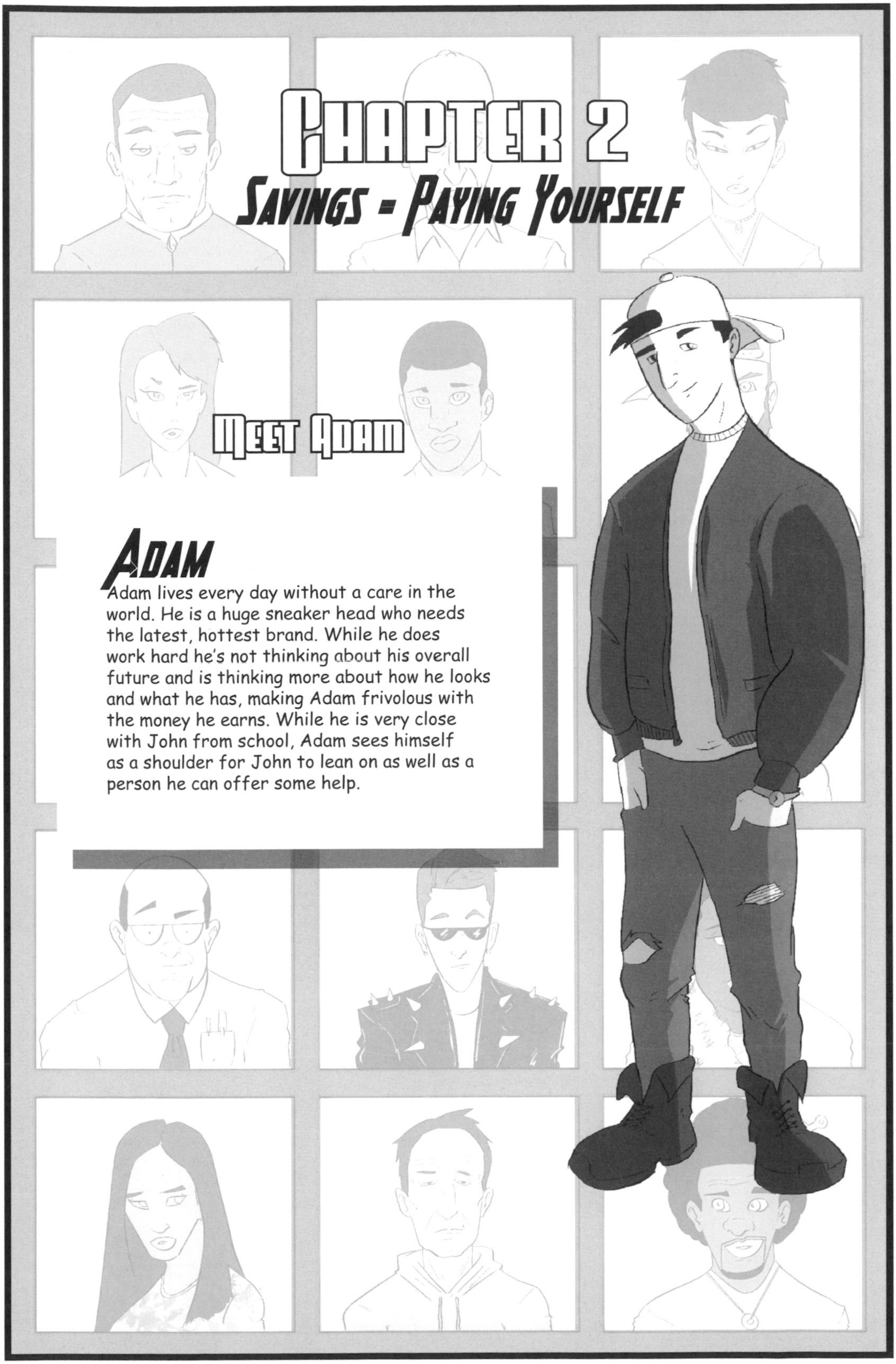

MEET ADAM

ADAM

Adam lives every day without a care in the world. He is a huge sneaker head who needs the latest, hottest brand. While he does work hard he's not thinking about his overall future and is thinking more about how he looks and what he has, making Adam frivolous with the money he earns. While he is very close with John from school, Adam sees himself as a shoulder for John to lean on as well as a person he can offer some help.

Chapter 2
Savings – Paying Yourself

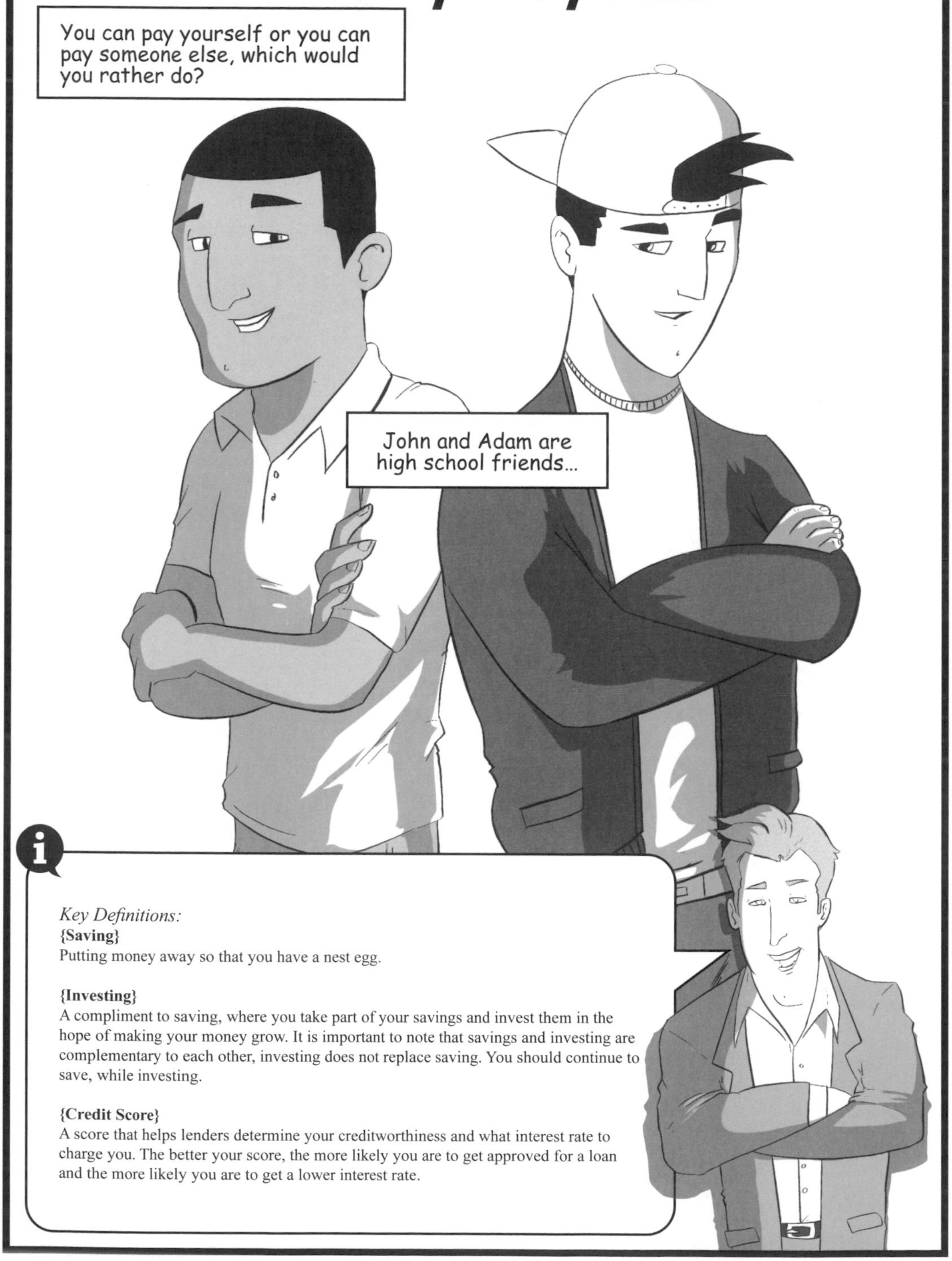
You can pay yourself or you can pay someone else, which would you rather do?
John and Adam are high school friends...

Key Definitions:

{Saving}
Putting money away so that you have a nest egg.

{Investing}
A compliment to saving, where you take part of your savings and invest them in the hope of making your money grow. It is important to note that savings and investing are complementary to each other, investing does not replace saving. You should continue to save, while investing.

{Credit Score}
A score that helps lenders determine your creditworthiness and what interest rate to charge you. The better your score, the more likely you are to get approved for a loan and the more likely you are to get a lower interest rate.

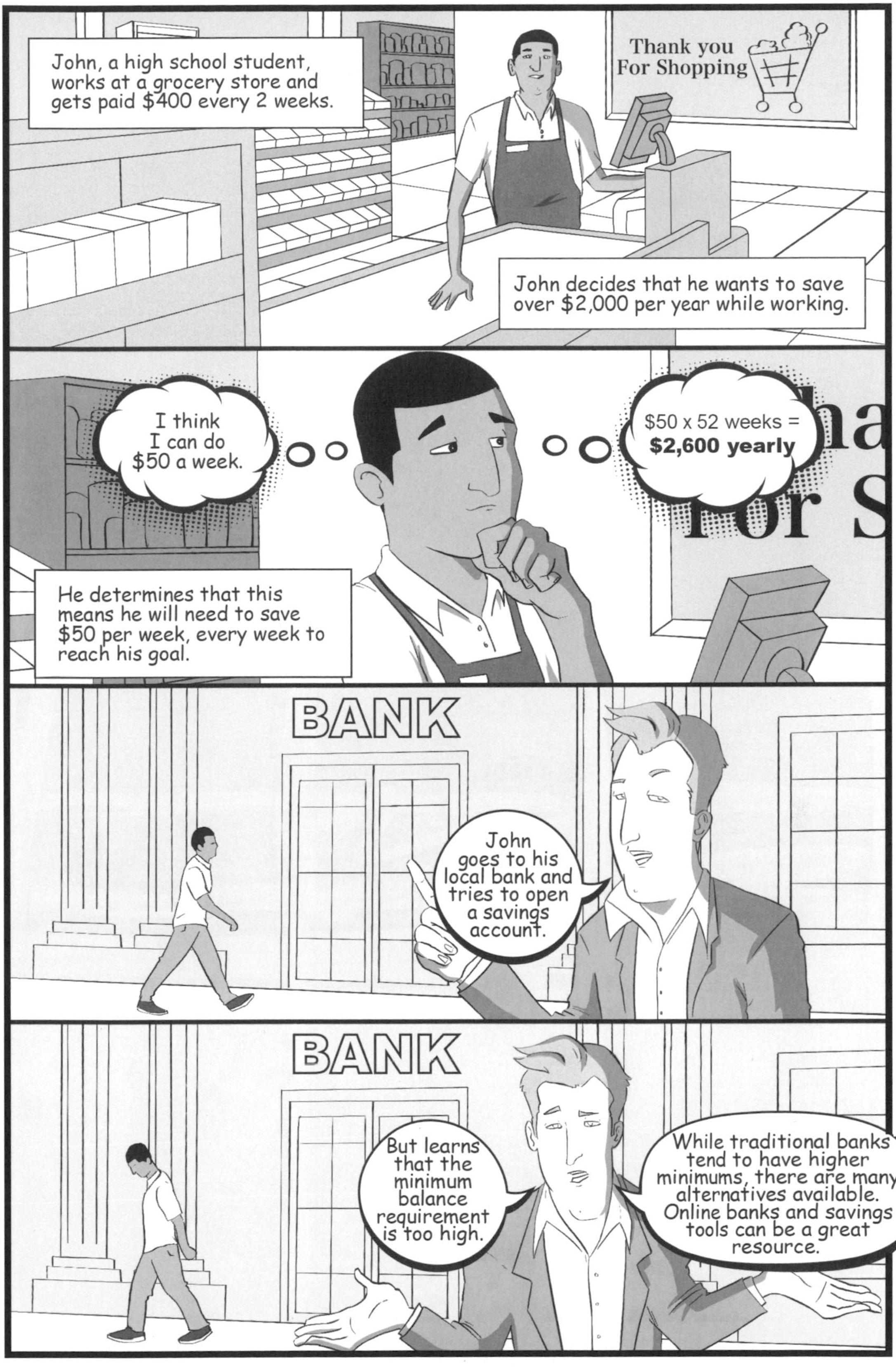
John, a high school student, works at a grocery store and gets paid $400 every 2 weeks.
Thank you For Shopping
John decides that he wants to save over $2,000 per year while working.
I think I can do $50 a week.
$50 x 52 weeks = **$2,600 yearly**
He determines that this means he will need to save $50 per week, every week to reach his goal.
BANK
John goes to his local bank and tries to open a savings account.
BANK
But learns that the minimum balance requirement is too high.
While traditional banks tend to have higher minimums, there are many alternatives available. Online banks and savings tools can be a great resource.

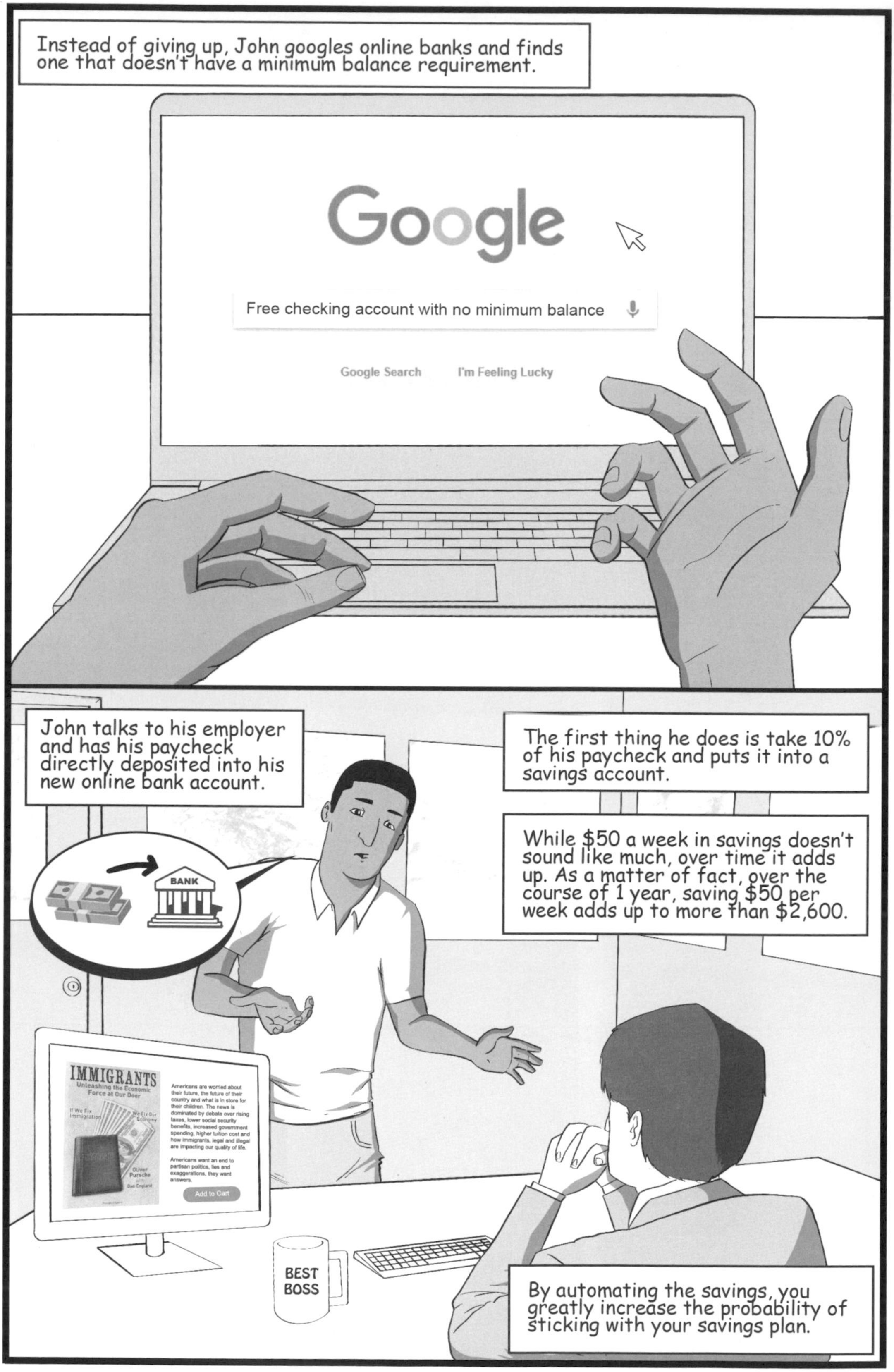
Instead of giving up, John googles online banks and finds one that doesn't have a minimum balance requirement.
Google
Free checking account with no minimum balance
Google Search
I'm Feeling Lucky
John talks to his employer and has his paycheck directly deposited into his new online bank account.
BANK
The first thing he does is take 10% of his paycheck and puts it into a savings account.
While $50 a week in savings doesn't sound like much, over time it adds up. As a matter of fact, over the course of 1 year, saving $50 per week adds up to more than $2,600.
IMMIGRANTS
Unleashing the Economic Force at Our Door
Add to Cart
BEST BOSS
By automating the savings, you greatly increase the probability of sticking with your savings plan.

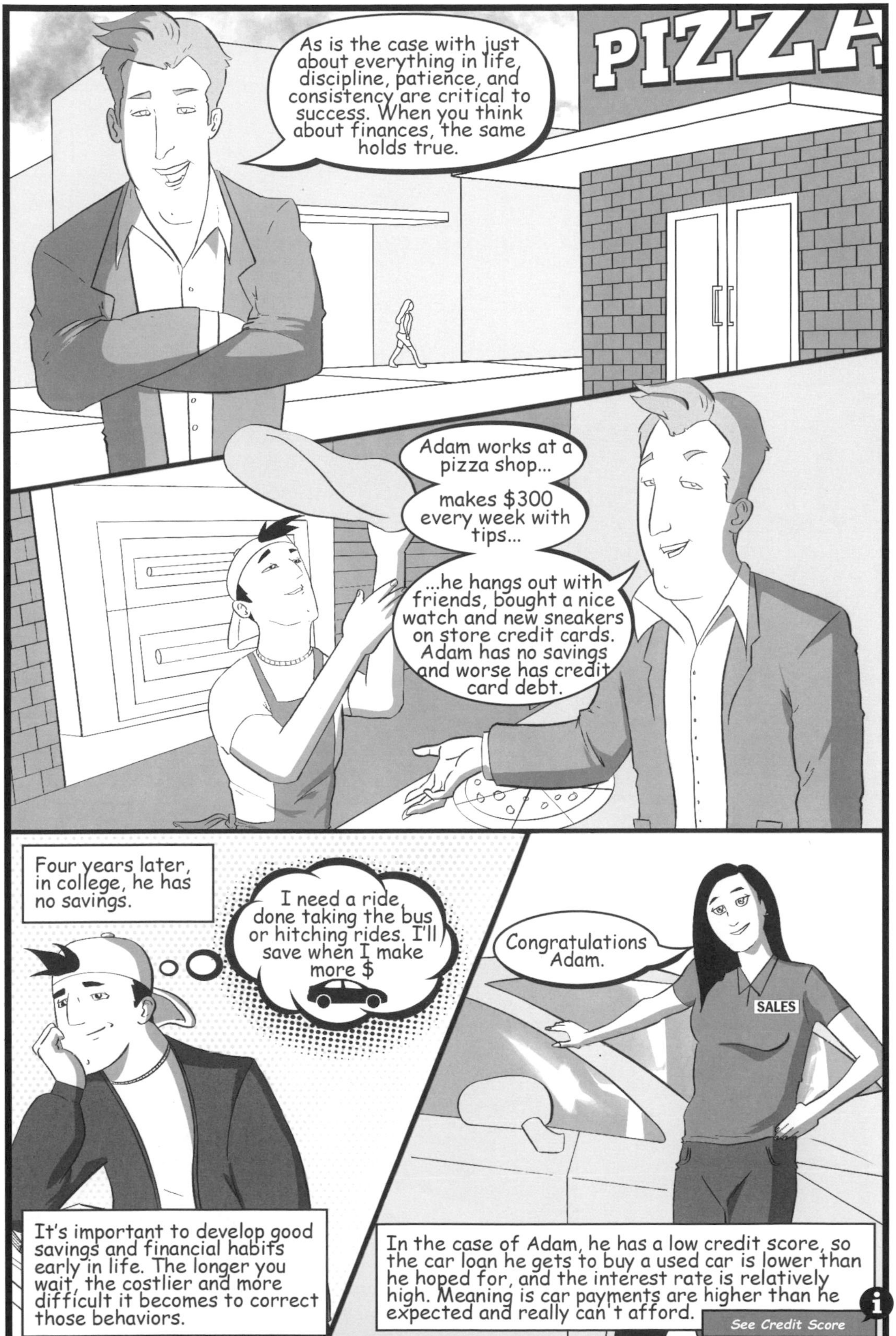
PIZZA
As is the case with just about everything in life, discipline, patience, and consistency are critical to success. When you think about finances, the same holds true.
Adam works at a pizza shop...
makes $300 every week with tips...
...he hangs out with friends, bought a nice watch and new sneakers on store credit cards. Adam has no savings and worse has credit card debt.
Four years later, in college, he has no savings.
I need a ride, done taking the bus or hitching rides. I'll save when I make more $
It's important to develop good savings and financial habits early in life. The longer you wait, the costlier and more difficult it becomes to correct those behaviors.
Congratulations Adam.
SALES
In the case of Adam, he has a low credit score, so the car loan he gets to buy a used car is lower than he hoped for, and the interest rate is relatively high. Meaning is car payments are higher than he expected and really can't afford.
See Credit Score

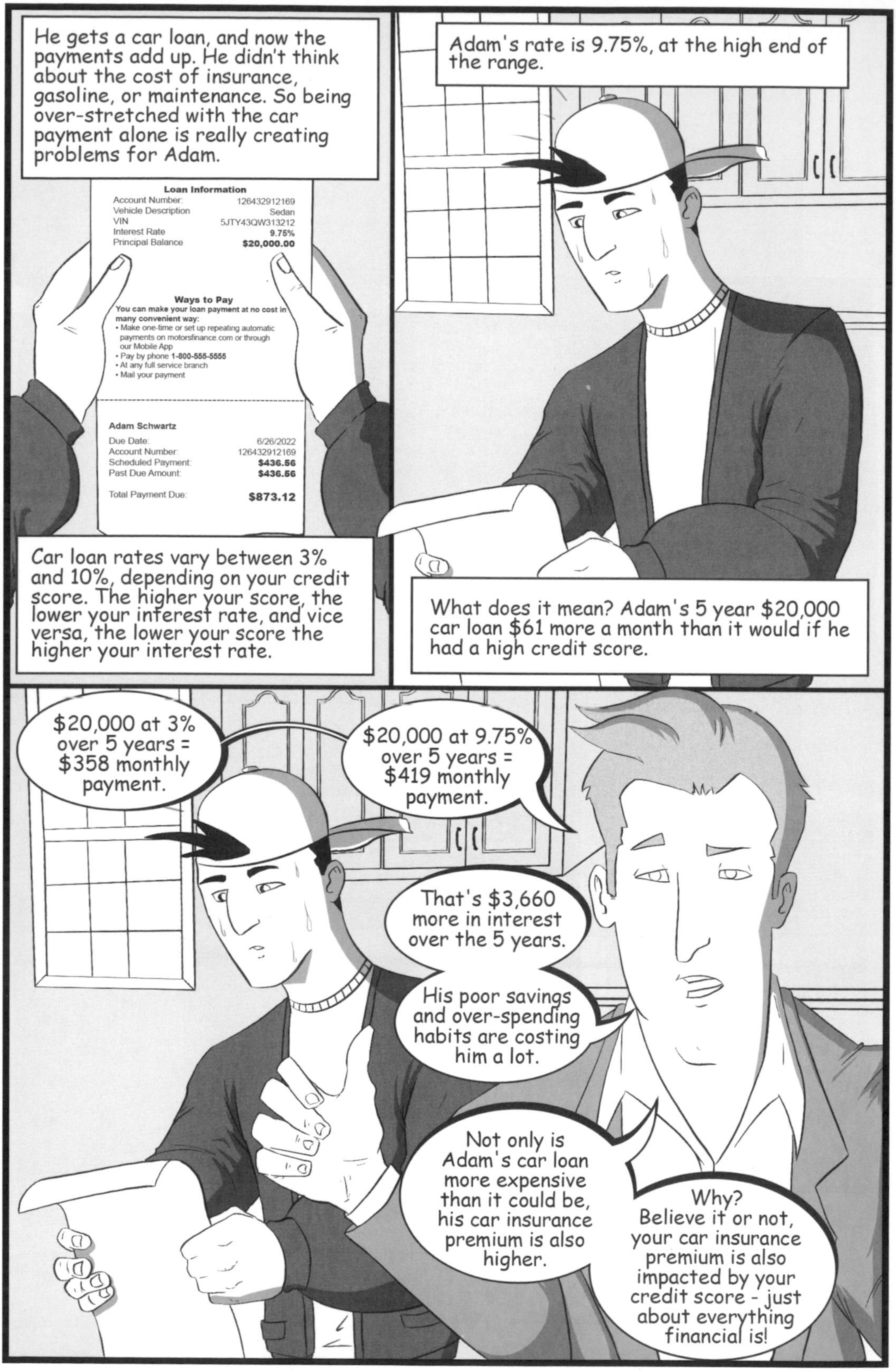
He gets a car loan, and now the payments add up. He didn't think about the cost of insurance, gasoline, or maintenance. So being over-stretched with the car payment alone is really creating problems for Adam.
Loan Information
Account Number: 126432912169
Vehicle Description Sedan
VIN 5JTY43QW313212
Interest Rate 9.75%
Principal Balance $20,000.00
Ways to Pay
You can make your loan payment at no cost in many convenient way:
• Make one-time or set up repeating automatic payments on motorsfinance.com or through our Mobile App
• Pay by phone 1-800-555-5555
• At any full service branch
• Mail your payment
Adam Schwartz
Due Date: 6/26/2022
Account Number: 126432912169
Scheduled Payment: $436.56
Past Due Amount: $436.56
Total Payment Due: $873.12
Car loan rates vary between 3% and 10%, depending on your credit score. The higher your score, the lower your interest rate, and vice versa, the lower your score the higher your interest rate.
Adam's rate is 9.75%, at the high end of the range.
What does it mean? Adam's 5 year $20,000 car loan $61 more a month than it would if he had a high credit score.
$20,000 at 3% over 5 years = $358 monthly payment.
$20,000 at 9.75% over 5 years = $419 monthly payment.
That's $3,660 more in interest over the 5 years.
His poor savings and over-spending habits are costing him a lot.
Not only is Adam's car loan more expensive than it could be, his car insurance premium is also higher.
Why? Believe it or not, your car insurance premium is also impacted by your credit score - just about everything financial is!

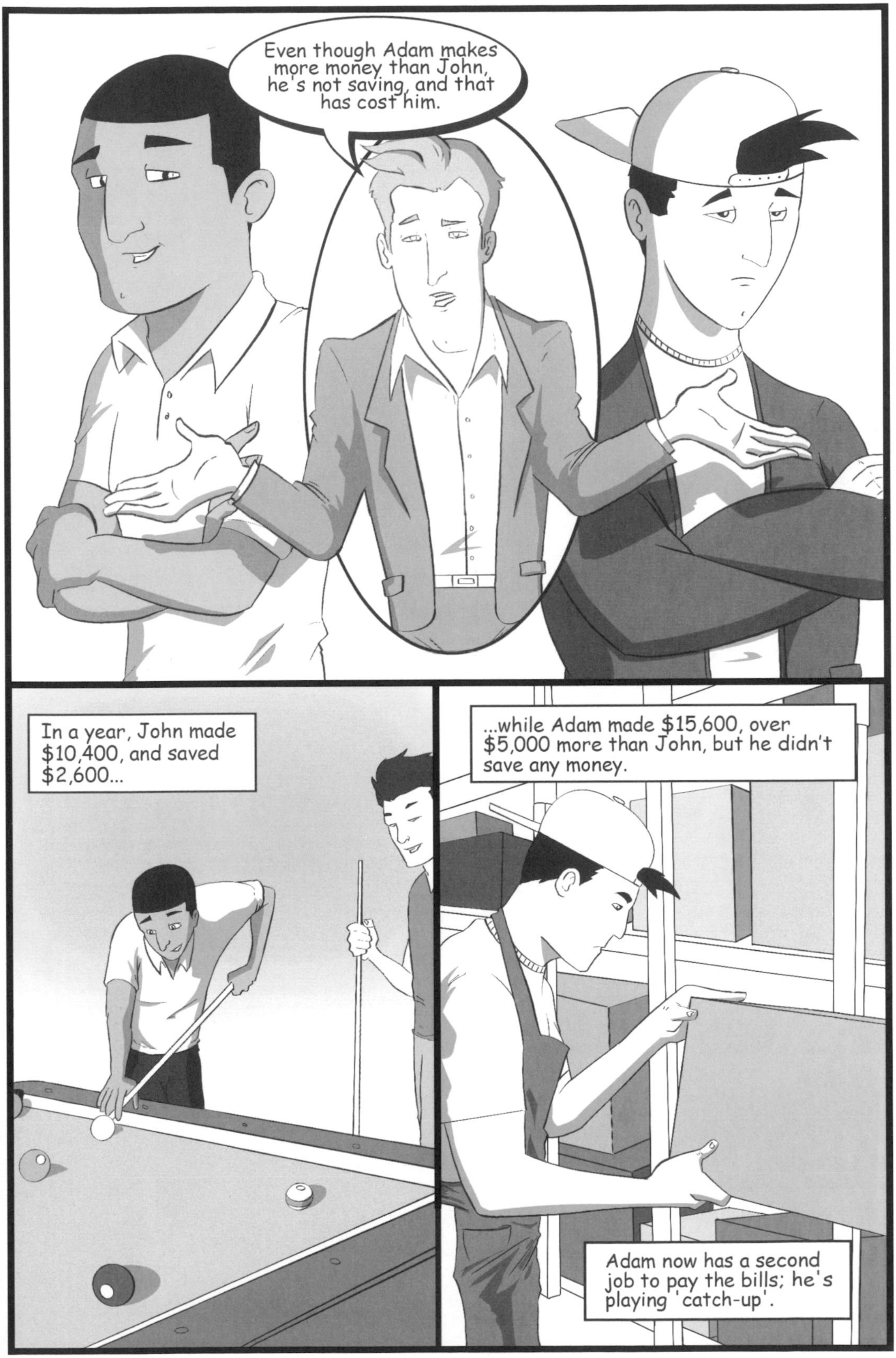
Even though Adam makes more money than John, he's not saving, and that has cost him.
In a year, John made $10,400, and saved $2,600...
...while Adam made $15,600, over $5,000 more than John, but he didn't save any money.
Adam now has a second job to pay the bills; he's playing 'catch-up'.

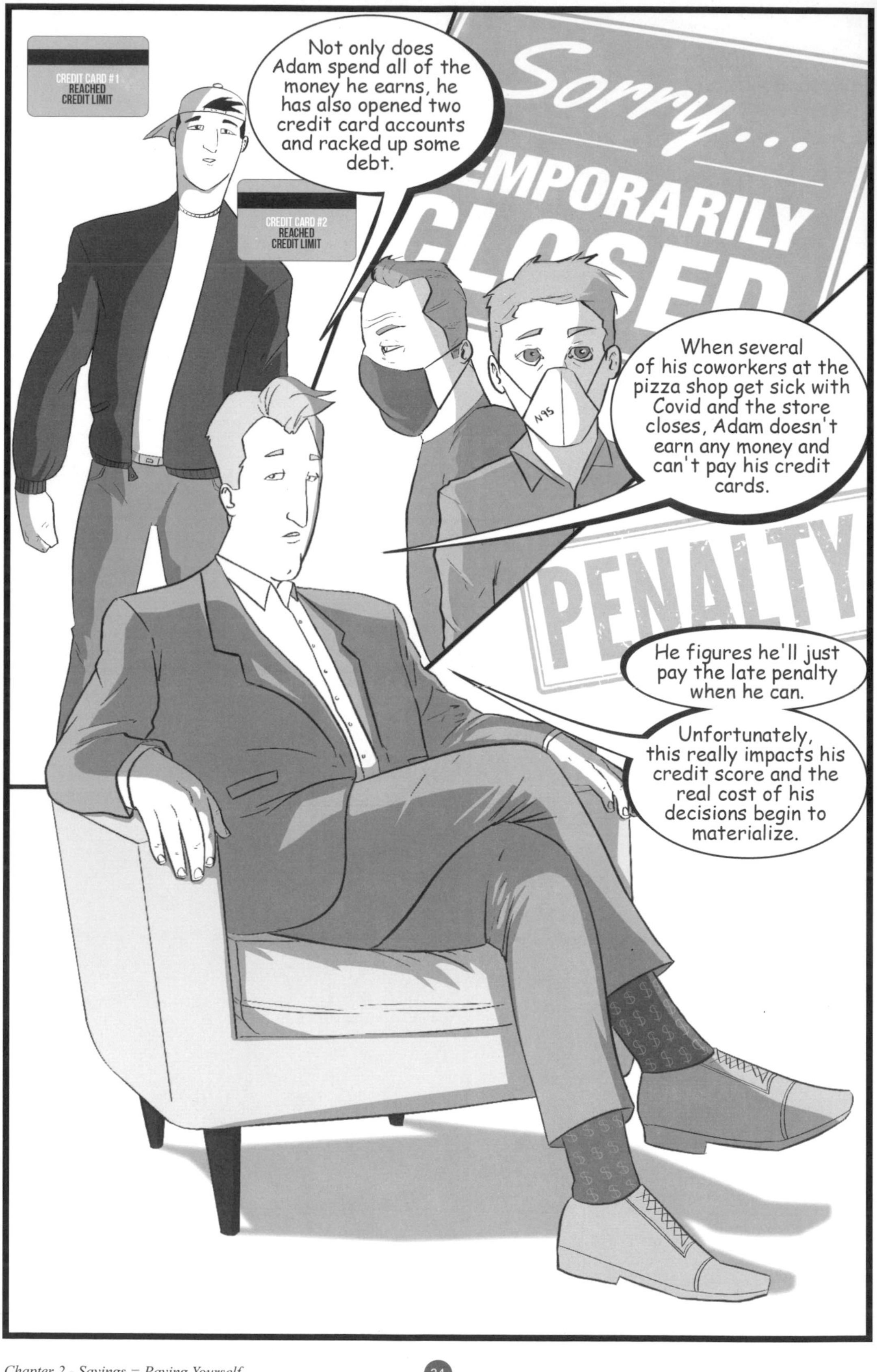
CREDIT CARD #1
REACHED
CREDIT LIMIT
Not only does Adam spend all of the money he earns, he has also opened two credit card accounts and racked up some debt.
Sorry...
EMPORARILY
CLOSED
CREDIT CARD #2
REACHED
CREDIT LIMIT
N95
When several of his coworkers at the pizza shop get sick with Covid and the store closes, Adam doesn't earn any money and can't pay his credit cards.
PENALTY
He figures he'll just pay the late penalty when he can.
Unfortunately, this really impacts his credit score and the real cost of his decisions begin to materialize.

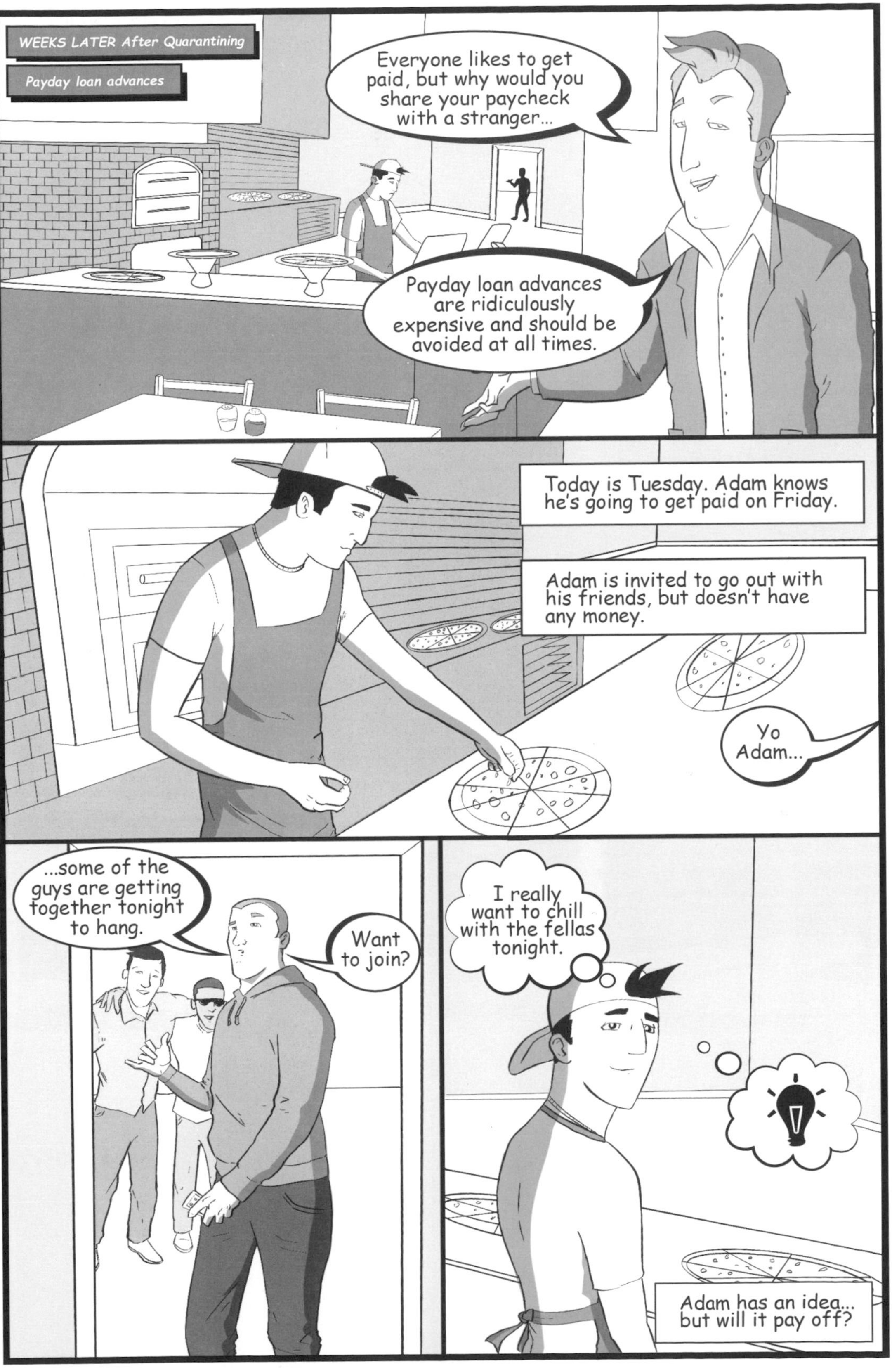
WEEKS LATER After Quarantining
Payday loan advances
Everyone likes to get paid, but why would you share your paycheck with a stranger...
Payday loan advances are ridiculously expensive and should be avoided at all times.
Today is Tuesday. Adam knows he's going to get paid on Friday.
Adam is invited to go out with his friends, but doesn't have any money.
Yo Adam...
...some of the guys are getting together tonight to hang.
Want to join?
I really want to chill with the fellas tonight.
Adam has an idea... but will it pay off?

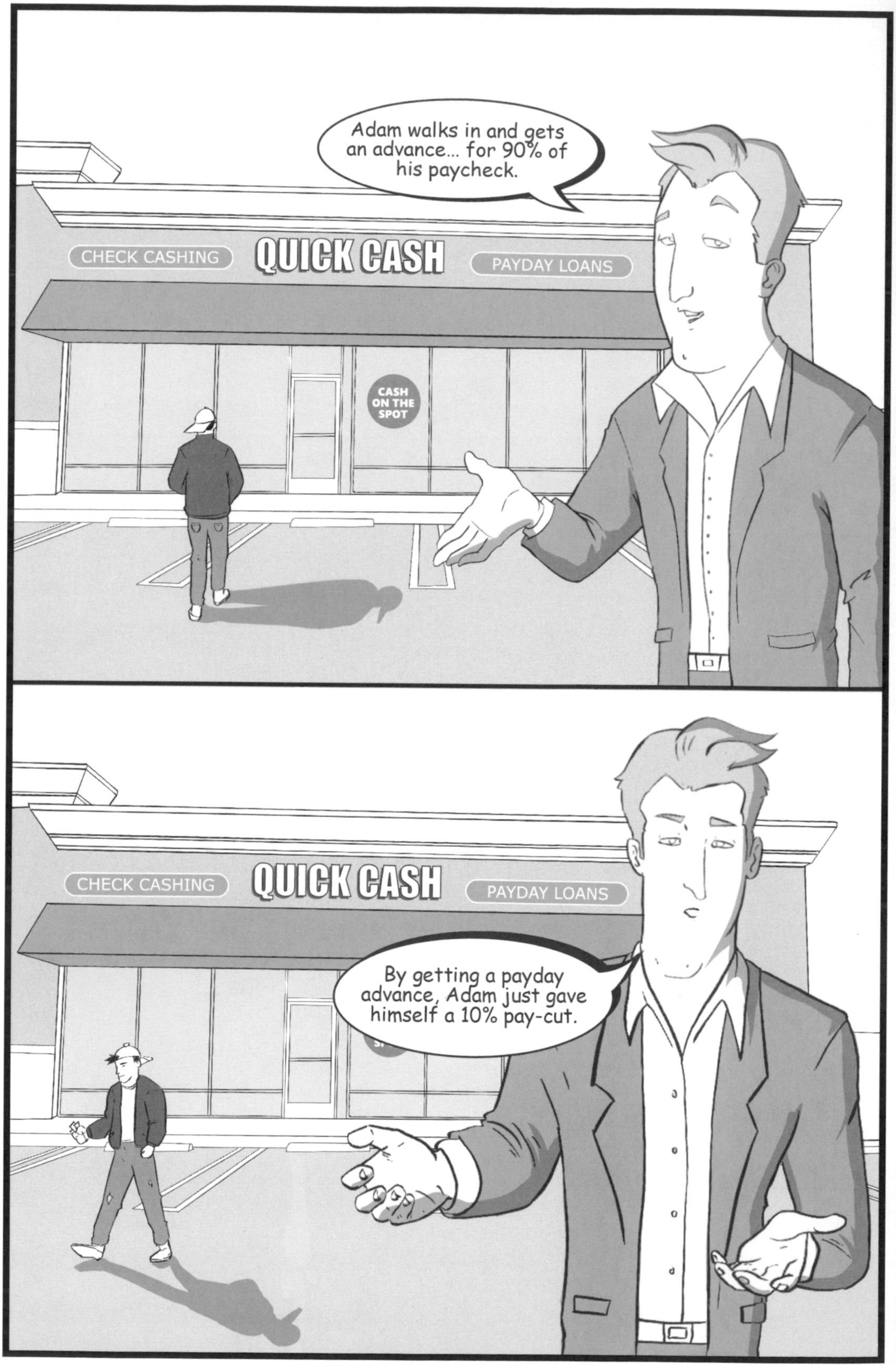

Adam walks in and gets an advance... for 90% of his paycheck.
CHECK CASHING
QUICK CASH
PAYDAY LOANS
CASH ON THE SPOT
CHECK CASHING
QUICK CASH
PAYDAY LOANS
By getting a payday advance, Adam just gave himself a 10% pay-cut.

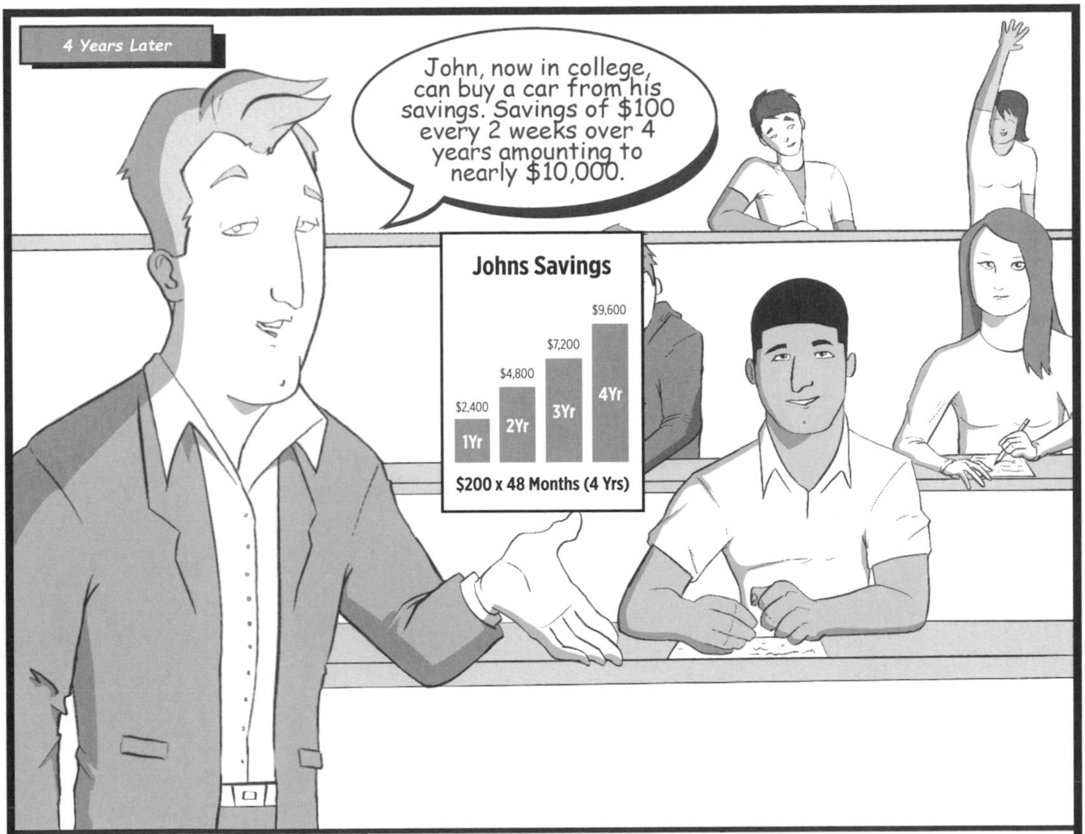
4 Years Later
John, now in college, can buy a car from his savings. Savings of $100 every 2 weeks over 4 years amounting to nearly $10,000.
Johns Savings
$2,400
1Yr
$4,800
2Yr
$7,200
3Yr
$9,600
4Yr
$200 x 48 Months (4 Yrs)

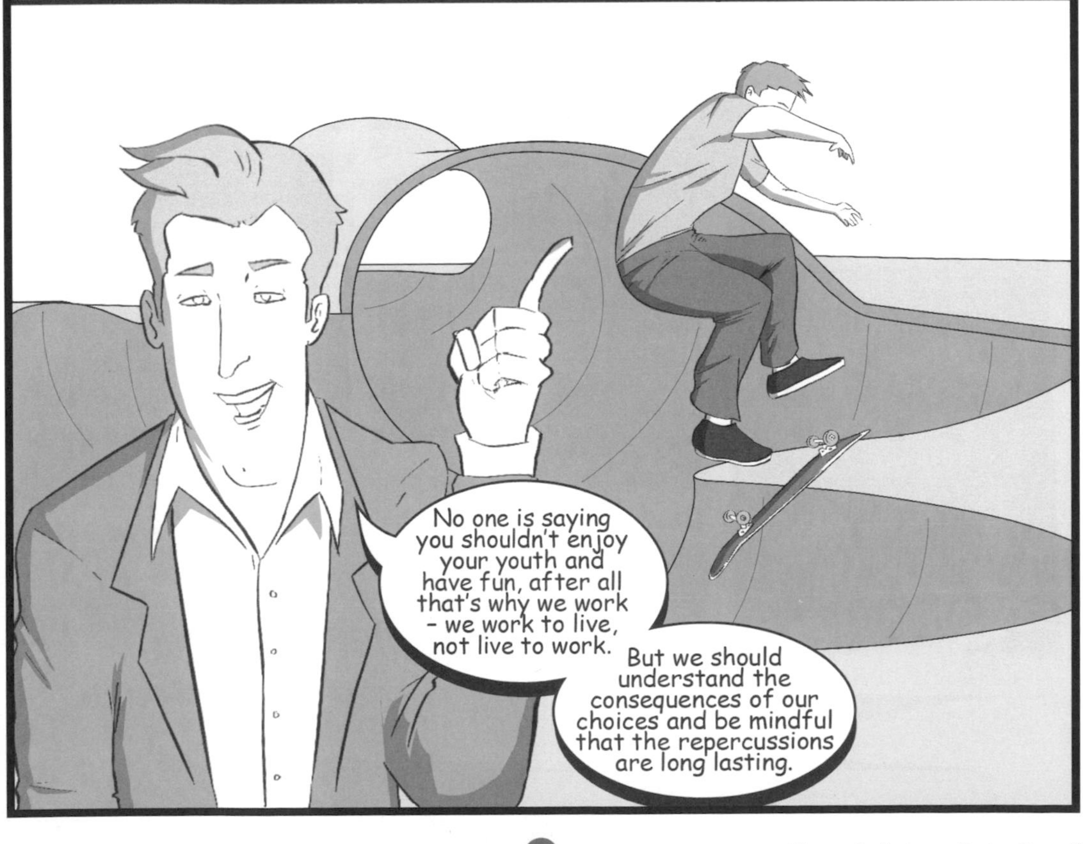
No one is saying you shouldn't enjoy your youth and have fun, after all that's why we work - we work to live, not live to work.
But we should understand the consequences of our choices and be mindful that the repercussions are long lasting.

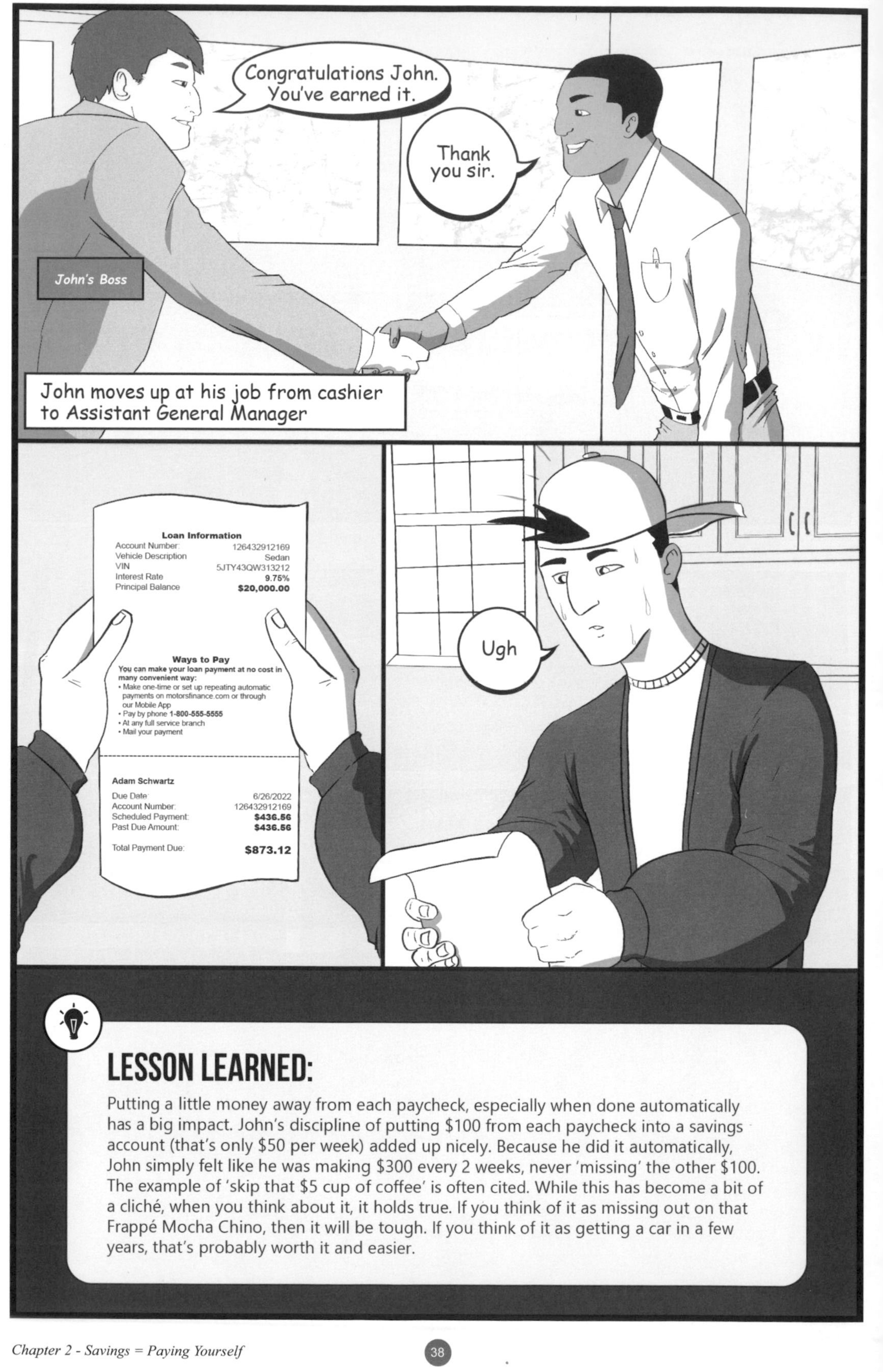
Congratulations John. You've earned it.
Thank you sir.
John's Boss
John moves up at his job from cashier to Assistant General Manager
Loan Information
Account Number: 126432912169
Vehicle Description Sedan
VIN 5JTY43QW313212
Interest Rate 9.75%
Principal Balance $20,000.00
Ways to Pay
You can make your loan payment at no cost in many convenient way:
• Make one-time or set up repeating automatic payments on motorsfinance.com or through our Mobile App
• Pay by phone 1-800-555-5555
• At any full service branch
• Mail your payment
Adam Schwartz
Due Date 6/26/2022
Account Number: 126432912169
Scheduled Payment: $436.56
Past Due Amount: $436.56
Total Payment Due: $873.12
Ugh

LESSON LEARNED:

Putting a little money away from each paycheck, especially when done automatically has a big impact. John's discipline of putting $100 from each paycheck into a savings account (that's only $50 per week) added up nicely. Because he did it automatically, John simply felt like he was making $300 every 2 weeks, never 'missing' the other $100. The example of 'skip that $5 cup of coffee' is often cited. While this has become a bit of a cliché, when you think about it, it holds true. If you think of it as missing out on that Frappé Mocha Chino, then it will be tough. If you think of it as getting a car in a few years, that's probably worth it and easier.

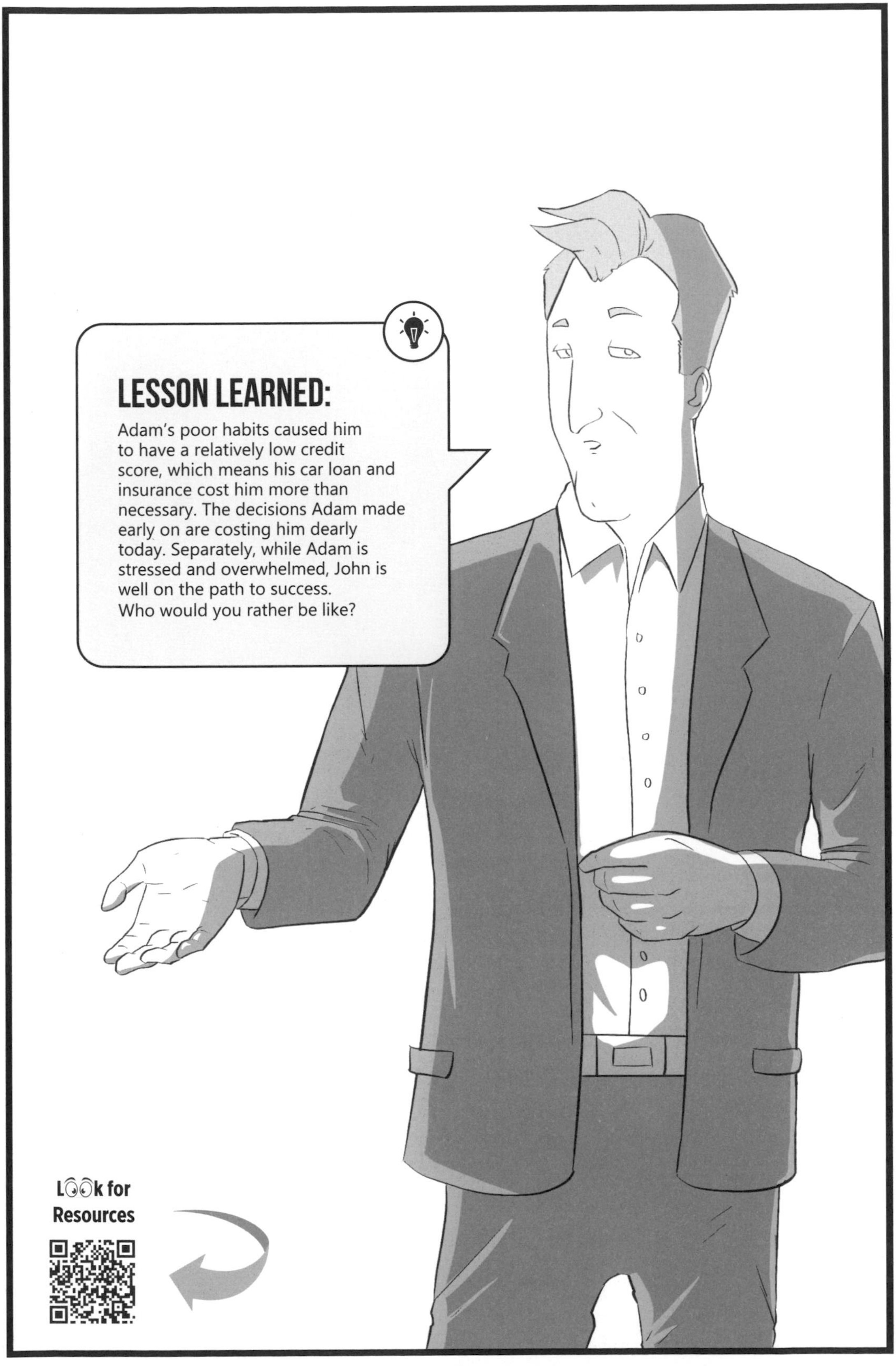
LESSON LEARNED:
Adam's poor habits caused him to have a relatively low credit score, which means his car loan and insurance cost him more than necessary. The decisions Adam made early on are costing him dearly today. Separately, while Adam is stressed and overwhelmed, John is well on the path to success. Who would you rather be like?
Look for Resources

CHAPTER 3

BUILDING A BUDGET, INCOME STATEMENT & BALANCE SHEET

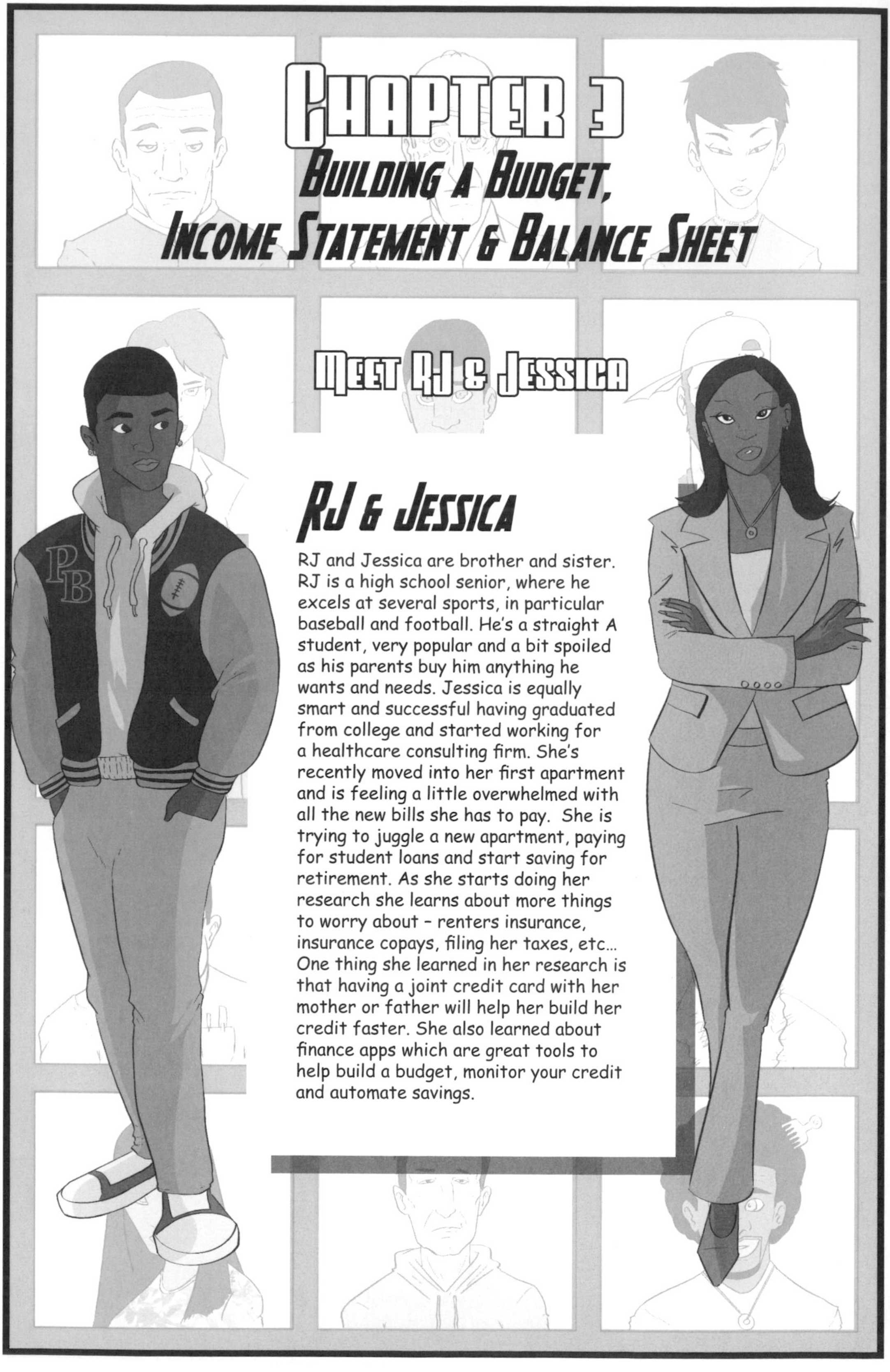

MEET RJ & JESSICA

RJ & JESSICA

RJ and Jessica are brother and sister. RJ is a high school senior, where he excels at several sports, in particular baseball and football. He's a straight A student, very popular and a bit spoiled as his parents buy him anything he wants and needs. Jessica is equally smart and successful having graduated from college and started working for a healthcare consulting firm. She's recently moved into her first apartment and is feeling a little overwhelmed with all the new bills she has to pay. She is trying to juggle a new apartment, paying for student loans and start saving for retirement. As she starts doing her research she learns about more things to worry about - renters insurance, insurance copays, filing her taxes, etc... One thing she learned in her research is that having a joint credit card with her mother or father will help her build her credit faster. She also learned about finance apps which are great tools to help build a budget, monitor your credit and automate savings.

CHAPTER 3

BUILDING A BUDGET, INCOME STATEMENT & BALANCE SHEET

Monthly Budget

Projected Monthly Income	
Income 1	$4,300.00
Extra income	$300.00
Total monthly income	**$4,600.00**

Actual Monthly Income	
Income 1	$4,000.00
Extra income	$300.00
Total monthly income	**$4,300.00**

Projected Balance (Projected income minus expenses)	$3,405.00
Actual Balance (Actual income minus expenses)	$3,064.00
Difference (Actual minus projected)	($341.00)

HOUSING	Projected Cost	Actual Cost	Difference
Mortgage or rent	$1,000.00	$1,000.00	$0.00
Phone	$54.00	$100.00	-$46.00
Electricity	$44.00	$56.00	-$12.00
Gas	$22.00	$28.00	-$6.00
Water and sewer	$8.00	$8.00	$0.00
Cable	$34.00	$34.00	$0.00
Waste removal	$10.00	$10.00	$0.00
Maintenance or repairs	$23.00	$0.00	$23.00
Supplies	$0.00	$0.00	$0.00
Other	$0.00	$0.00	$0.00
Subtotal			-$41.00

TRANSPORTATION	Projected Cost	Actual Cost	Difference
Vehicle payment			$560.00
Bus/taxi fare			$0.00
Insurance			$150.00

ENTERTAINMENT	Projected Cost	Actual Cost	Difference
Streaming Services			$26.00
Movies			$50.00
Concerts			$0.00
Sporting events			$250.00
Live theater			$0.00
Other			$0.00
Other			$0.00
Other			$0.00
Other			$0.00
Subtotal			$326.00

LOANS	Projected Cost	Actual Cost	Difference
Personal			$0.00
Student			$0.00
Credit card			$0.00
Credit card			$0.00
			$0.00
			$0.00
			$0.00

	Projected Cost		Difference
			$0.00
			$0.00
			$0.00
			$0.00
			$0.00

Key Definitions:

{Assets}
What you own and their worth.

{Liabilities}
What you owe / debts; i.e. car loan, credit card balances, mortgages, etc.

{Balance Sheet}
A summary of your assets and liabilities.

{Income Statement}
How much you earn, less withholdings such as taxes.

{Non-Discretionary Spending}
Things you have to spend money on, not want to. For instance, rent, utilities, car insurance, health insurance.

{Discretionary Spending}
Things you want to spend money on, but don't need. For instance, streaming services, dinner at a fancy restaurant, a new phone.

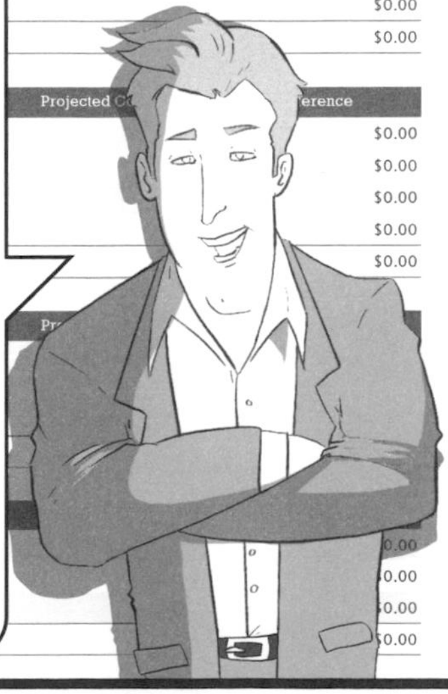

Grooming	$0.00

BALANCE SHEET EXAMPLE

> Your balance sheet is a summary of everything you own and everything you owe.

ASSETS

Current Assets

Checking Account	$5,000
Savings Account	$12,000
401(k)	$100,000
Brokerage Account	$42,000
529 Plan	$16,000
Total Current Assets	**175,000**

Property

Land	$150,000

Other Assets

Computer	$3,000
Total Assets	**328,000**

LIABILITIES & EQUITY

Current Liabilities

Accounts Payable	$40,000
Credit Card	$12,000
Total Current Liabilities	**52,000**

Noncurrent Liabilities

Long-term Debt (loan)	$60,000
Total Liabilities	**112,000**

Equity

Common Stock	$100,000
Retaining Earnings	$200,000
Total Equity	**300,000**
Total Liabilities & Equity	**412,000**

ASSETS - LIABILITIES = NET WORTH

See Balance Sheet ⓘ

INCOME STATEMENT EXAMPLE

> Your income statement and budget is a summary of what you earn and what you spend – pretty simple, right?

REVENUE

Income

Gross Wages	$6,000
Paid Time Off	$104
Dividend Income	$1,000
RMDs	$500
Total Income	**7,604**

EXPENSES

Housing

Rent/Mortgage	$1,800
Utilities	$600
Total Housing	**2,400**

Transportation

Car Payment	$300
Fuel	$150
Repairs	$750
Car Insurance	$75
Total Transportation	**1,275**

Household Expense

Groceries	$500
Supplies	$200
Total Household Expenses	**700**
Total Expenses	**4,375**

See Income Statement ⓘ

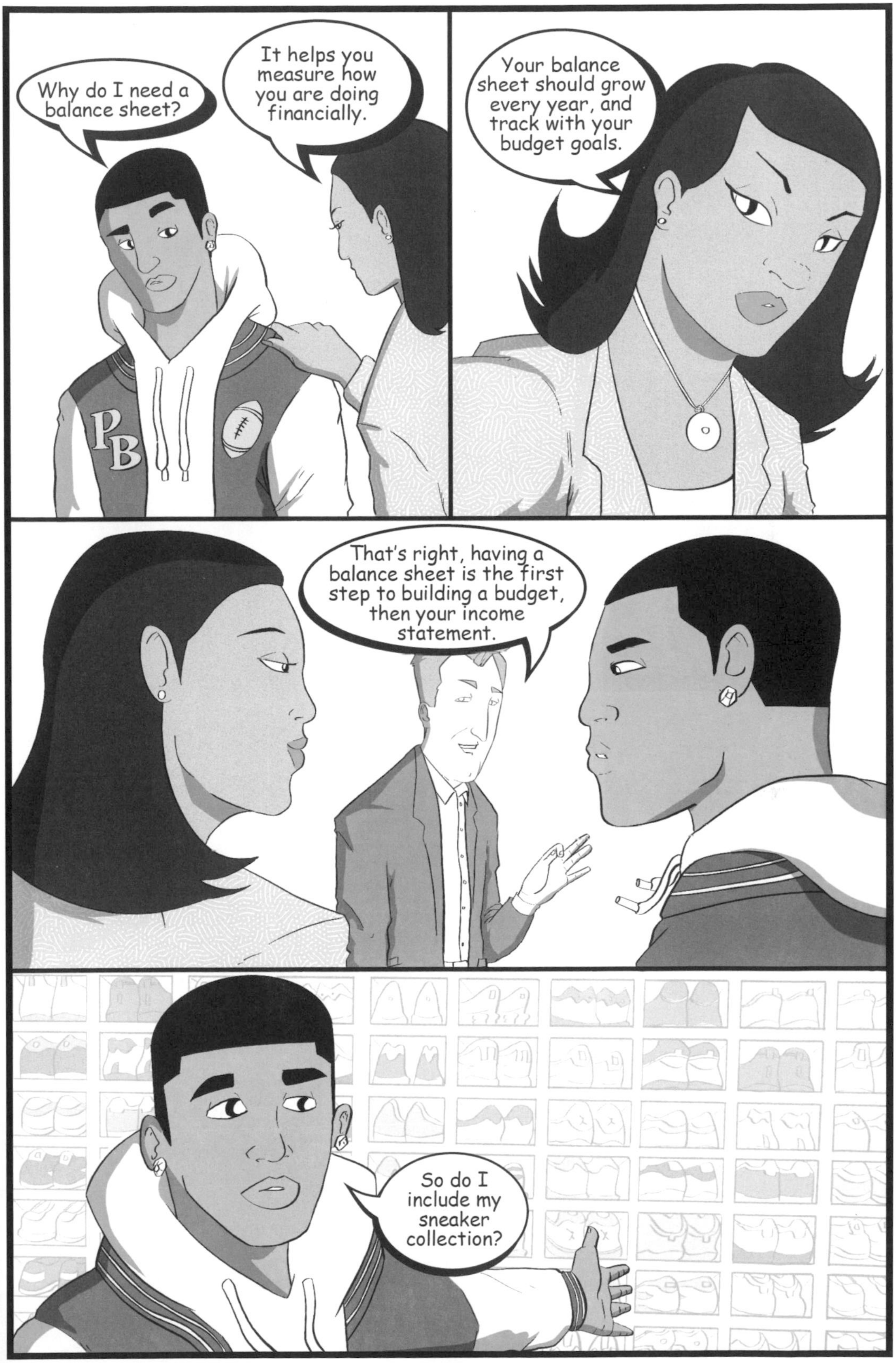
Why do I need a balance sheet?
It helps you measure how you are doing financially.
Your balance sheet should grow every year, and track with your budget goals.
PB
That's right, having a balance sheet is the first step to building a budget, then your income statement.
So do I include my sneaker collection?

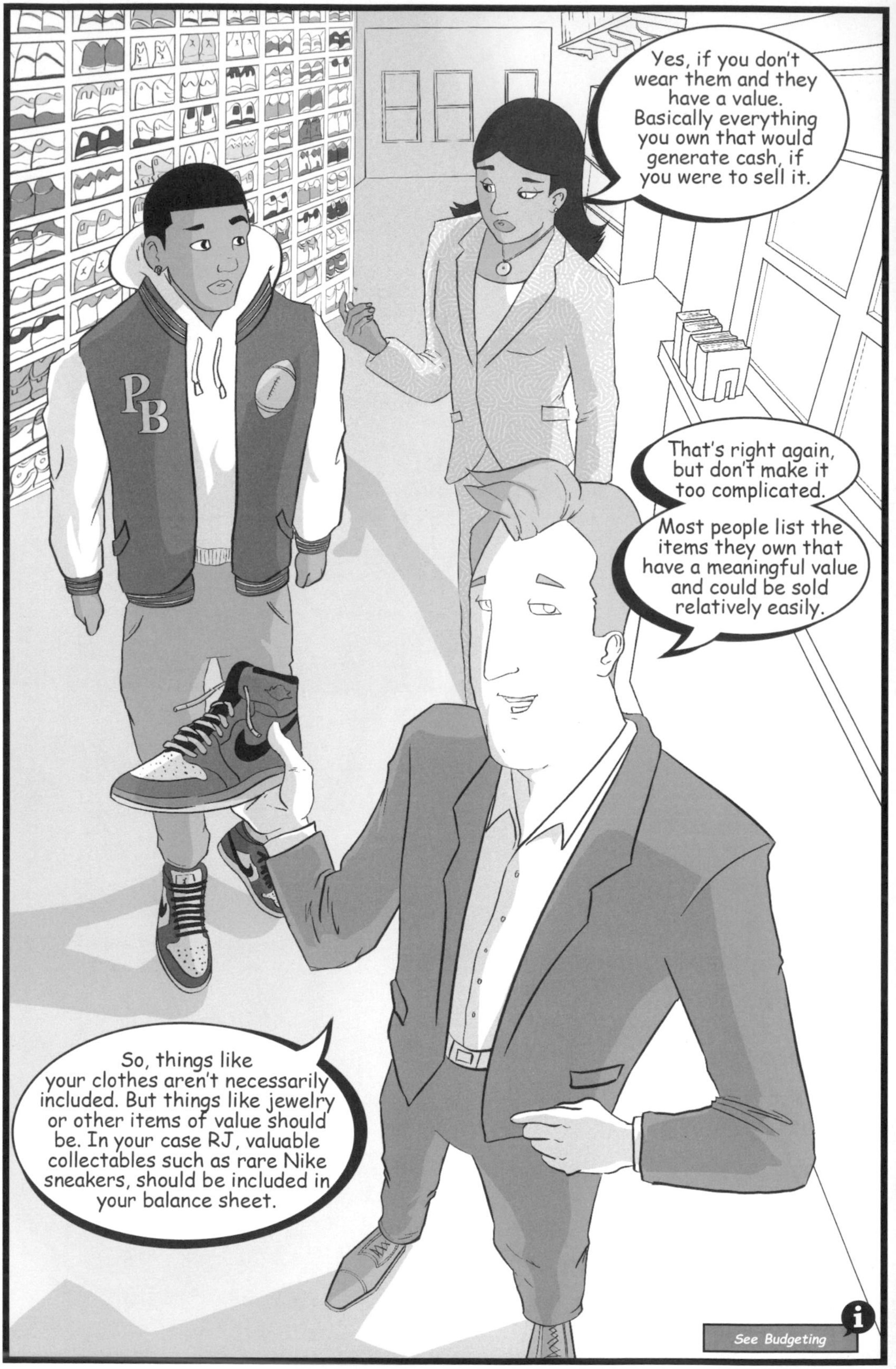
Yes, if you don't wear them and they have a value. Basically everything you own that would generate cash, if you were to sell it.
That's right again, but don't make it too complicated.
Most people list the items they own that have a meaningful value and could be sold relatively easily.
So, things like your clothes aren't necessarily included. But things like jewelry or other items of value should be. In your case RJ, valuable collectables such as rare Nike sneakers, should be included in your balance sheet.
PB
See Budgeting

INCOME STATEMENT EXAMPLE

Now that you've put together your balance sheet, you are easily able to see your net-worth and how your assets and debts are distributed.

REVENUE

Income	
Gross Wages	$6,000
Paid Time Off	$104
Dividend Income	$1,000
Total Income	**7,104**

Your income statement should be pretty straight forward, at least for now. Simply speaking, this is what you earn before and after taxes. Additionally, as you start investing, you will also add dividends, interest and realized gains from investments.

EXPENSES

Housing	
Rent/Mortgage	$1,800
Utilities	$600
Total Housing	**2,400**
Transportation	
Car Payment	$300
Fuel	$150
Repairs	$750
Car Insurance	$75
Total Transportation	**1,275**
Household Expense	
Groceries	$500
Supplies	$200
Total Household Expenses	**700**
Total Expenses	**4,375**

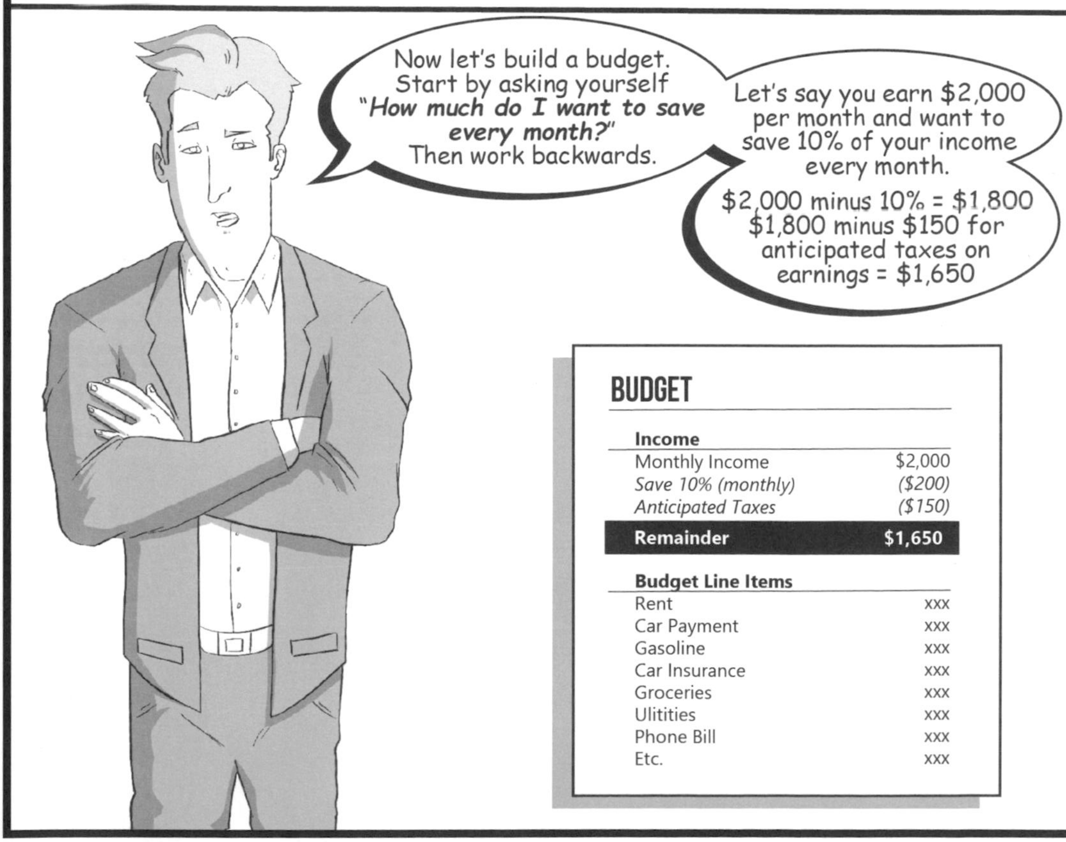
Now let's build a budget. Start by asking yourself "How much do I want to save every month?" Then work backwards.
Let's say you earn $2,000 per month and want to save 10% of your income every month.
$2,000 minus 10% = $1,800 $1,800 minus $150 for anticipated taxes on earnings = $1,650

BUDGET

Income	
Monthly Income	$2,000
Save 10% (monthly)	*($200)*
Anticipated Taxes	*($150)*
Remainder	**$1,650**
Budget Line Items	
Rent	xxx
Car Payment	xxx
Gasoline	xxx
Car Insurance	xxx
Groceries	xxx
Ulitities	xxx
Phone Bill	xxx
Etc.	xxx

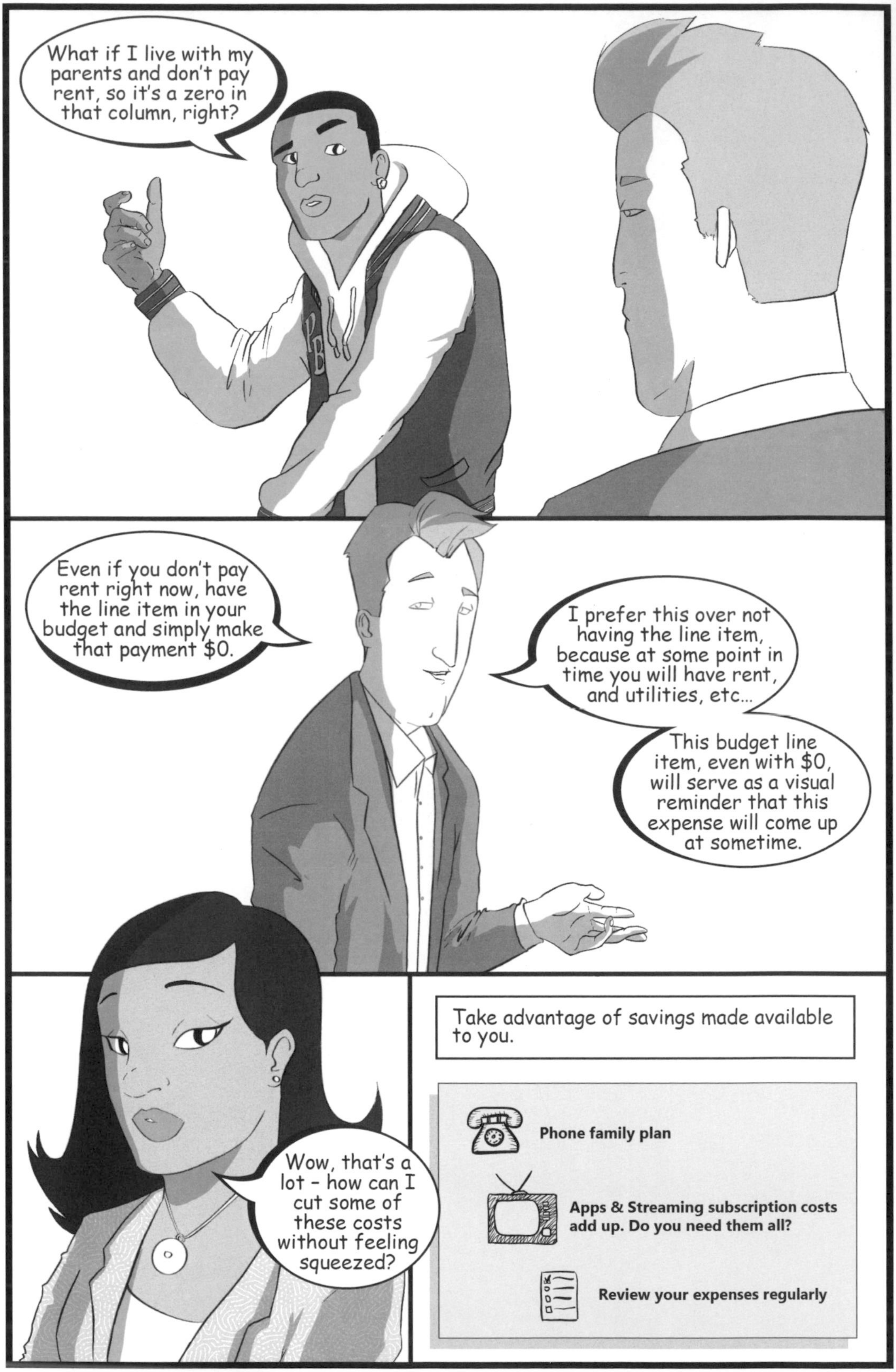
What if I live with my parents and don't pay rent, so it's a zero in that column, right?
Even if you don't pay rent right now, have the line item in your budget and simply make that payment $0.
I prefer this over not having the line item, because at some point in time you will have rent, and utilities, etc...
This budget line item, even with $0, will serve as a visual reminder that this expense will come up at sometime.
Wow, that's a lot - how can I cut some of these costs without feeling squeezed?
Take advantage of savings made available to you.
Phone family plan
Apps & Streaming subscription costs add up. Do you need them all?
Review your expenses regularly

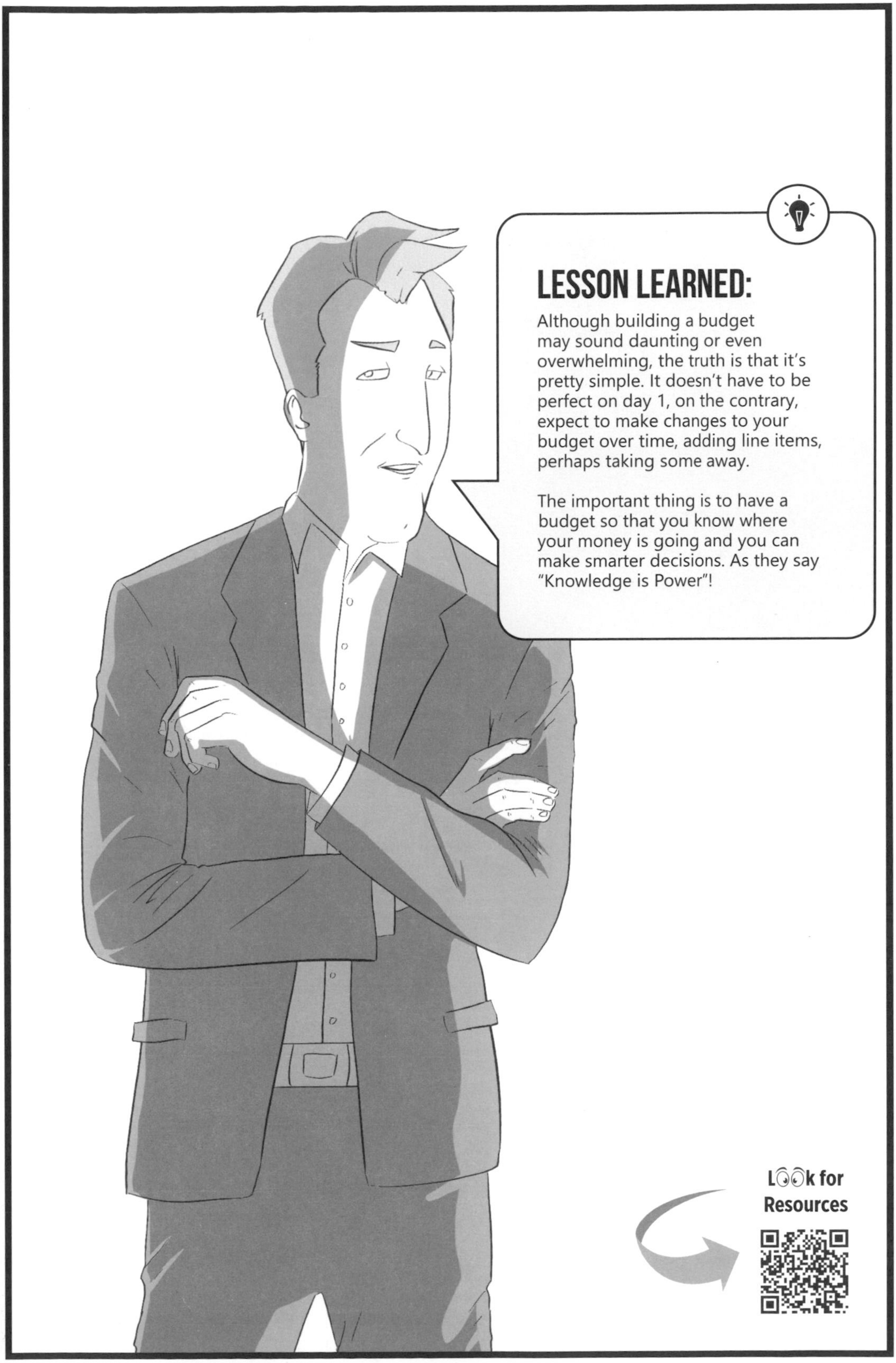
LESSON LEARNED:
Although building a budget may sound daunting or even overwhelming, the truth is that it's pretty simple. It doesn't have to be perfect on day 1, on the contrary, expect to make changes to your budget over time, adding line items, perhaps taking some away.
The important thing is to have a budget so that you know where your money is going and you can make smarter decisions. As they say "Knowledge is Power"!
Look for Resources

CHAPTER 4
SAVING VERSUS INVESTING

Key Definitions:
{Risk}
In the investing world risk is often defined as volatility and the probability of you losing money. The higher the expected return on investment, the high the risk and therefore the probability of losing money.

{Mutual Fund & ETF}
A pooled investment vehicle that allows you to invest in a diversified portfolio alongside other investors with much less money than would be required to own the same stocks or bonds individually.

{Return on Investment (ROI)}
Is a performance measure used to evaluate the efficiency or profitability of an investment or compare the efficiency of a number of different investments.

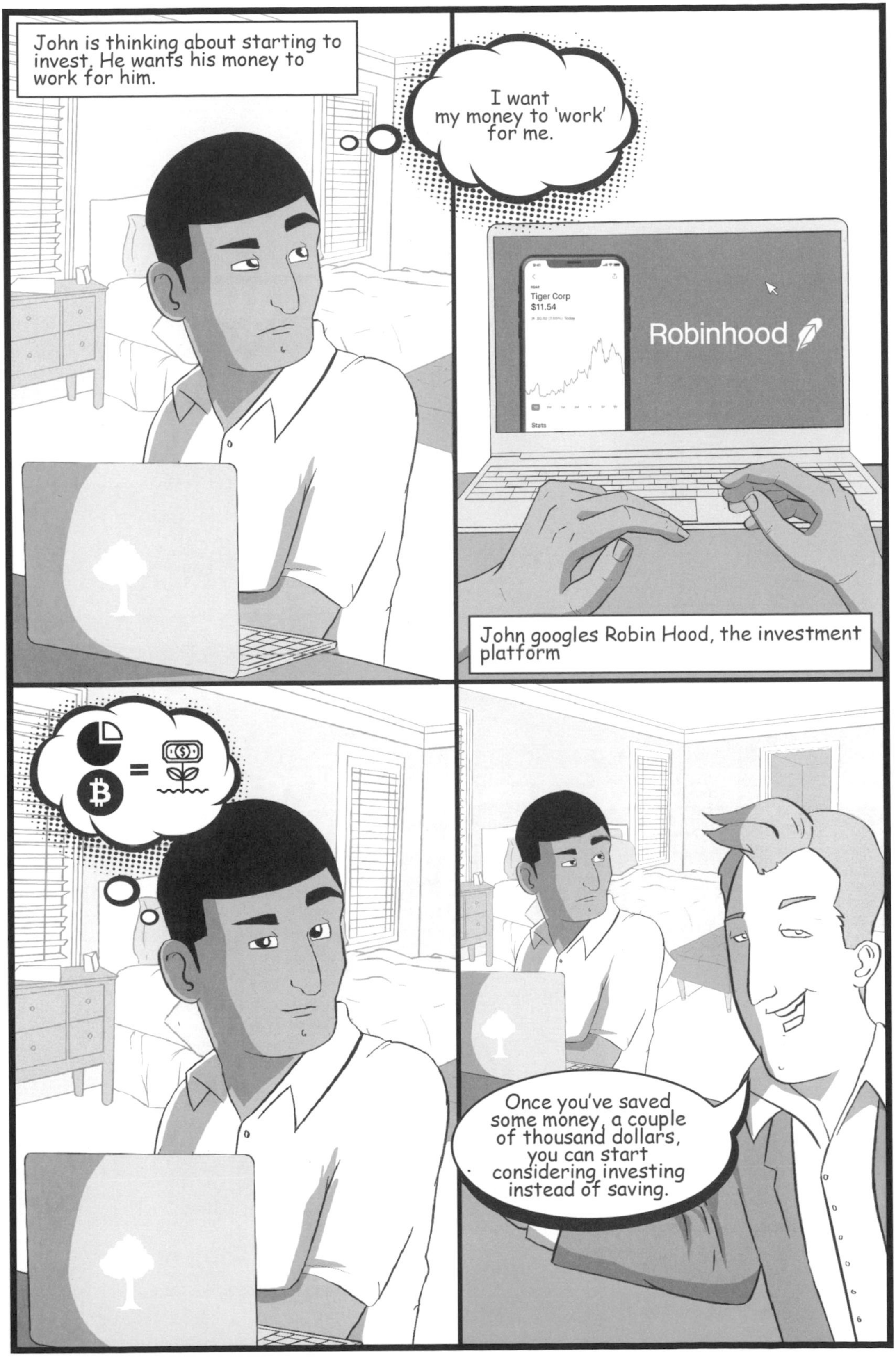
John is thinking about starting to invest. He wants his money to work for him.
I want my money to 'work' for me.
Tiger Corp
$11.54
Stats
Robinhood
John googles Robin Hood, the investment platform
Once you've saved some money, a couple of thousand dollars, you can start considering investing instead of saving.

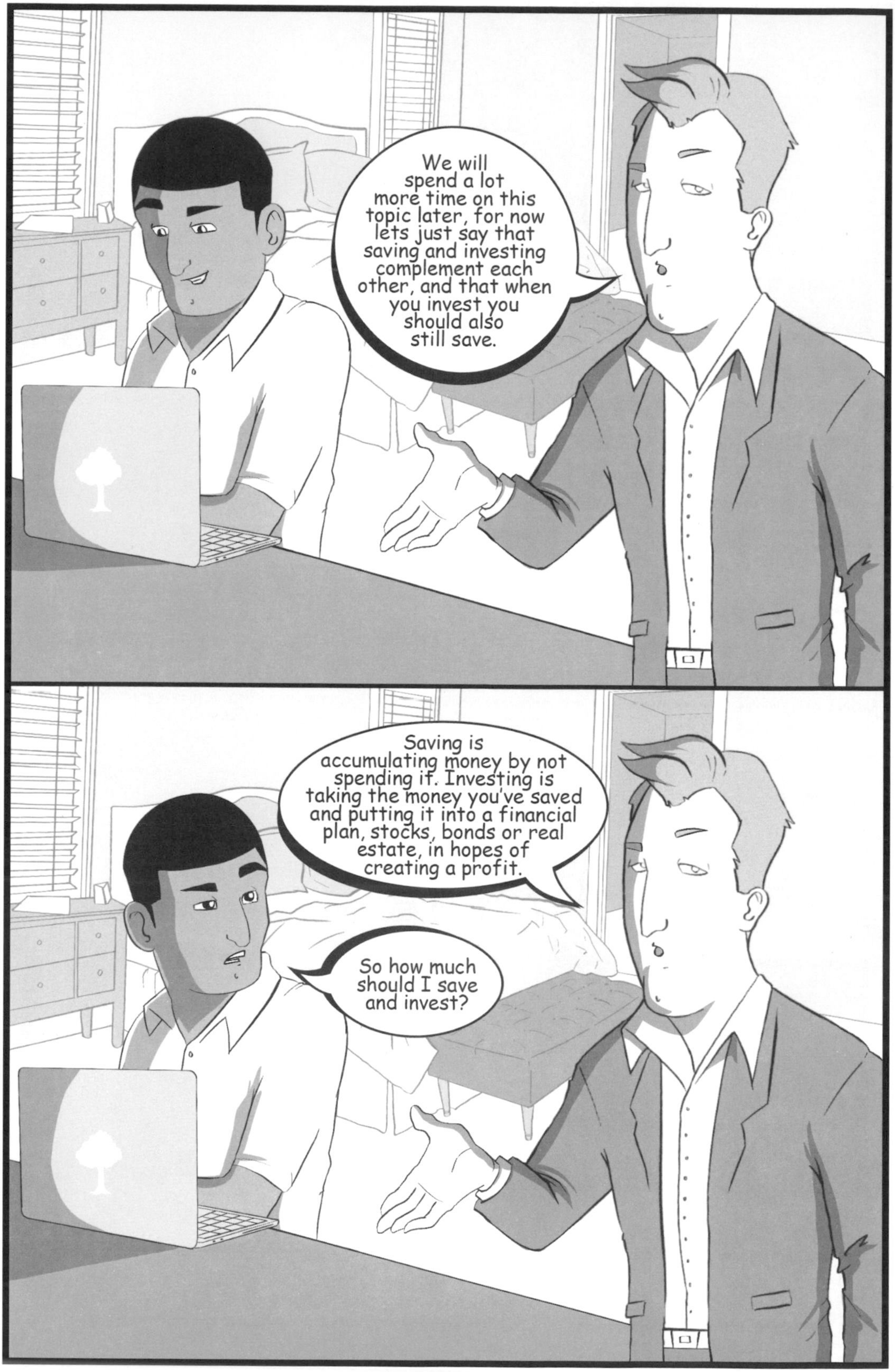
We will spend a lot more time on this topic later, for now lets just say that saving and investing complement each other, and that when you invest you should also still save.
Saving is accumulating money by not spending it. Investing is taking the money you've saved and putting it into a financial plan, stocks, bonds or real estate, in hopes of creating a profit.
So how much should I save and invest?

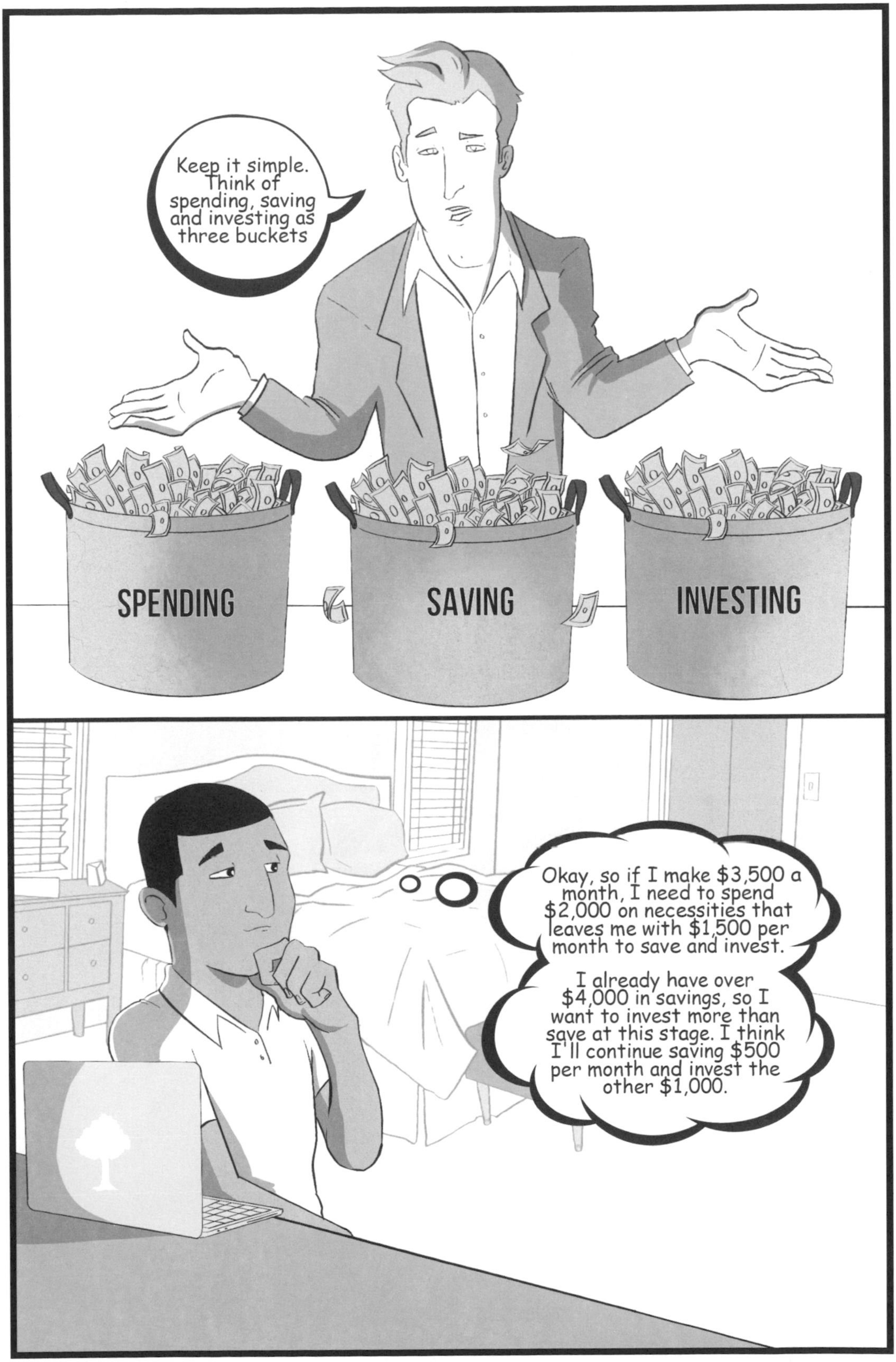
Keep it simple. Think of spending, saving and investing as three buckets
SPENDING
SAVING
INVESTING
Okay, so if I make $3,500 a month, I need to spend $2,000 on necessities that leaves me with $1,500 per month to save and invest.
I already have over $4,000 in savings, so I want to invest more than save at this stage. I think I'll continue saving $500 per month and invest the other $1,000.

These are the five different types of investment accounts everyone should consider.

5 TYPES OF INVESTMENT ACCOUNTS

BROKERAGE

This is a broad investment account, which is typically taxable, and allows you to make a wide array of investments and does not restrict withdrawals or changes of investments.

401(K)

This is a retirement account offered by most employers. You can choose to have money taken out of your paycheck and invested directly into the investments of your choice.

There is also a Roth 401 (k) option, which allows for tax free withdrawals when you retire (more on this later).

IRA

This is a self-directed retirement account. There is much flexibility and choice with these, including Roth options.

HEALTH SAVINGS ACCOUNT (HSA)

This is an account that allows for tax deductible contributions and tax free withdrawals for qualified medical expenses.

529 PLAN

This is a college savings account, with tax deferred growth and depending on the selection of plan, tax incentives.

You can use a 529 plan to pay for K-12 tuition, college tuition, apprenticeship programs, and student loan repayments

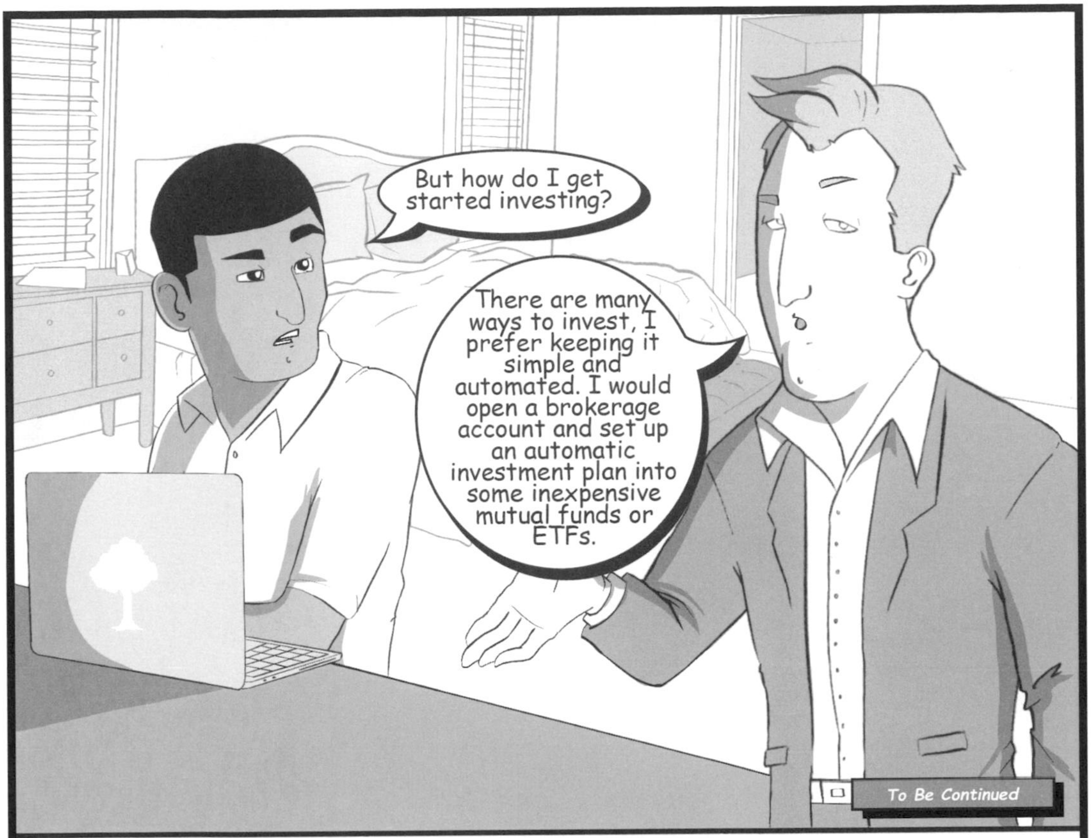
But how do I get started investing?
There are many ways to invest, I prefer keeping it simple and automated. I would open a brokerage account and set up an automatic investment plan into some inexpensive mutual funds or ETFs.
To Be Continued

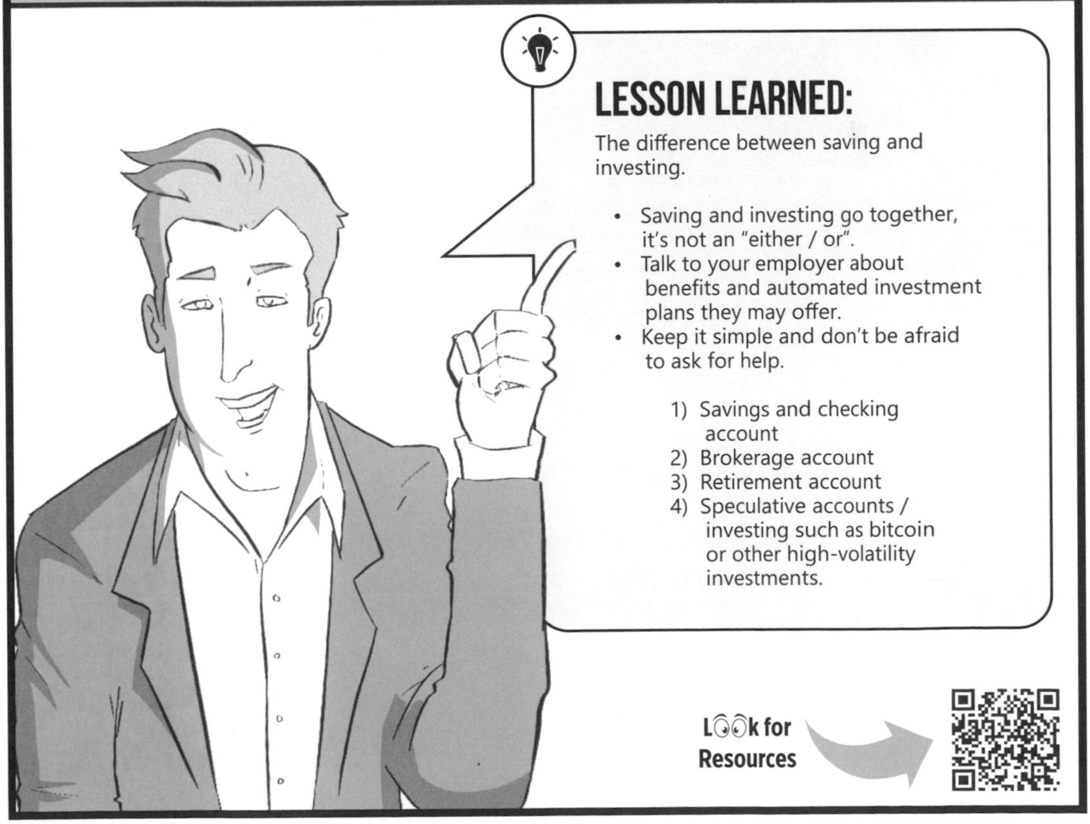
LESSON LEARNED:
The difference between saving and investing.
• Saving and investing go together, it's not an "either / or".
• Talk to your employer about benefits and automated investment plans they may offer.
• Keep it simple and don't be afraid to ask for help.
1) Savings and checking account
2) Brokerage account
3) Retirement account
4) Speculative accounts / investing such as bitcoin or other high-volatility investments.
Look for Resources

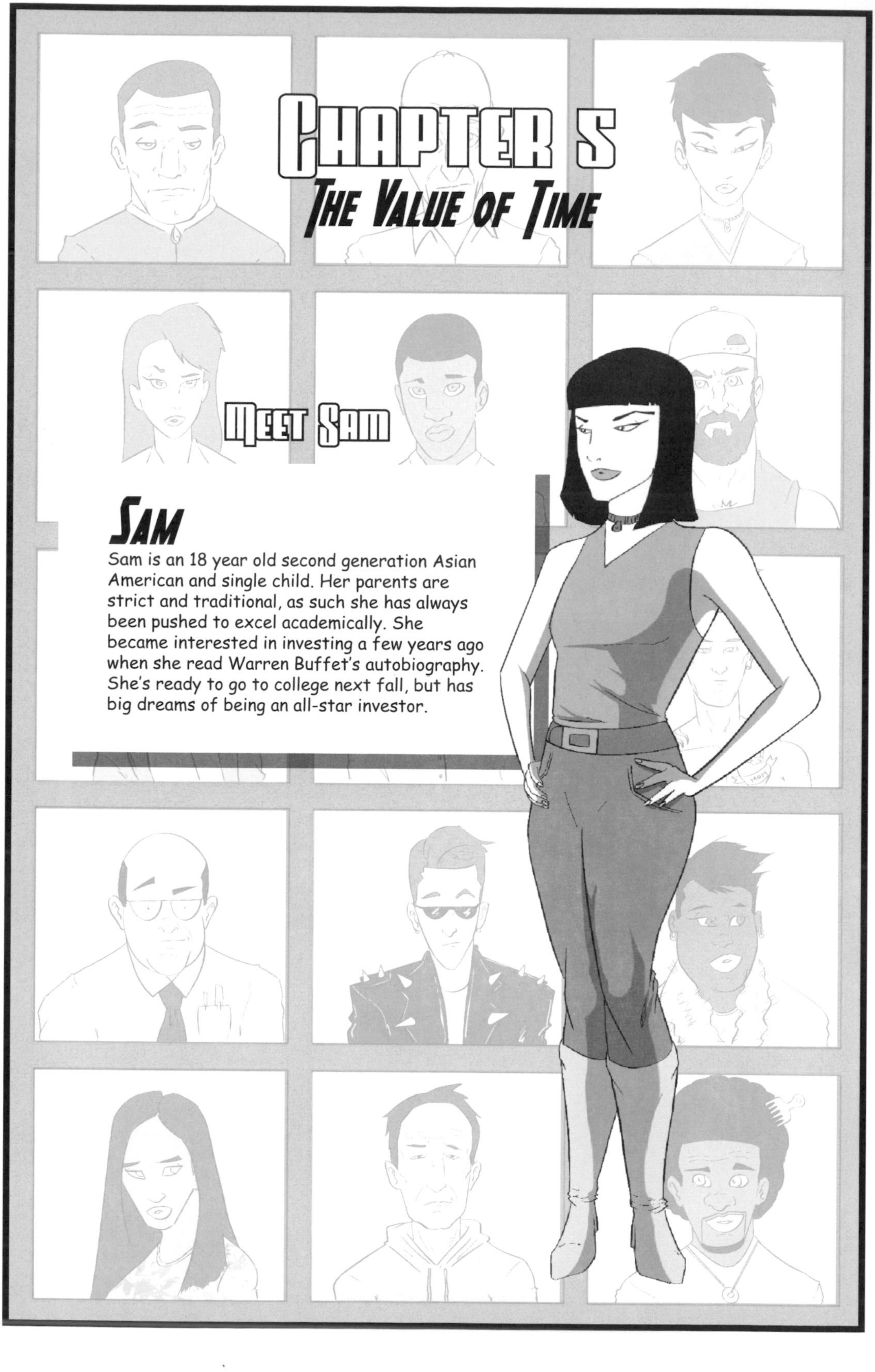
CHAPTER 5
THE VALUE OF TIME
MEET SAM
SAM
Sam is an 18 year old second generation Asian American and single child. Her parents are strict and traditional, as such she has always been pushed to excel academically. She became interested in investing a few years ago when she read Warren Buffet's autobiography. She's ready to go to college next fall, but has big dreams of being an all-star investor.

CHAPTER 5
THE VALUE OF TIME

Key Definitions:
{Asset Allocation}
The mix of stocks, bonds, real estate, crypto currencies and other investments that make up the entirety of your portfolio. Knowing your asset allocation helps understand your risks and expected returns.

{Compounding Returns}
Earning money on 'earned' money. For instance, you save and invest $1,000, which grows to $1,100 because your investment appreciated by 10%. The next year, the investment rises by another 10%, meaning you now have $1,210 - your initial $1,000, the $100 you earned last year, the $100 you earned on your initial investment this year, plus the $10 you earned on last year's $100 earnings.

{Inflation}
A general persistent rise in the price of goods and services, making them more expensive and therefore reducing the value of money. $1,000 50 years ago was worth a lot more than $1,000 today - because of inflation.

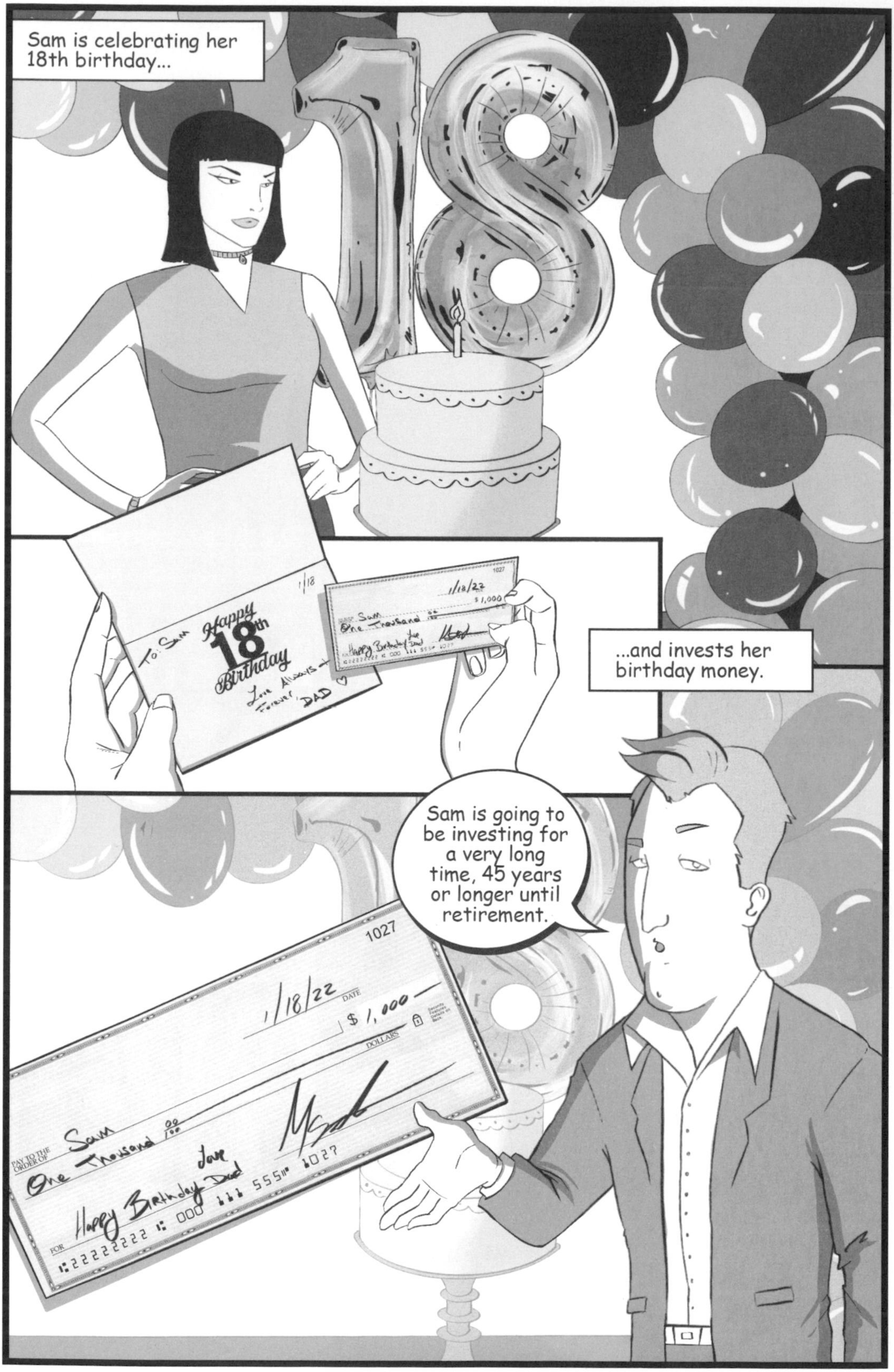
Sam is celebrating her 18th birthday...
...and invests her birthday money.
Sam is going to be investing for a very long time, 45 years or longer until retirement.

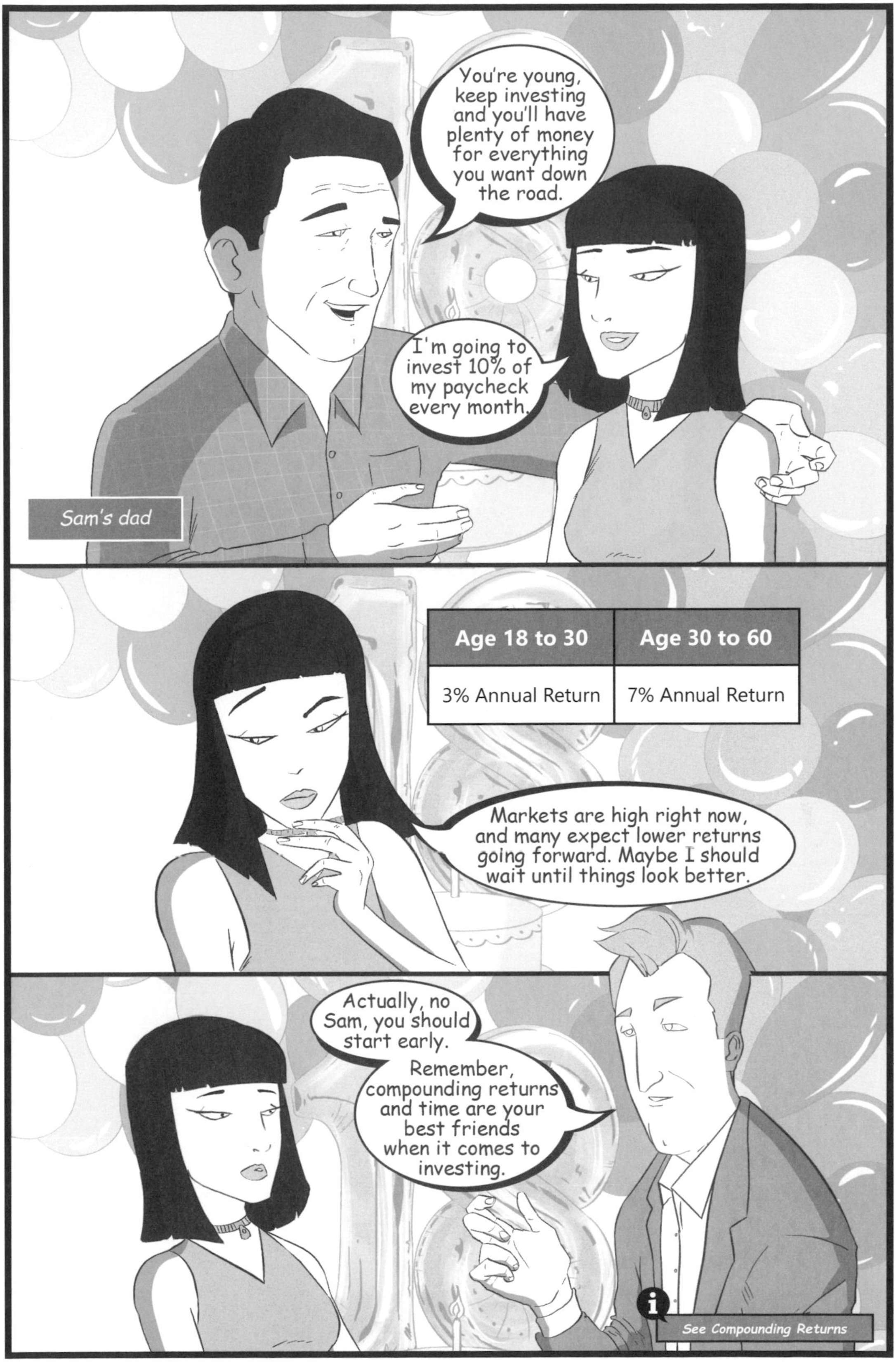
You're young, keep investing and you'll have plenty of money for everything you want down the road.
I'm going to invest 10% of my paycheck every month.
Sam's dad
Age 18 to 30
3% Annual Return
Age 30 to 60
7% Annual Return
Markets are high right now, and many expect lower returns going forward. Maybe I should wait until things look better.
Actually, no Sam, you should start early.
Remember, compounding returns and time are your best friends when it comes to investing.
See Compounding Returns

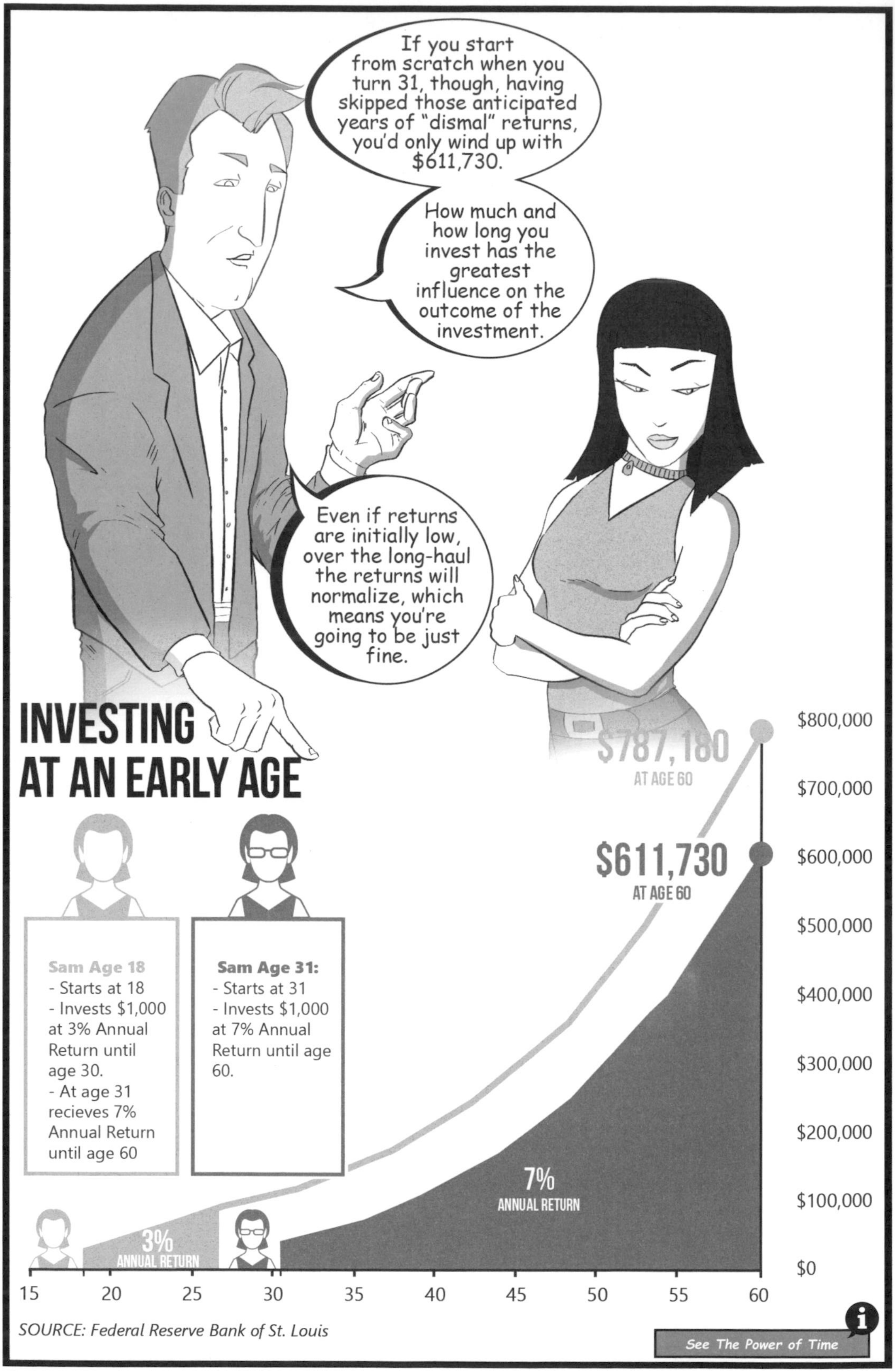

If you start from scratch when you turn 31, though, having skipped those anticipated years of "dismal" returns, you'd only wind up with $611,730.
How much and how long you invest has the greatest influence on the outcome of the investment.
Even if returns are initially low, over the long-haul the returns will normalize, which means you're going to be just fine.
INVESTING AT AN EARLY AGE
$787,180
AT AGE 60
$611,730
AT AGE 60
Sam Age 18
- Starts at 18
- Invests $1,000 at 3% Annual Return until age 30.
- At age 31 recieves 7% Annual Return until age 60
Sam Age 31:
- Starts at 31
- Invests $1,000 at 7% Annual Return until age 60.
3%
ANNUAL RETURN
7%
ANNUAL RETURN
$800,000
$700,000
$600,000
$500,000
$400,000
$300,000
$200,000
$100,000
$0
15
20
25
30
35
40
45
50
55
60
SOURCE: Federal Reserve Bank of St. Louis
See The Power of Time

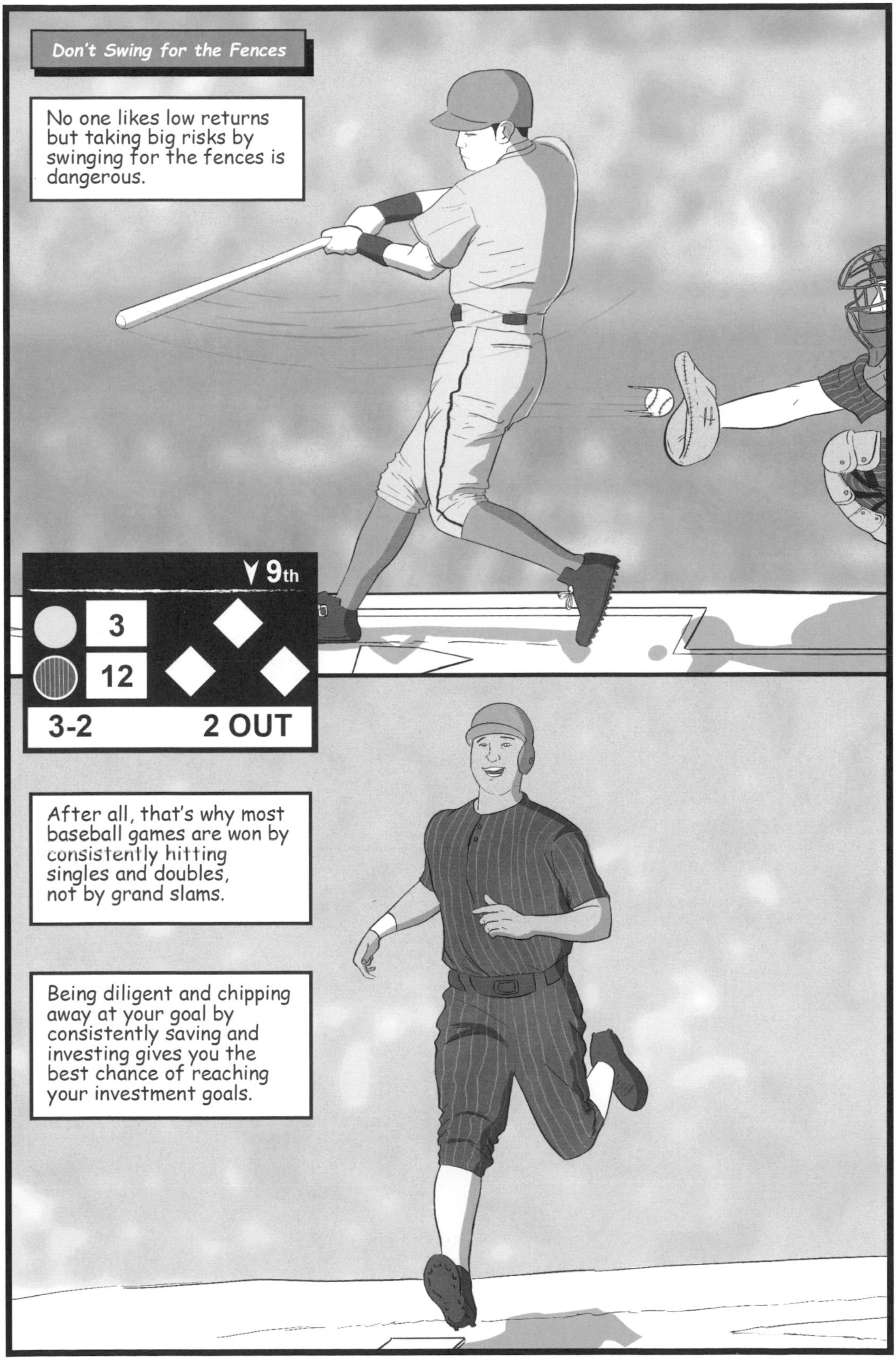
Don't Swing for the Fences
No one likes low returns but taking big risks by swinging for the fences is dangerous.
9th
3
12
3-2
2 OUT
After all, that's why most baseball games are won by consistently hitting singles and doubles, not by grand slams.
Being diligent and chipping away at your goal by consistently saving and investing gives you the best chance of reaching your investment goals.

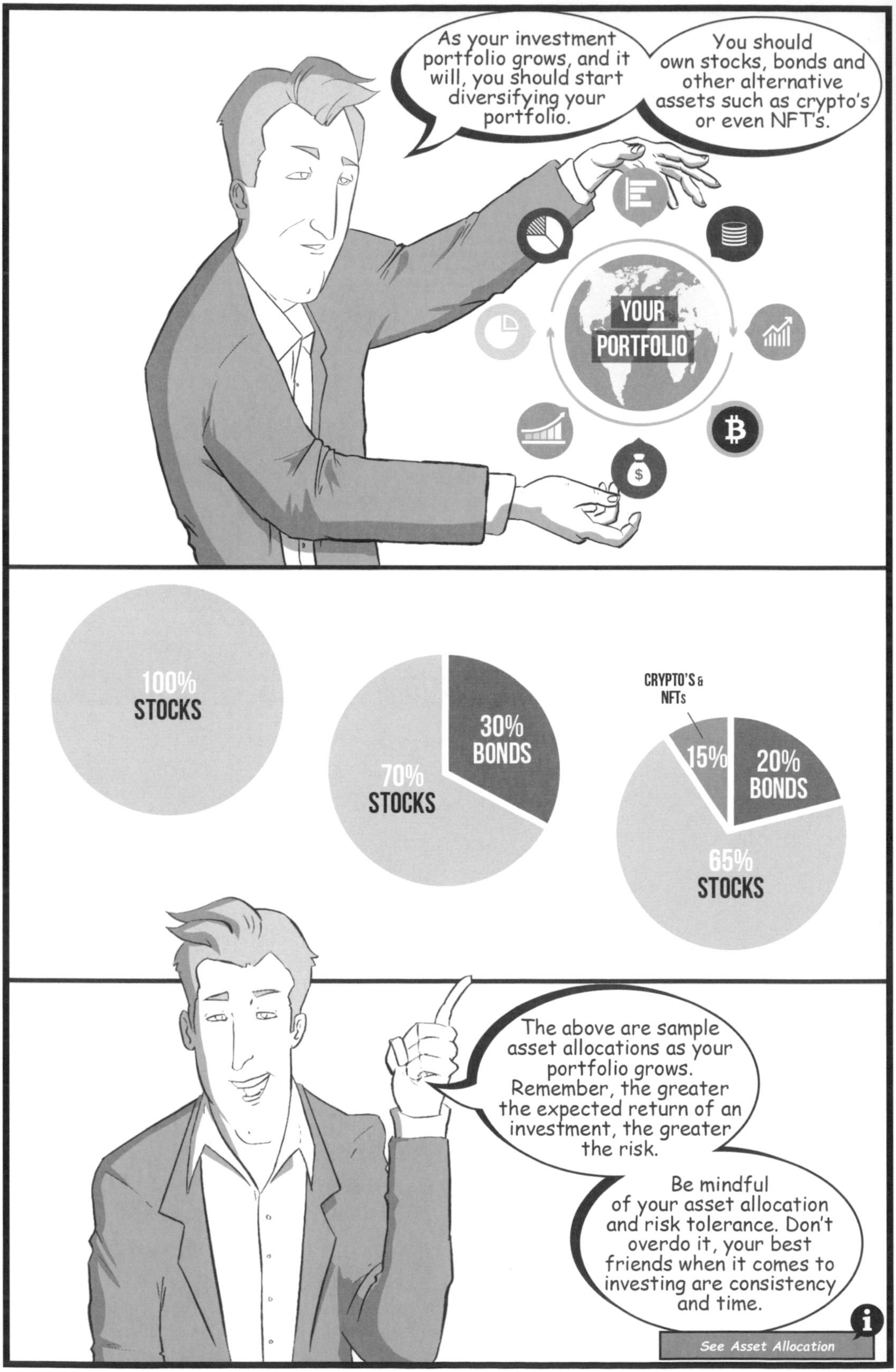

As your investment portfolio grows, and it will, you should start diversifying your portfolio.
You should own stocks, bonds and other alternative assets such as crypto's or even NFT's.
YOUR PORTFOLIO
100% STOCKS
30% BONDS
70% STOCKS
CRYPTO'S & NFTs
15%
20% BONDS
65% STOCKS
The above are sample asset allocations as your portfolio grows. Remember, the greater the expected return of an investment, the greater the risk.
Be mindful of your asset allocation and risk tolerance. Don't overdo it, your best friends when it comes to investing are consistency and time.
See Asset Allocation

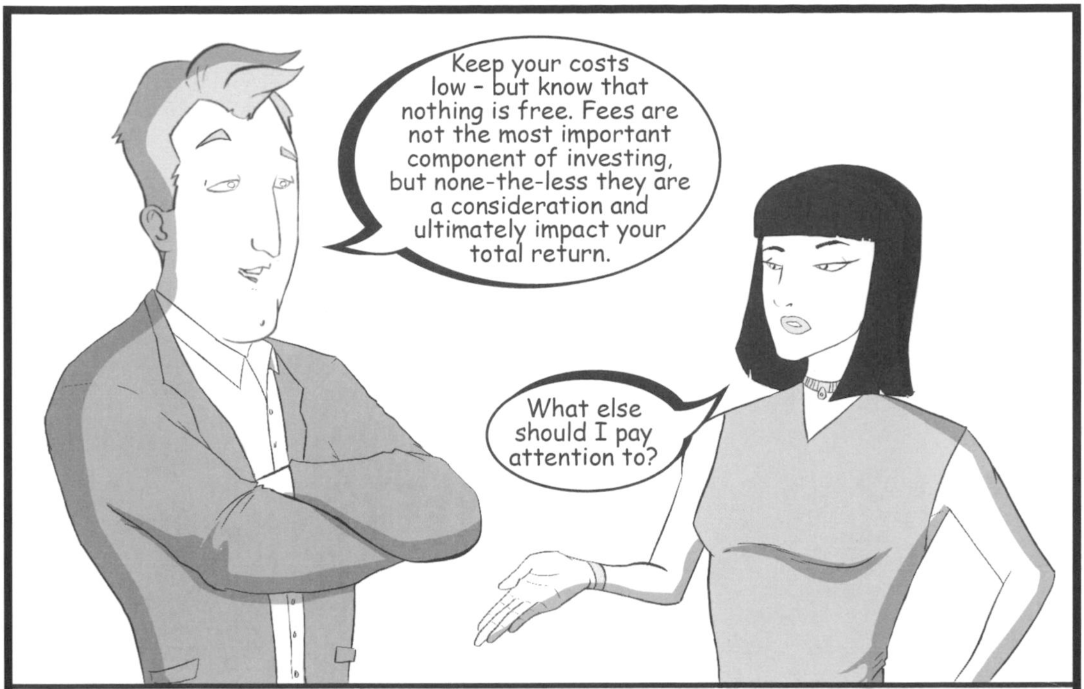
Keep your costs low - but know that nothing is free. Fees are not the most important component of investing, but none-the-less they are a consideration and ultimately impact your total return.
What else should I pay attention to?

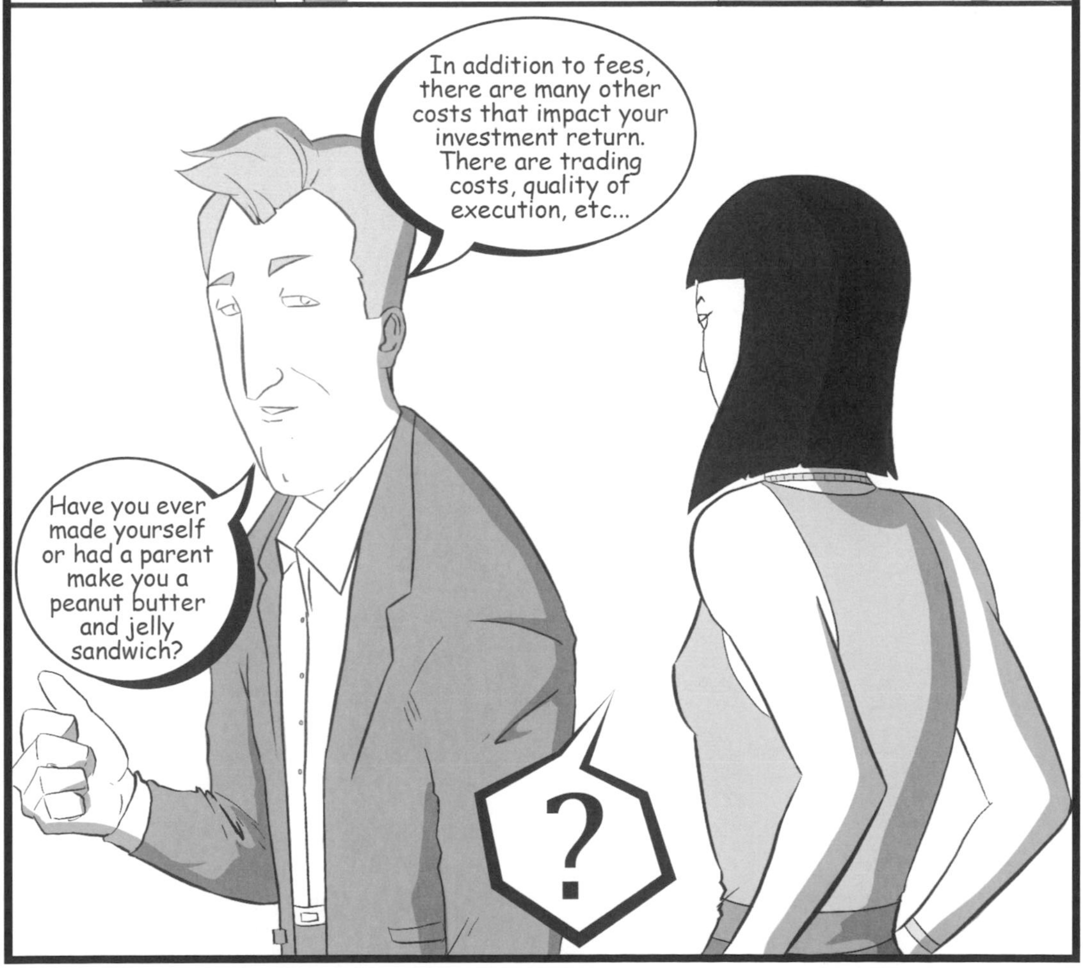
In addition to fees, there are many other costs that impact your investment return. There are trading costs, quality of execution, etc...
Have you ever made yourself or had a parent make you a peanut butter and jelly sandwich?
?

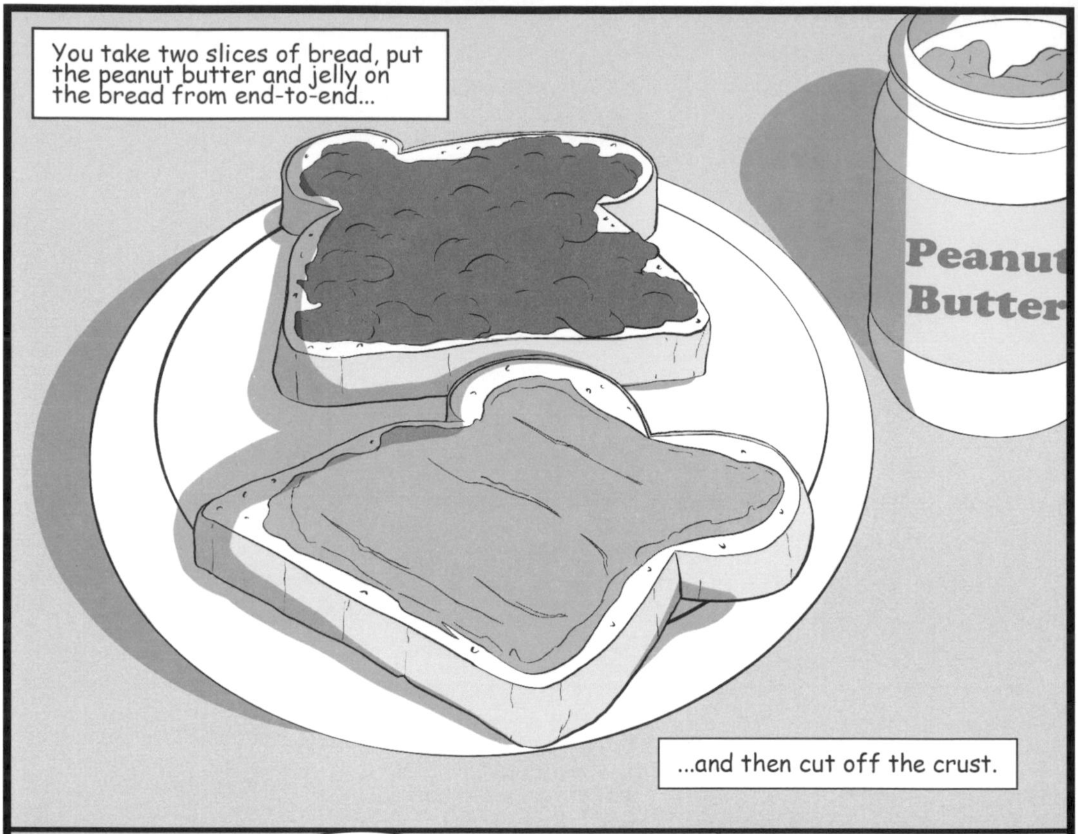
You take two slices of bread, put the peanut butter and jelly on the bread from end-to-end...
Peanut Butter
...and then cut off the crust.

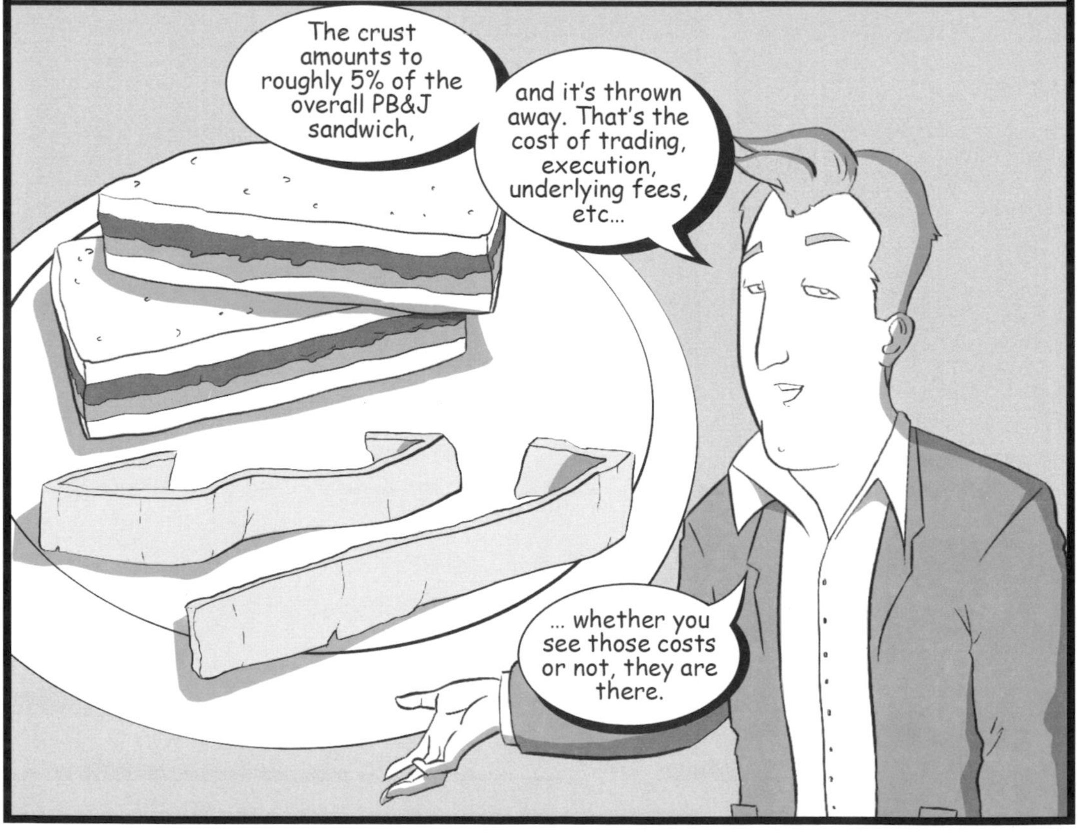
The crust amounts to roughly 5% of the overall PB&J sandwich,
and it's thrown away. That's the cost of trading, execution, underlying fees, etc...
... whether you see those costs or not, they are there.

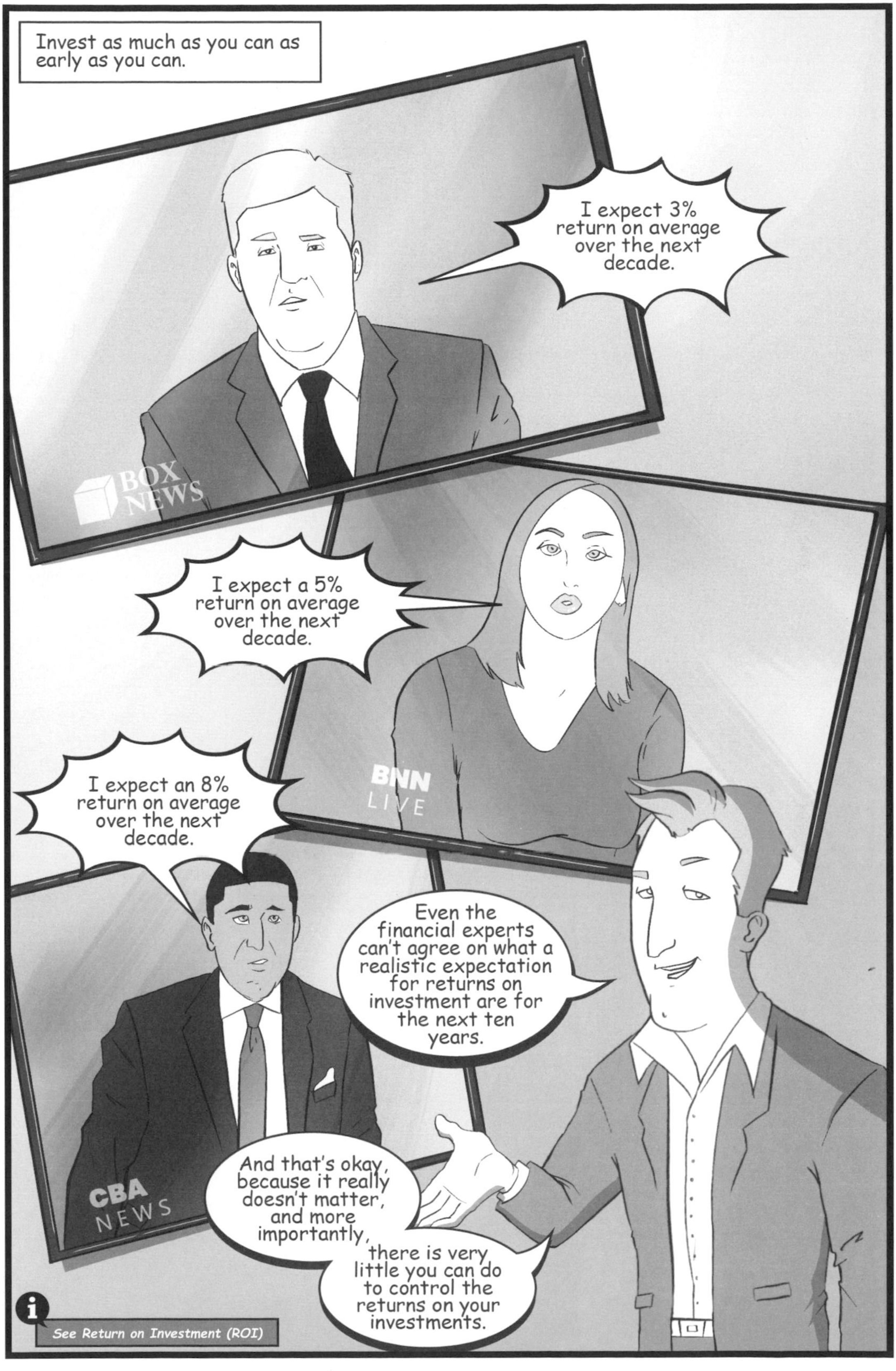
Invest as much as you can as early as you can.
I expect 3% return on average over the next decade.
BOX NEWS
I expect a 5% return on average over the next decade.
BNN LIVE
I expect an 8% return on average over the next decade.
Even the financial experts can't agree on what a realistic expectation for returns on investment are for the next ten years.
CBA NEWS
And that's okay, because it really doesn't matter, and more importantly,
there is very little you can do to control the returns on your investments.
See Return on Investment (ROI)

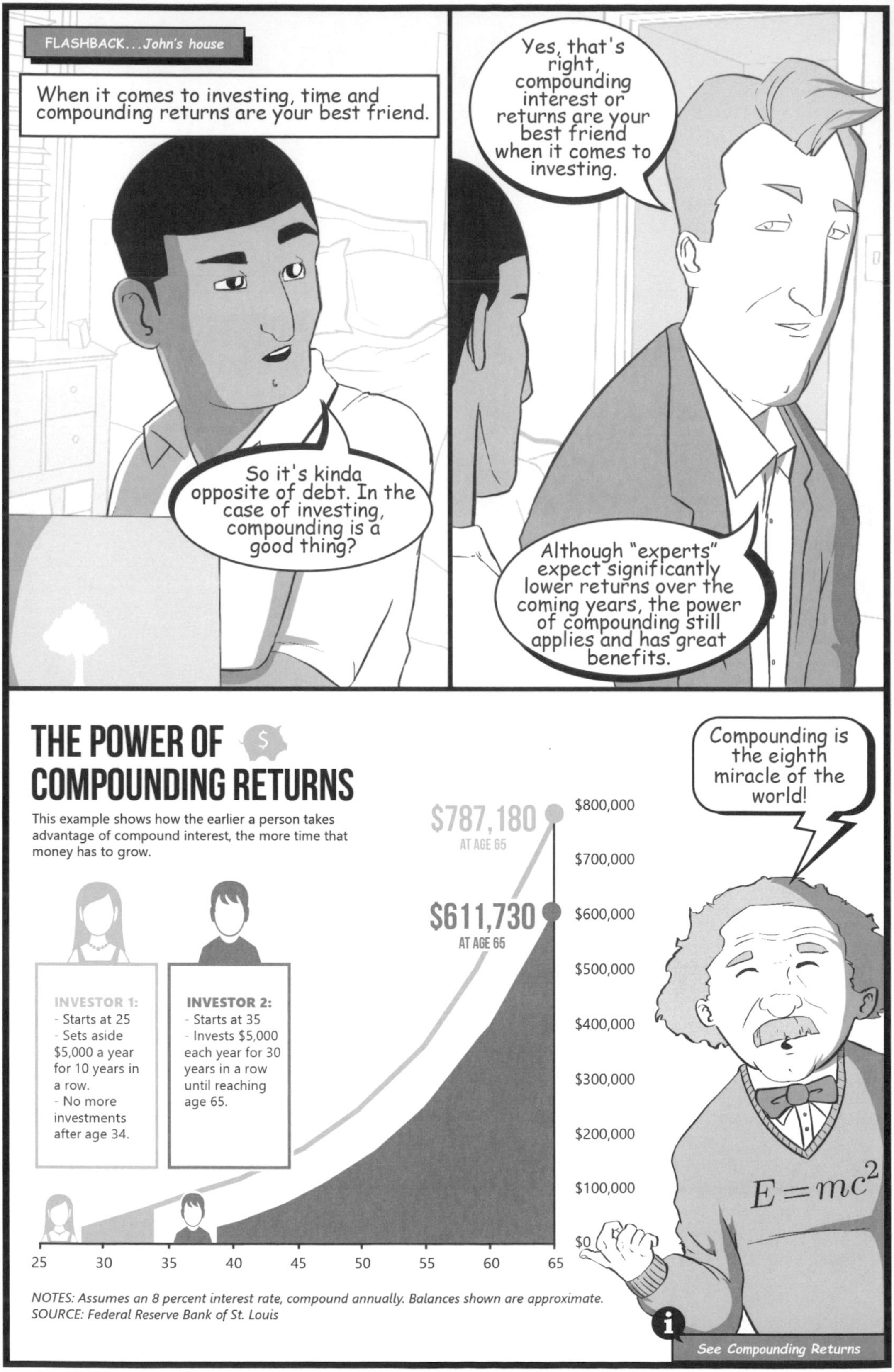
FLASHBACK...John's house
When it comes to investing, time and compounding returns are your best friend.
So it's kinda opposite of debt. In the case of investing, compounding is a good thing?
Yes, that's right, compounding interest or returns are your best friend when it comes to investing.
Although "experts" expect significantly lower returns over the coming years, the power of compounding still applies and has great benefits.
THE POWER OF COMPOUNDING RETURNS
This example shows how the earlier a person takes advantage of compound interest, the more time that money has to grow.
INVESTOR 1:
- Starts at 25
- Sets aside $5,000 a year for 10 years in a row.
- No more investments after age 34.
INVESTOR 2:
- Starts at 35
- Invests $5,000 each year for 30 years in a row until reaching age 65.
$787,180 AT AGE 65
$611,730 AT AGE 65
$800,000
$700,000
$600,000
$500,000
$400,000
$300,000
$200,000
$100,000
$0
25 30 35 40 45 50 55 60 65
NOTES: Assumes an 8 percent interest rate, compound annually. Balances shown are approximate.
SOURCE: Federal Reserve Bank of St. Louis
Compounding is the eighth miracle of the world!
E=mc2
See Compounding Returns

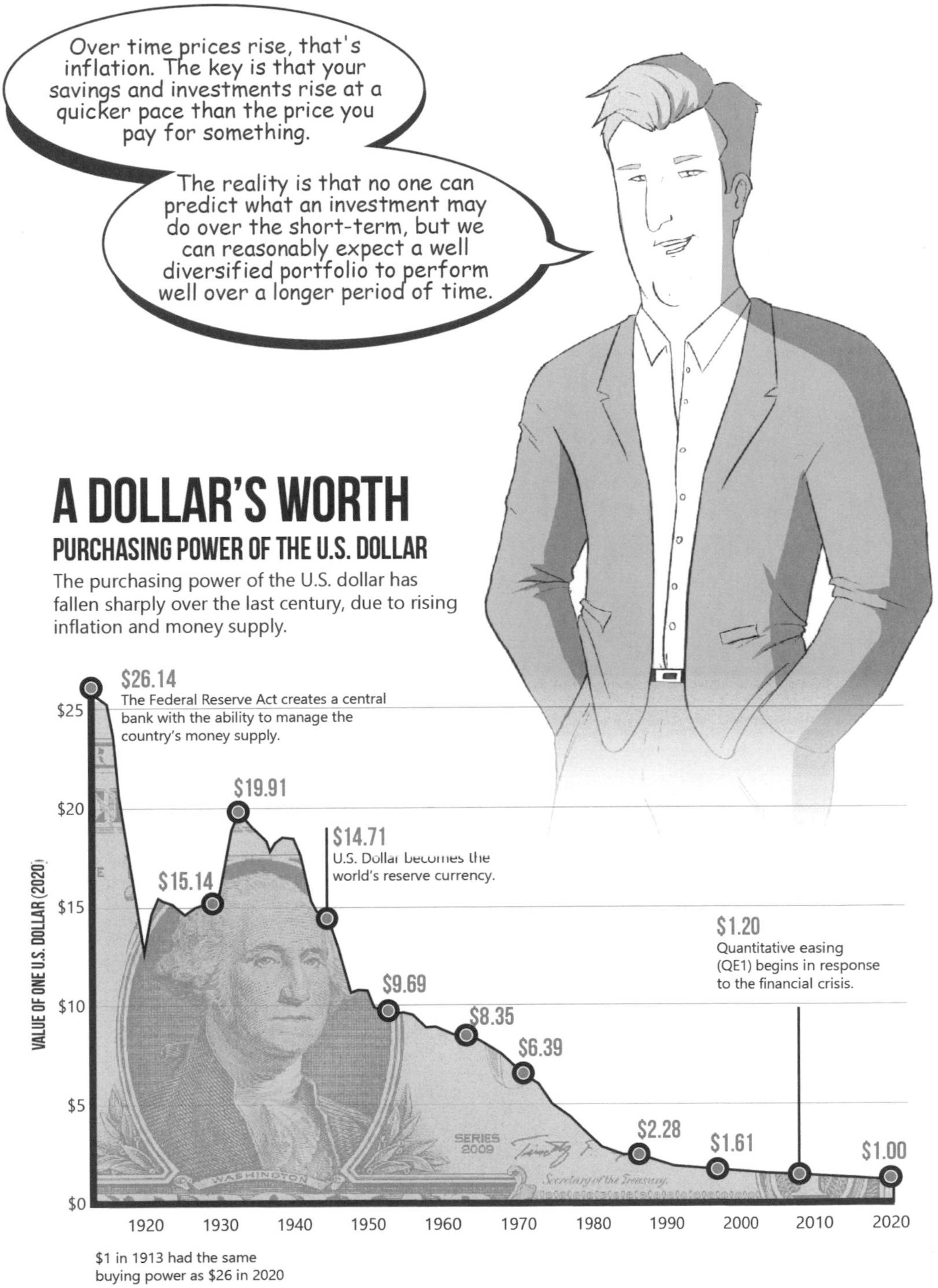

Over time prices rise, that's inflation. The key is that your savings and investments rise at a quicker pace than the price you pay for something.

The reality is that no one can predict what an investment may do over the short-term, but we can reasonably expect a well diversified portfolio to perform well over a longer period of time.

A DOLLAR'S WORTH

PURCHASING POWER OF THE U.S. DOLLAR

The purchasing power of the U.S. dollar has fallen sharply over the last century, due to rising inflation and money supply.

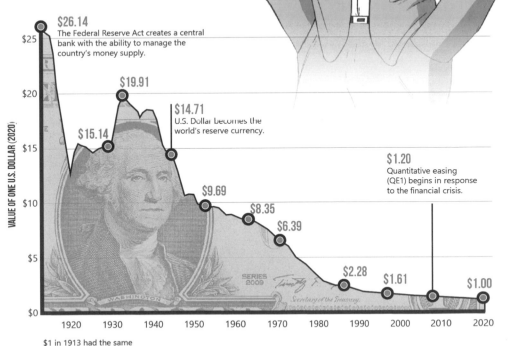

$26.14
The Federal Reserve Act creates a central bank with the ability to manage the country's money supply.

$19.91

$14.71
U.S. Dollar becomes the world's reserve currency.

$15.14

$1.20
Quantitative easing (QE1) begins in response to the financial crisis.

$9.69

$8.35

$6.39

$2.28

$1.61

$1.00

VALUE OF ONE U.S. DOLLAR (2020)

$25 $20 $15 $10 $5 $0

1920 1930 1940 1950 1960 1970 1980 1990 2000 2010 2020

$1 in 1913 had the same buying power as $26 in 2020

SOURCE: Bureau of Labor Statistics - Consumer Price Index, Morris County Library of Historic Prices

i

See Inflation

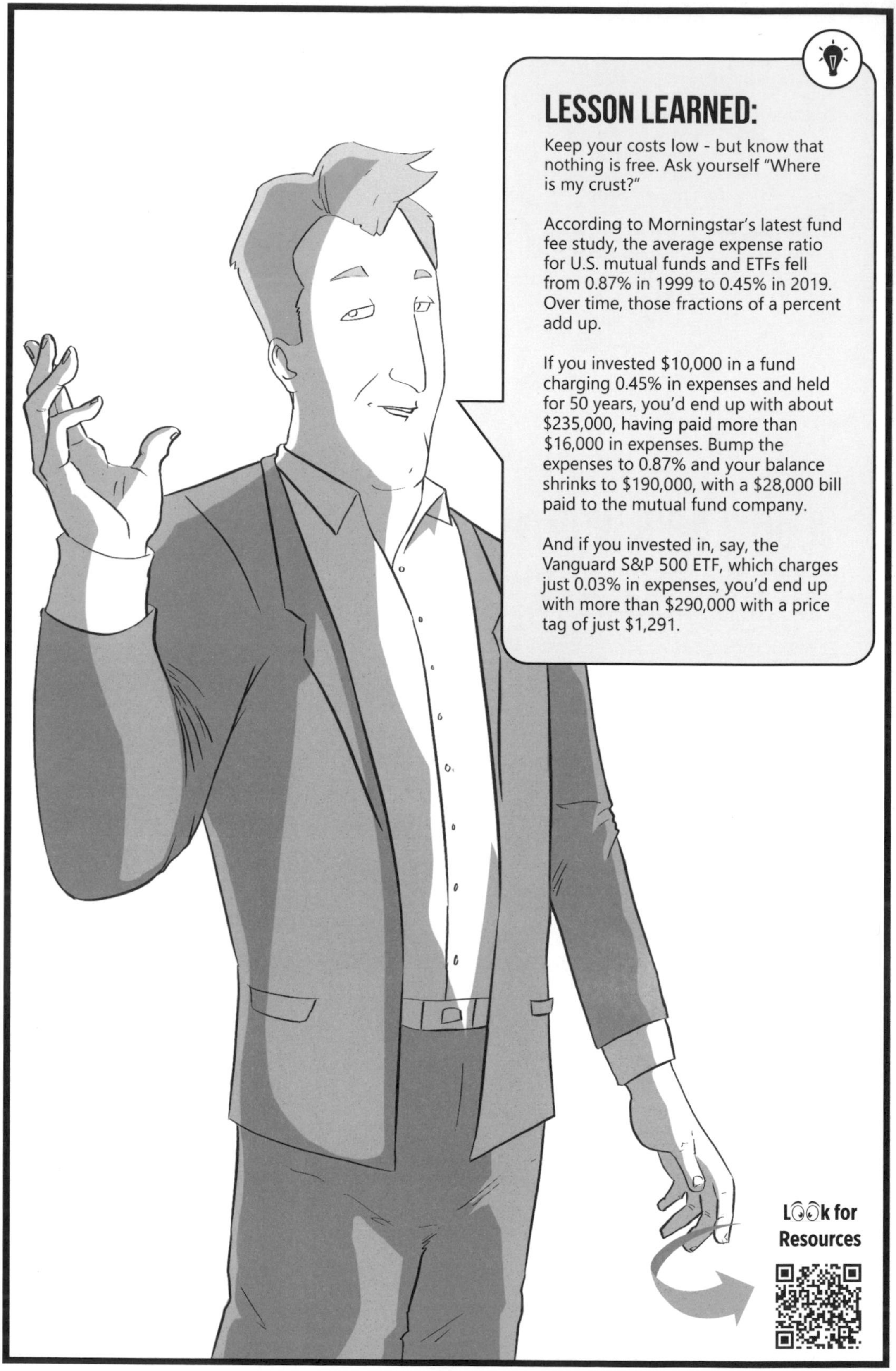
LESSON LEARNED:
Keep your costs low - but know that nothing is free. Ask yourself "Where is my crust?"
According to Morningstar's latest fund fee study, the average expense ratio for U.S. mutual funds and ETFs fell from 0.87% in 1999 to 0.45% in 2019. Over time, those fractions of a percent add up.
If you invested $10,000 in a fund charging 0.45% in expenses and held for 50 years, you'd end up with about $235,000, having paid more than $16,000 in expenses. Bump the expenses to 0.87% and your balance shrinks to $190,000, with a $28,000 bill paid to the mutual fund company.
And if you invested in, say, the Vanguard S&P 500 ETF, which charges just 0.03% in expenses, you'd end up with more than $290,000 with a price tag of just $1,291.
Look for Resources

CHAPTER 6
THE TEMPTATION OF
RENT-TO-OWN AND BUY NOW / PAY LATER

MEET EVA

EVA

Eva, and her four sisters were born into a rough home with divorced parents in East Los Angeles, California. They were surrounded by gang violence their entire youths; however, Eva was different from her sisters. She was a straight "A" student through high school, even though she got pregnant at age 16 and gave birth to her first daughter, Melissa, at age 17. She went to community college, but never found it possible to handle a young baby, work, and school. When she got pregnant with Juliet, her second, at 18 she focused on family and putting food on the table. She became an assistant at a law firm, and as her children grew older and began going to school full time, she got a night-shift job to make extra money. She saved as much as she could and was finally able to rent a larger three-bedroom apartment. Her dream is to eventually have a house with a back yard that she can enjoy with her daughters, now 10 and 8, as well as her pet rabbit and 2 cats.

Chapter 6
The Temptation of Rent-to-Own and Buy Now / Pay Later

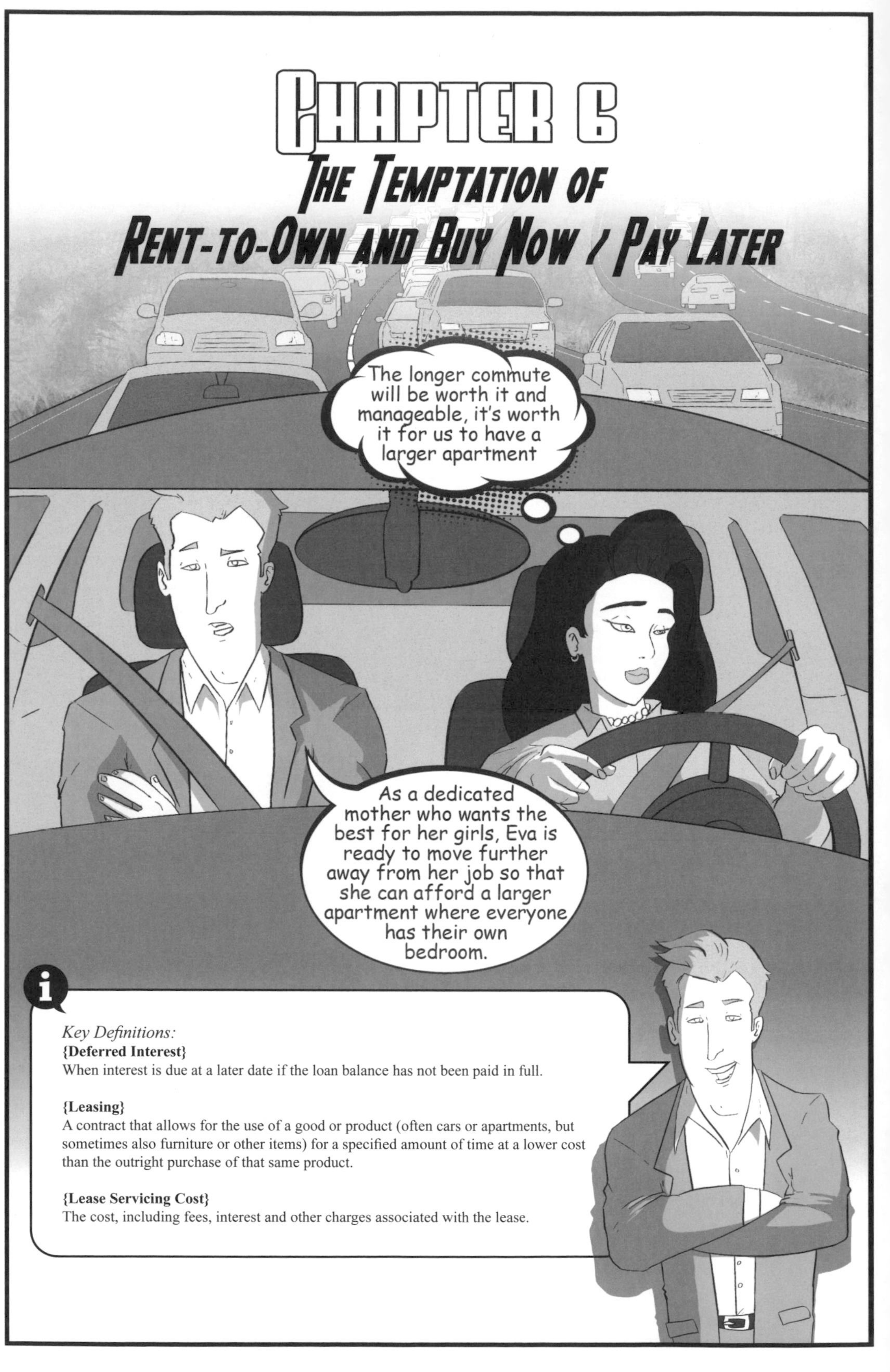
The longer commute will be worth it and manageable, it's worth it for us to have a larger apartment
As a dedicated mother who wants the best for her girls, Eva is ready to move further away from her job so that she can afford a larger apartment where everyone has their own bedroom.

Key Definitions:

{Deferred Interest}
When interest is due at a later date if the loan balance has not been paid in full.

{Leasing}
A contract that allows for the use of a good or product (often cars or apartments, but sometimes also furniture or other items) for a specified amount of time at a lower cost than the outright purchase of that same product.

{Lease Servicing Cost}
The cost, including fees, interest and other charges associated with the lease.

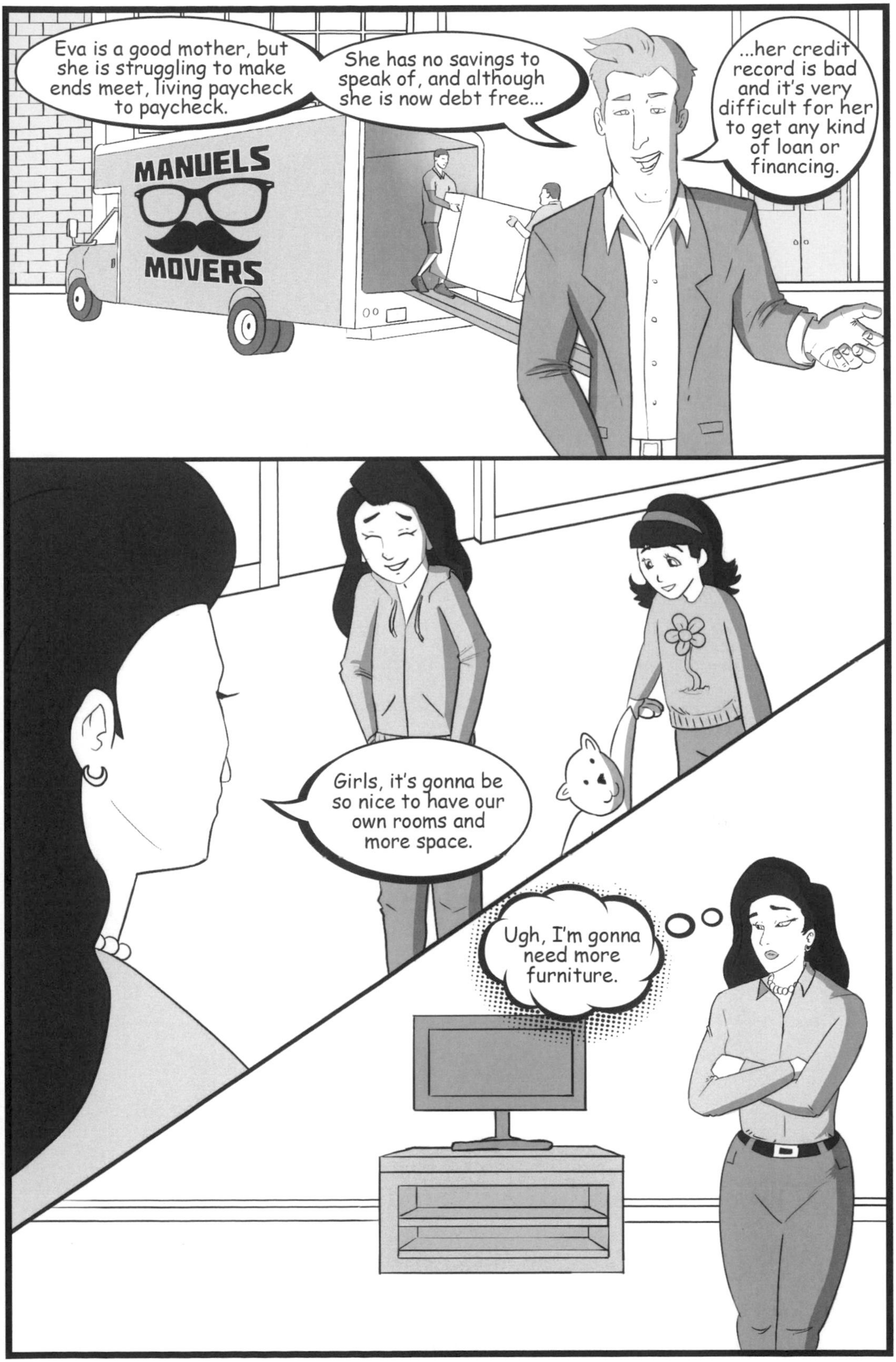
Eva is a good mother, but she is struggling to make ends meet, living paycheck to paycheck.
She has no savings to speak of, and although she is now debt free...
...her credit record is bad and it's very difficult for her to get any kind of loan or financing.
MANUELS
MOVERS
Girls, it's gonna be so nice to have our own rooms and more space.
Ugh, I'm gonna need more furniture.

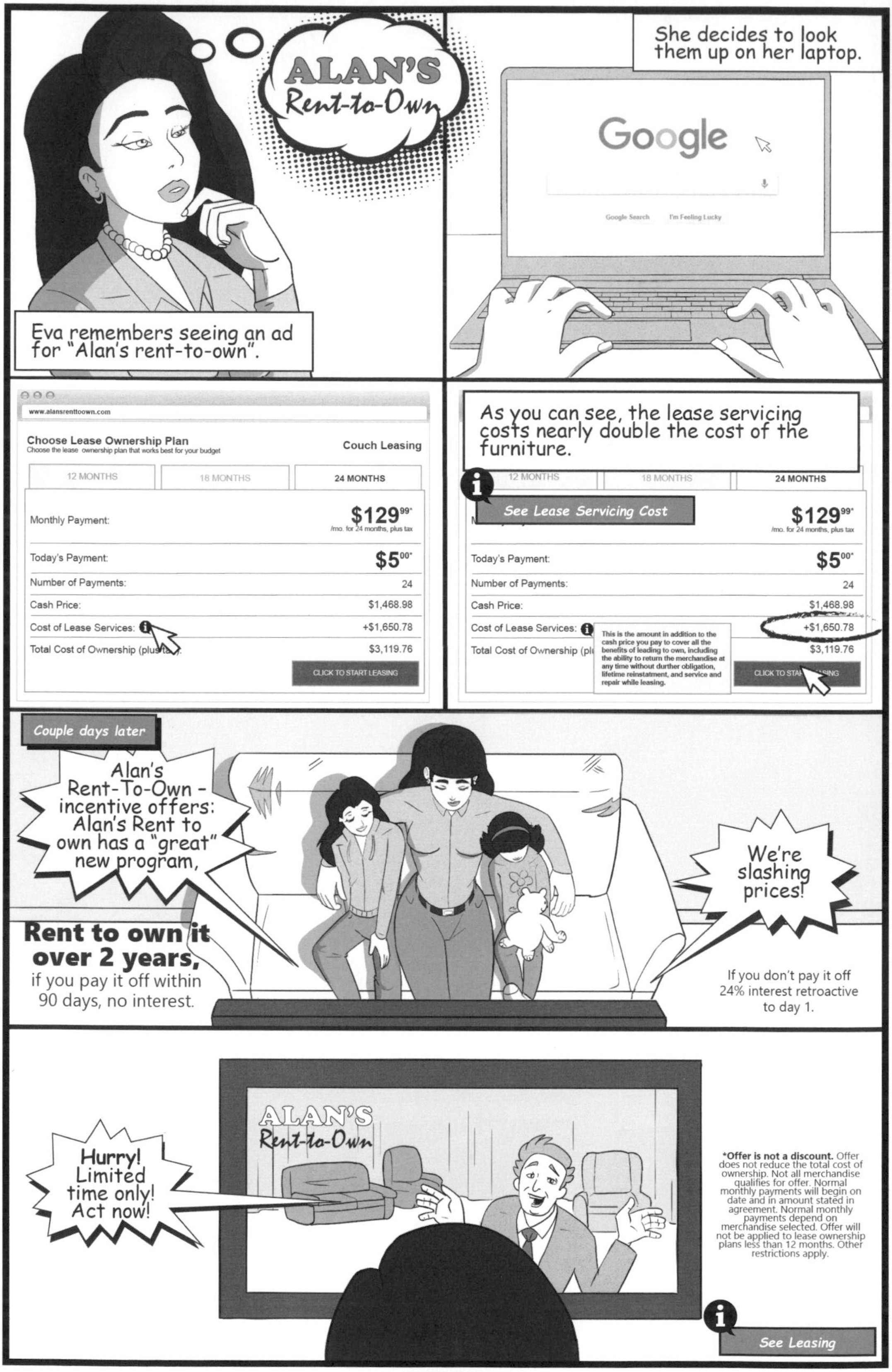
ALAN'S Rent-to-Own
Eva remembers seeing an ad for "Alan's rent-to-own".
She decides to look them up on her laptop.
Google
Google Search
I'm Feeling Lucky
www.alansrenttoown.com
Choose Lease Ownership Plan
Choose the lease ownership plan that works best for your budget
Couch Leasing
12 MONTHS
18 MONTHS
24 MONTHS
Monthly Payment: $129.99* /mo. for 24 months, plus tax
Today's Payment: $5.00*
Number of Payments: 24
Cash Price: $1,468.98
Cost of Lease Services: +$1,650.78
Total Cost of Ownership (plus tax): $3,119.76
CLICK TO START LEASING
As you can see, the lease servicing costs nearly double the cost of the furniture.
See Lease Servicing Cost
This is the amount in addition to the cash price you pay to cover all the benefits of leading to own, including the ability to return the merchandise at any time without durther obligation, lifetime reinstatment, and service and repair while leasing.
Couple days later
Alan's Rent-To-Own - incentive offers: Alan's Rent to own has a "great" new program,
Rent to own it over 2 years,
if you pay it off within 90 days, no interest.
We're slashing prices!
If you don't pay it off 24% interest retroactive to day 1.
ALAN'S Rent-to-Own
Hurry! Limited time only! Act now!
*Offer is not a discount. Offer does not reduce the total cost of ownership. Not all merchandise qualifies for offer. Normal monthly payments will begin on date and in amount stated in agreement. Normal monthly payments depend on merchandise selected. Offer will not be applied to lease ownership plans less than 12 months. Other restrictions apply.
See Leasing

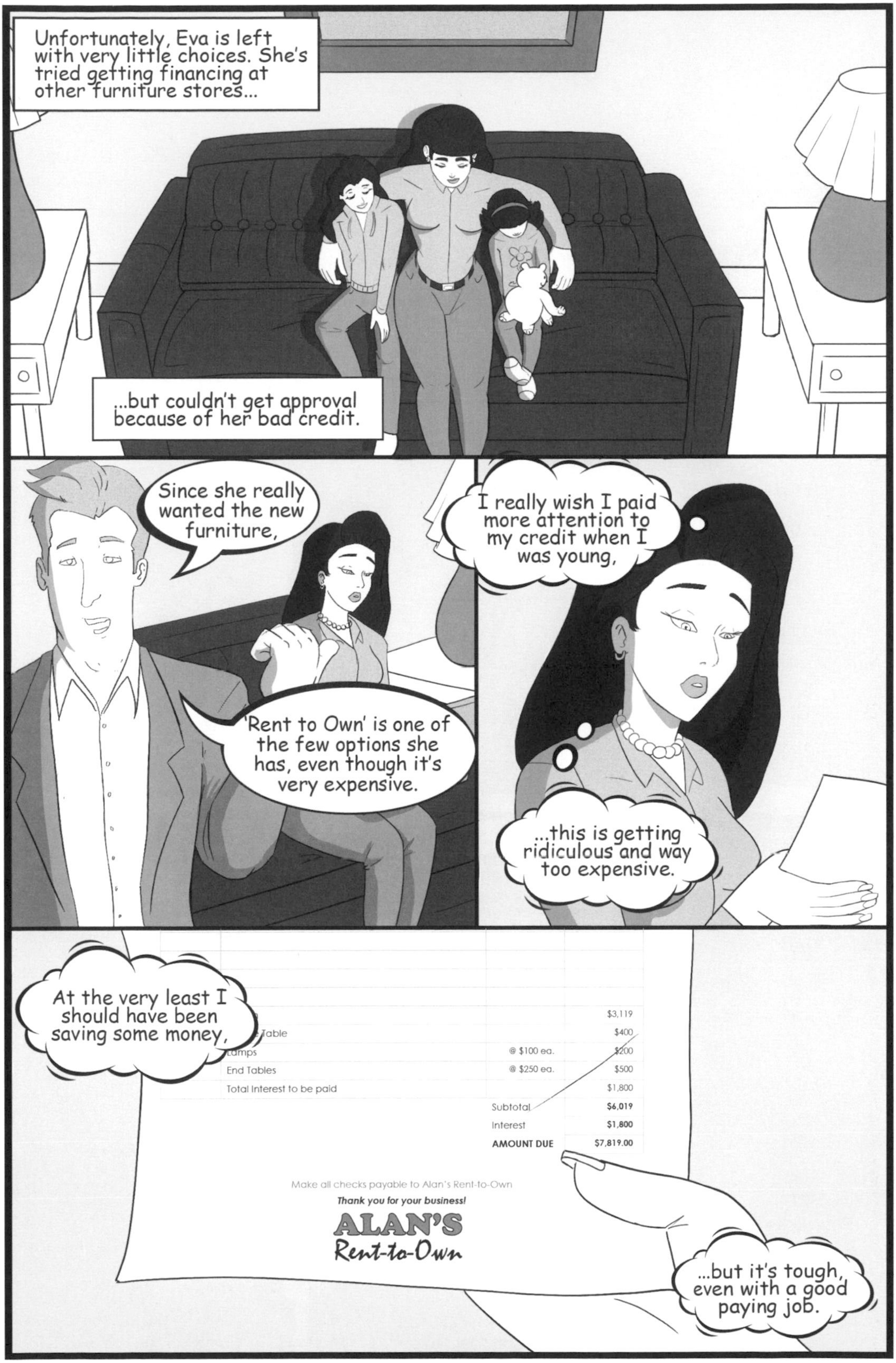

Unfortunately, Eva is left with very little choices. She's tried getting financing at other furniture stores...
...but couldn't get approval because of her bad credit.
Since she really wanted the new furniture,
'Rent to Own' is one of the few options she has, even though it's very expensive.
I really wish I paid more attention to my credit when I was young,
...this is getting ridiculous and way too expensive.
At the very least I should have been saving some money,
$3,119
Table $400
Lamps @ $100 ea. $200
End Tables @ $250 ea. $500
Total Interest to be paid $1,800
Subtotal $6,019
Interest $1,800
AMOUNT DUE $7,819.00
Make all checks payable to Alan's Rent-to-Own
Thank you for your business!
ALAN'S
Rent-to-Own
...but it's tough, even with a good paying job.

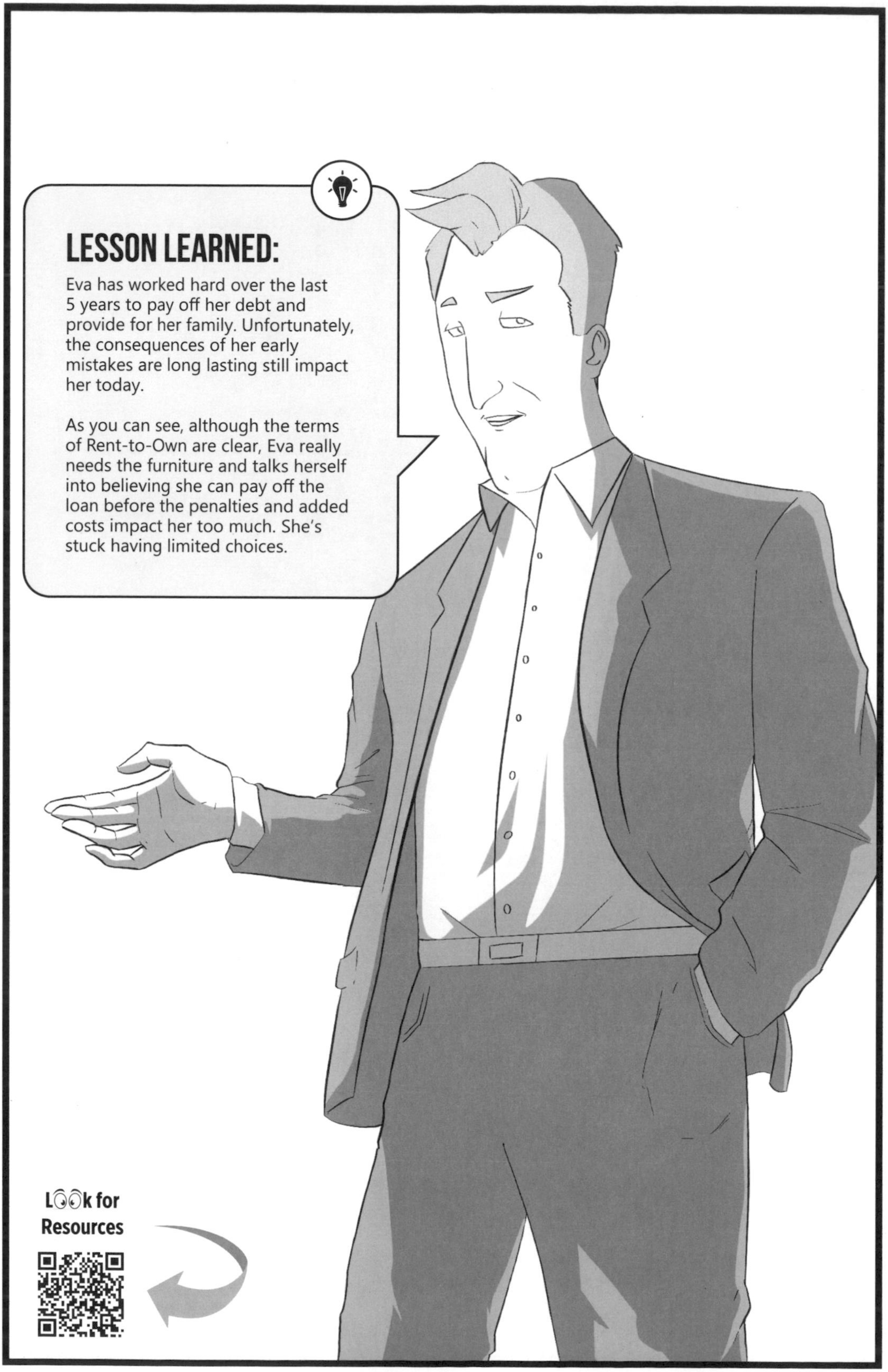
LESSON LEARNED:
Eva has worked hard over the last 5 years to pay off her debt and provide for her family. Unfortunately, the consequences of her early mistakes are long lasting still impact her today.
As you can see, although the terms of Rent-to-Own are clear, Eva really needs the furniture and talks herself into believing she can pay off the loan before the penalties and added costs impact her too much. She's stuck having limited choices.
LOOk for Resources

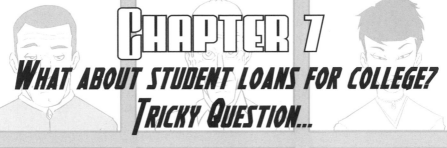

CHAPTER 7
WHAT ABOUT STUDENT LOANS FOR COLLEGE?
TRICKY QUESTION...

MEET MARY

MARY

Mary lives in Norwalk, CT with her parents. She has always been very smart and hard-working, but has never taken to school. She's always a C or B minus student in most subjects. Her two cousins own a garage, where they work as mechanics. Mary always loves spending time at the garage and has a real passion for cars. When she hears that a local detailing shop is hiring, she jumps on the chance.

Chapter 7
What about student loans for college? Tricky Question...

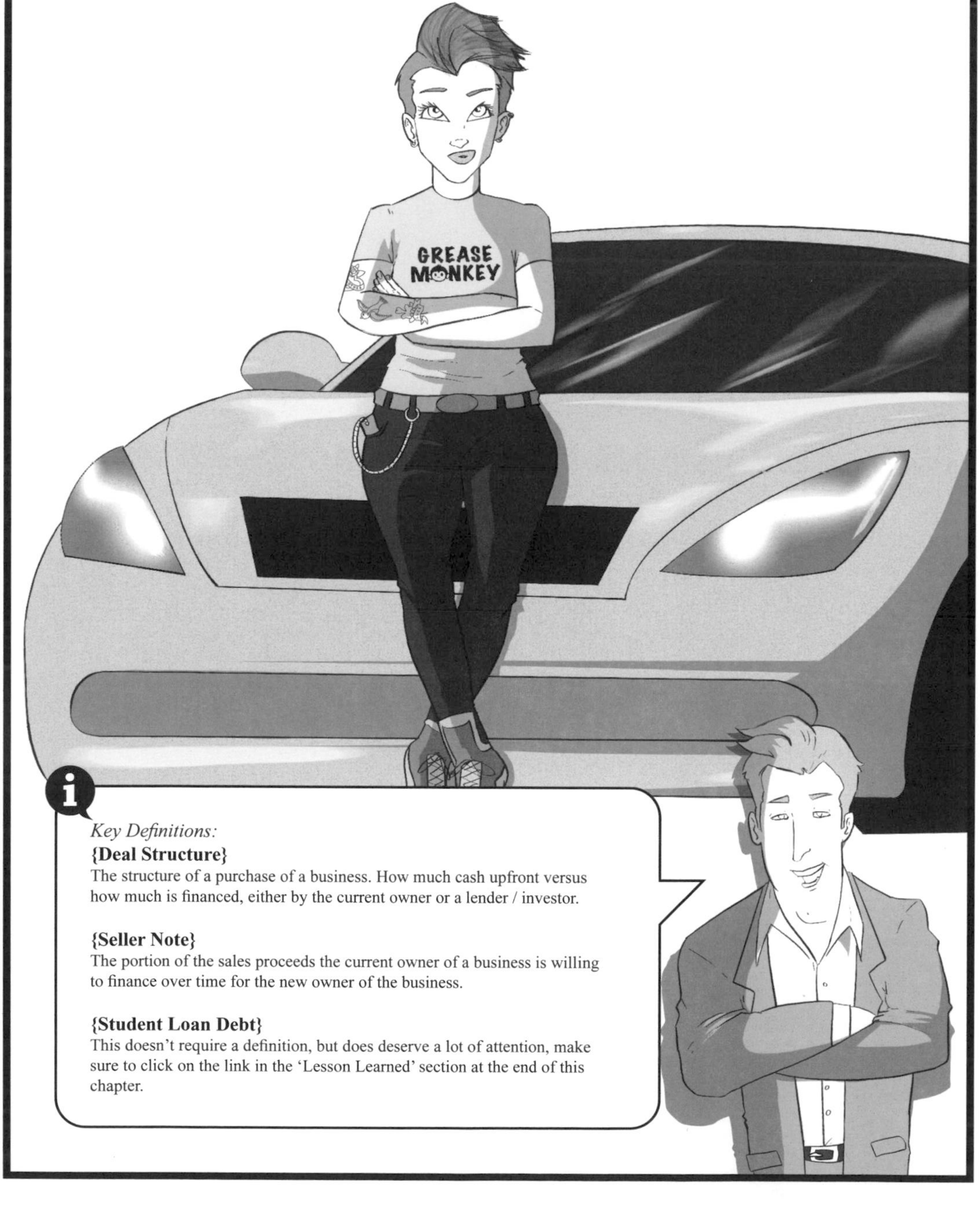
GREASE MONKEY
Key Definitions:
{Deal Structure}
The structure of a purchase of a business. How much cash upfront versus how much is financed, either by the current owner or a lender / investor.
{Seller Note}
The portion of the sales proceeds the current owner of a business is willing to finance over time for the new owner of the business.
{Student Loan Debt}
This doesn't require a definition, but does deserve a lot of attention, make sure to click on the link in the 'Lesson Learned' section at the end of this chapter.

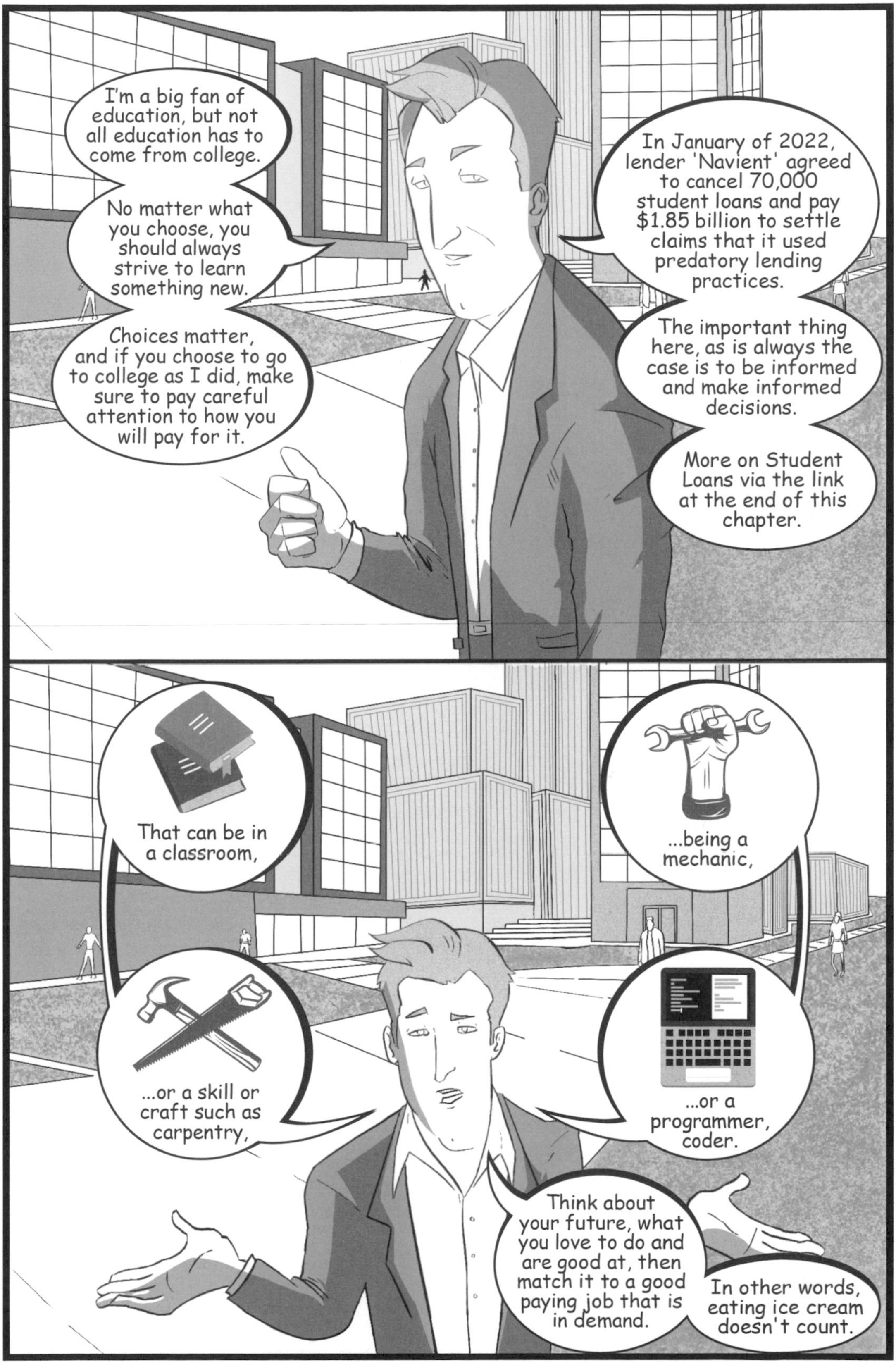
I'm a big fan of education, but not all education has to come from college.
No matter what you choose, you should always strive to learn something new.
Choices matter, and if you choose to go to college as I did, make sure to pay careful attention to how you will pay for it.
In January of 2022, lender 'Navient' agreed to cancel 70,000 student loans and pay $1.85 billion to settle claims that it used predatory lending practices.
The important thing here, as is always the case is to be informed and make informed decisions.
More on Student Loans via the link at the end of this chapter.
That can be in a classroom,
...being a mechanic,
...or a skill or craft such as carpentry,
...or a programmer, coder.
Think about your future, what you love to do and are good at, then match it to a good paying job that is in demand.
In other words, eating ice cream doesn't count.

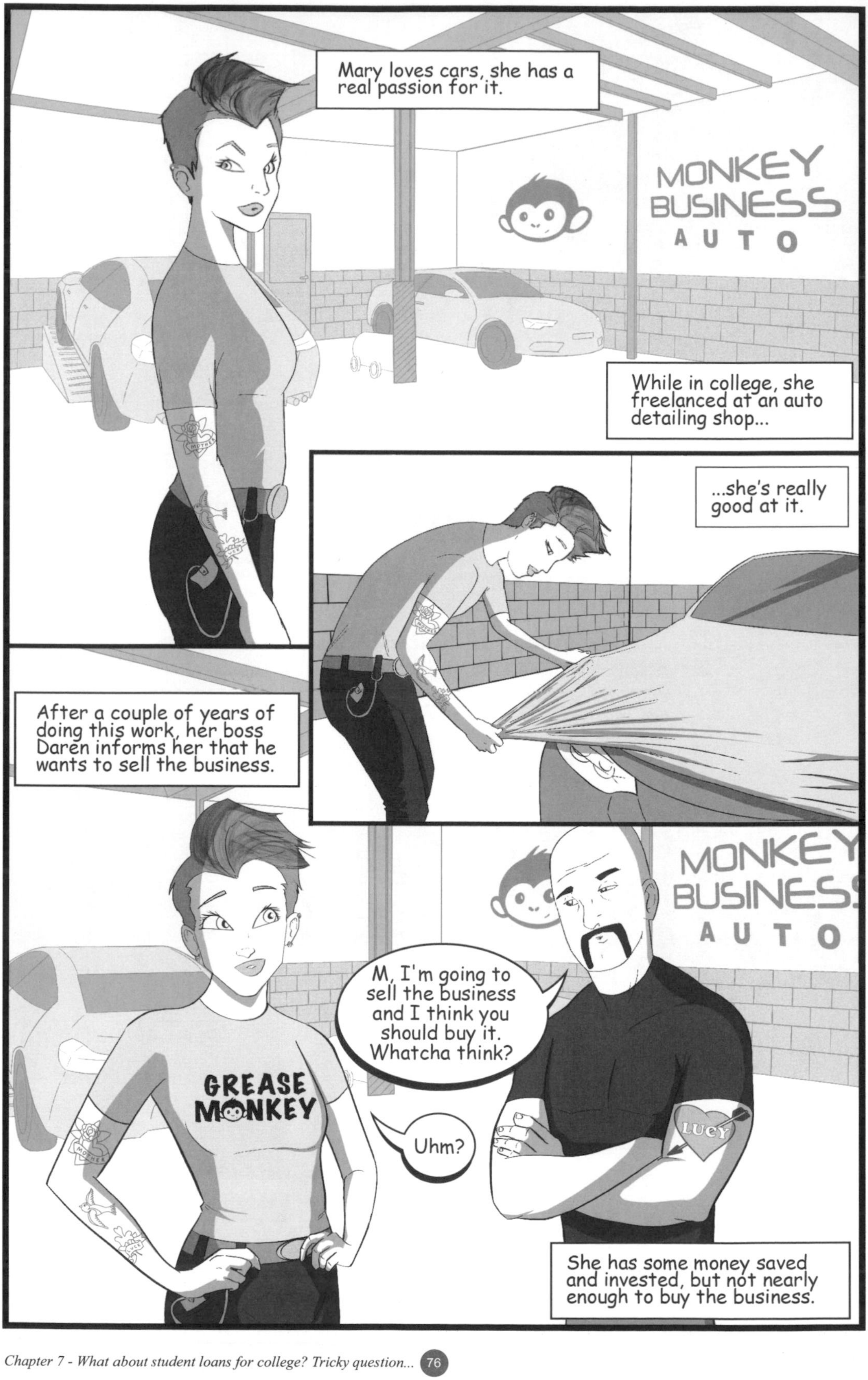
Mary loves cars, she has a real passion for it.
MONKEY BUSINESS AUTO
While in college, she freelanced at an auto detailing shop...
...she's really good at it.
After a couple of years of doing this work, her boss Daren informs her that he wants to sell the business.
MONKEY BUSINESS AUTO
M, I'm going to sell the business and I think you should buy it. Whatcha think?
GREASE MONKEY
Uhm?
LUCY
She has some money saved and invested, but not nearly enough to buy the business.

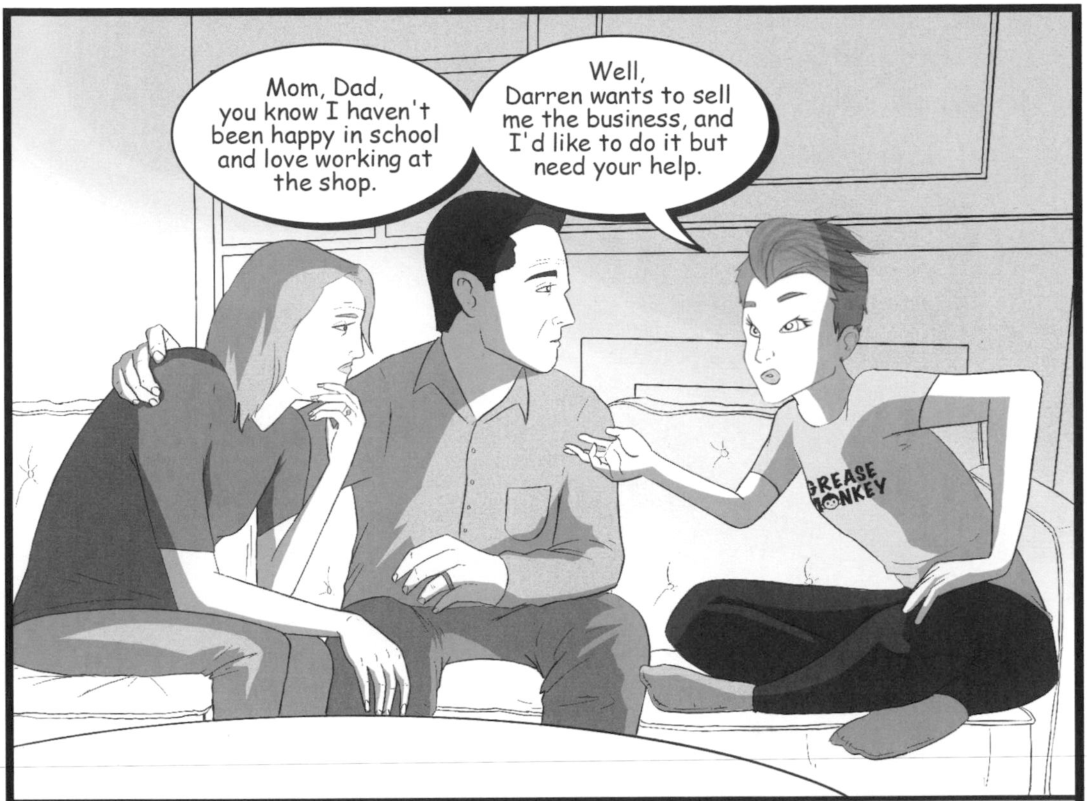
Mom, Dad, you know I haven't been happy in school and love working at the shop.
Well, Darren wants to sell me the business, and I'd like to do it but need your help.
GREASE MONKEY

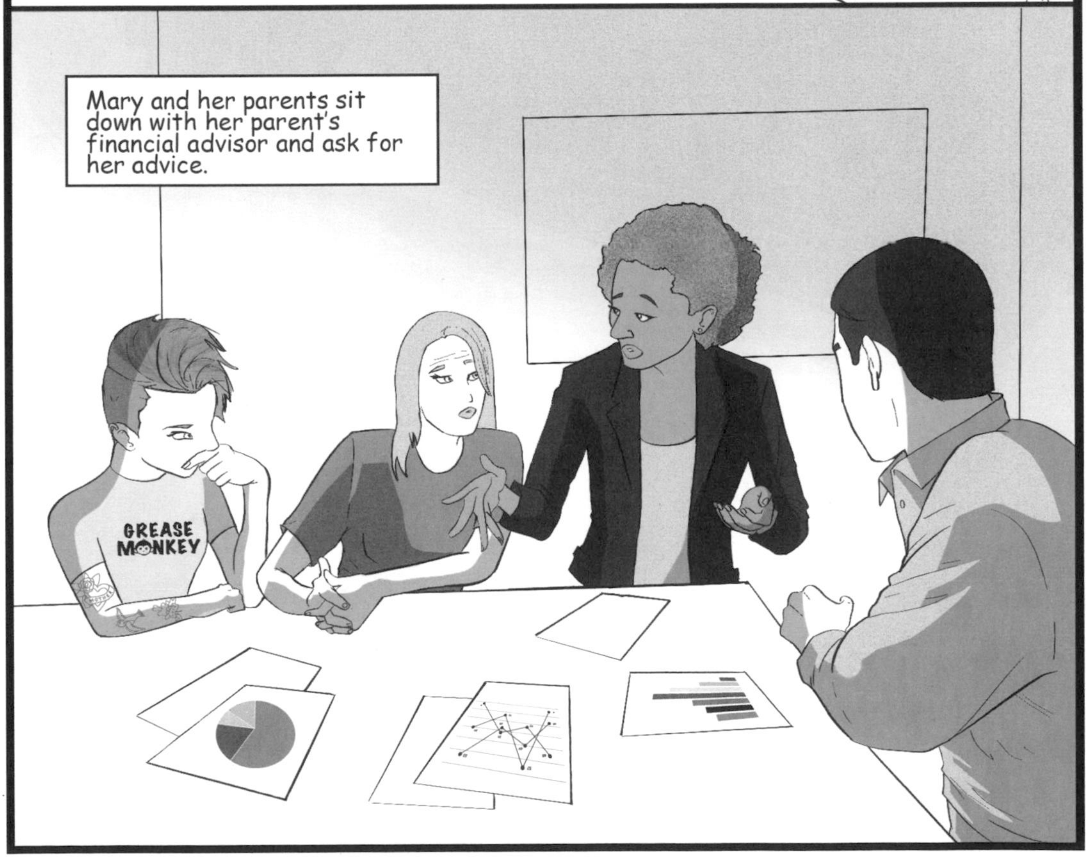
Mary and her parents sit down with her parent's financial advisor and ask for her advice.
GREASE MONKEY

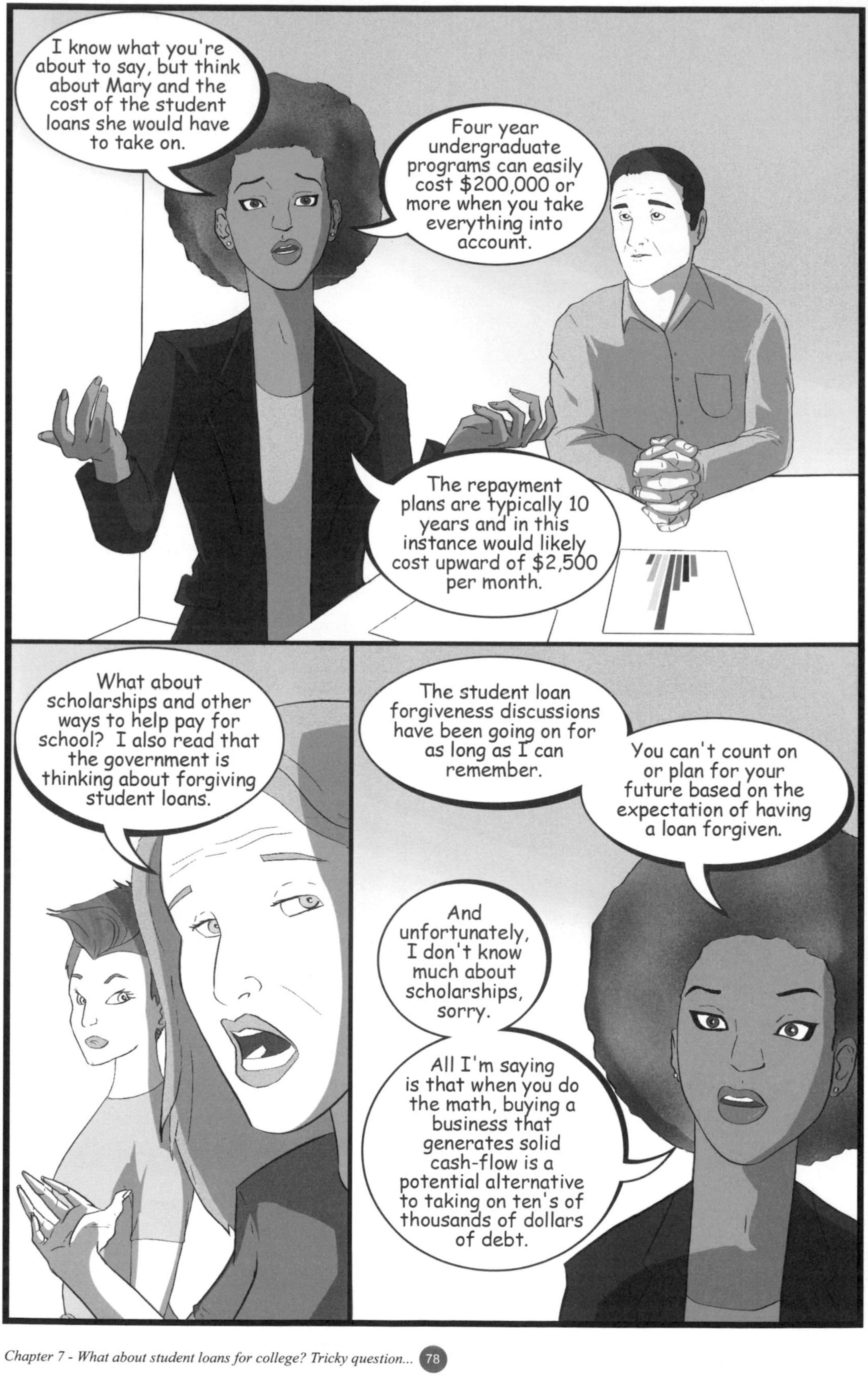
I know what you're about to say, but think about Mary and the cost of the student loans she would have to take on.
Four year undergraduate programs can easily cost $200,000 or more when you take everything into account.
The repayment plans are typically 10 years and in this instance would likely cost upward of $2,500 per month.
What about scholarships and other ways to help pay for school? I also read that the government is thinking about forgiving student loans.
The student loan forgiveness discussions have been going on for as long as I can remember.
You can't count on or plan for your future based on the expectation of having a loan forgiven.
And unfortunately, I don't know much about scholarships, sorry.
All I'm saying is that when you do the math, buying a business that generates solid cash-flow is a potential alternative to taking on ten's of thousands of dollars of debt.

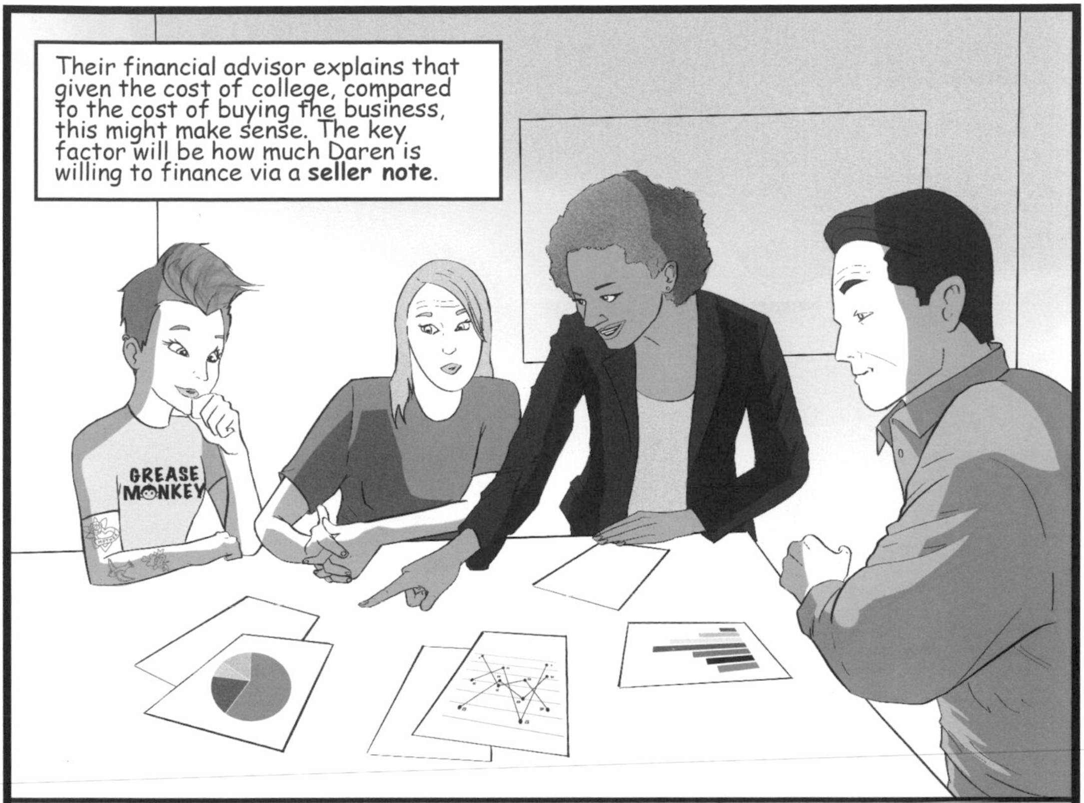
Their financial advisor explains that given the cost of college, compared to the cost of buying the business, this might make sense. The key factor will be how much Daren is willing to finance via a **seller note**.
GREASE MONKEY

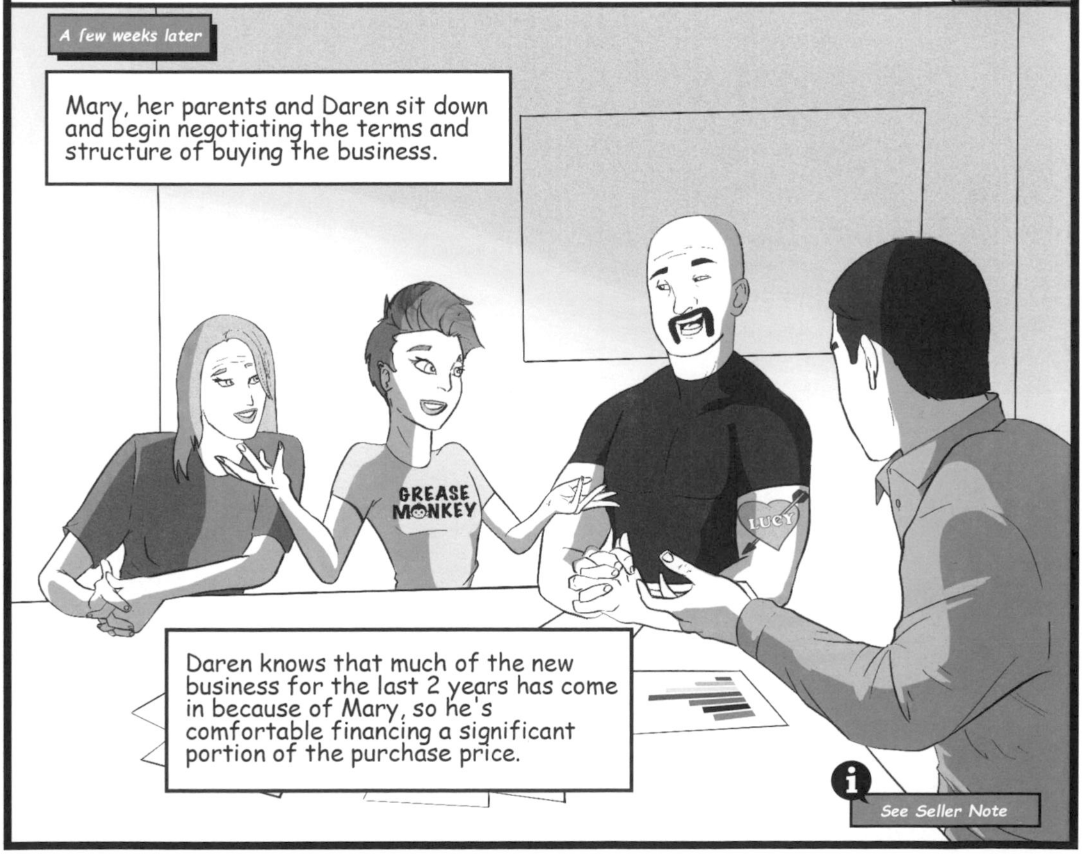
A few weeks later
Mary, her parents and Daren sit down and begin negotiating the terms and structure of buying the business.
GREASE MONKEY
LUCY
Daren knows that much of the new business for the last 2 years has come in because of Mary, so he's comfortable financing a significant portion of the purchase price.
See Seller Note

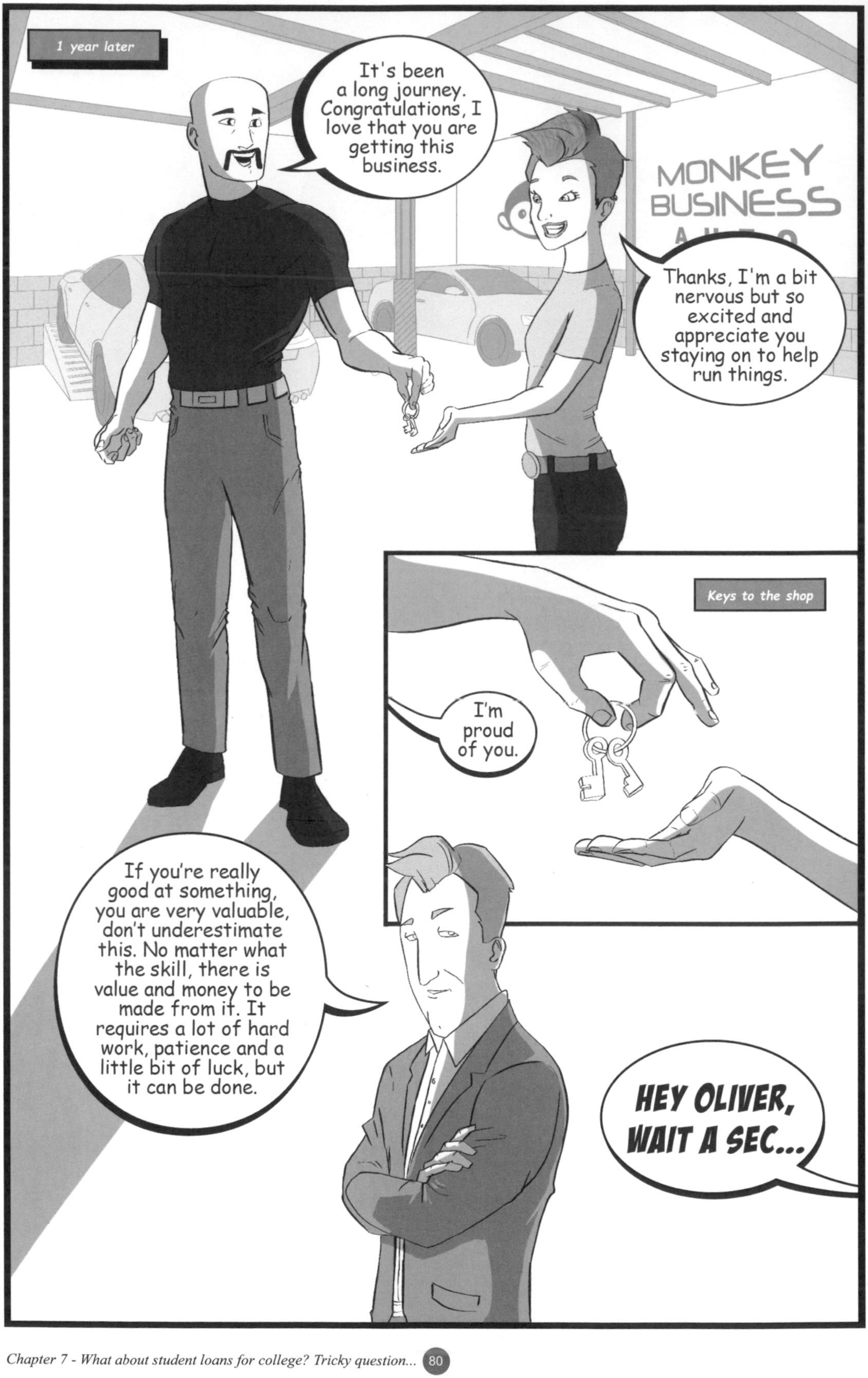
1 year later
It's been a long journey. Congratulations, I love that you are getting this business.
MONKEY BUSINESS
Thanks, I'm a bit nervous but so excited and appreciate you staying on to help run things.
Keys to the shop
I'm proud of you.
If you're really good at something, you are very valuable, don't underestimate this. No matter what the skill, there is value and money to be made from it. It requires a lot of hard work, patience and a little bit of luck, but it can be done.
HEY OLIVER, WAIT A SEC...

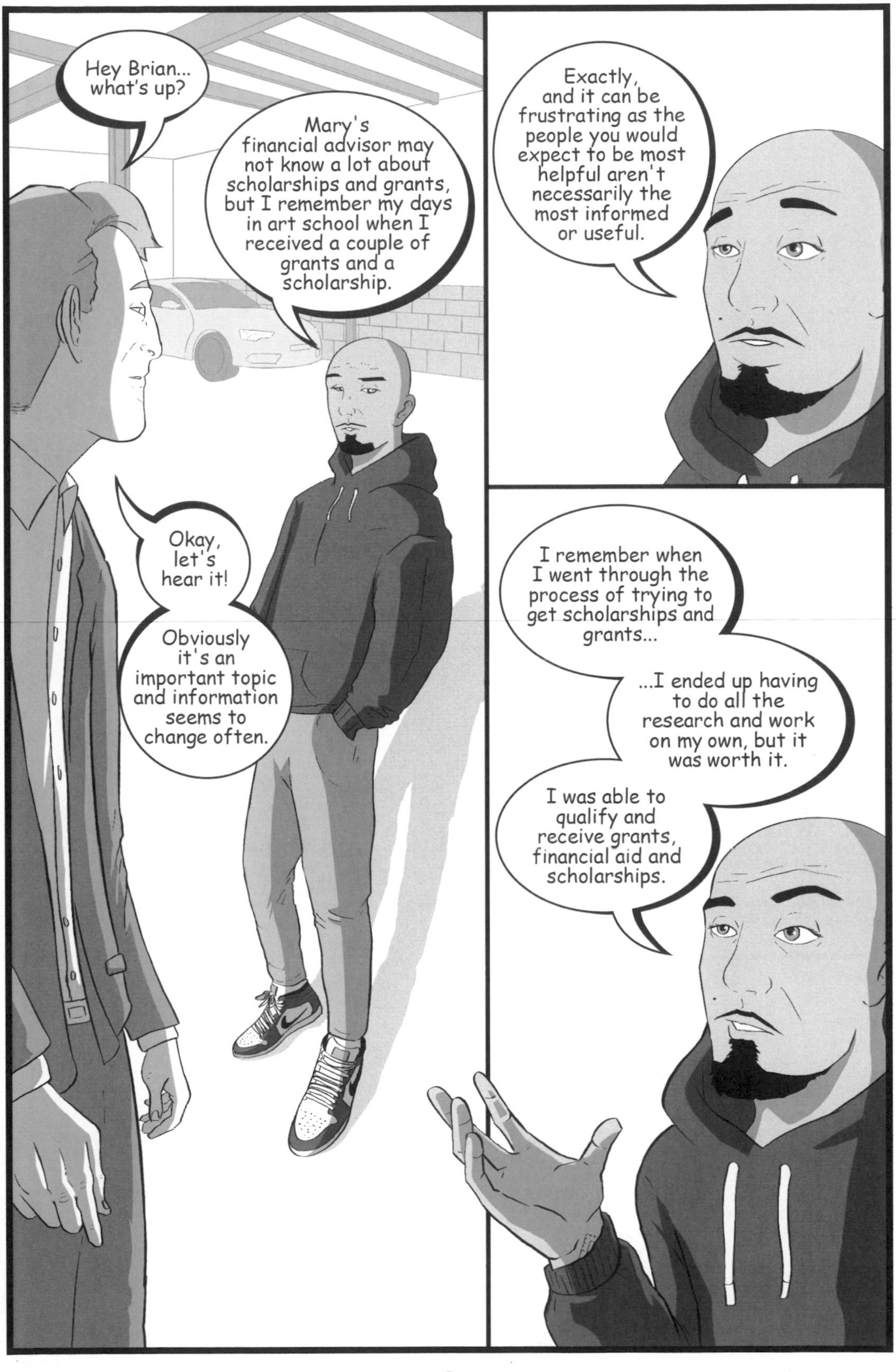
Hey Brian... what's up?
Mary's financial advisor may not know a lot about scholarships and grants, but I remember my days in art school when I received a couple of grants and a scholarship.
Okay, let's hear it!
Obviously it's an important topic and information seems to change often.
Exactly, and it can be frustrating as the people you would expect to be most helpful aren't necessarily the most informed or useful.
I remember when I went through the process of trying to get scholarships and grants...
...I ended up having to do all the research and work on my own, but it was worth it.
I was able to qualify and receive grants, financial aid and scholarships.

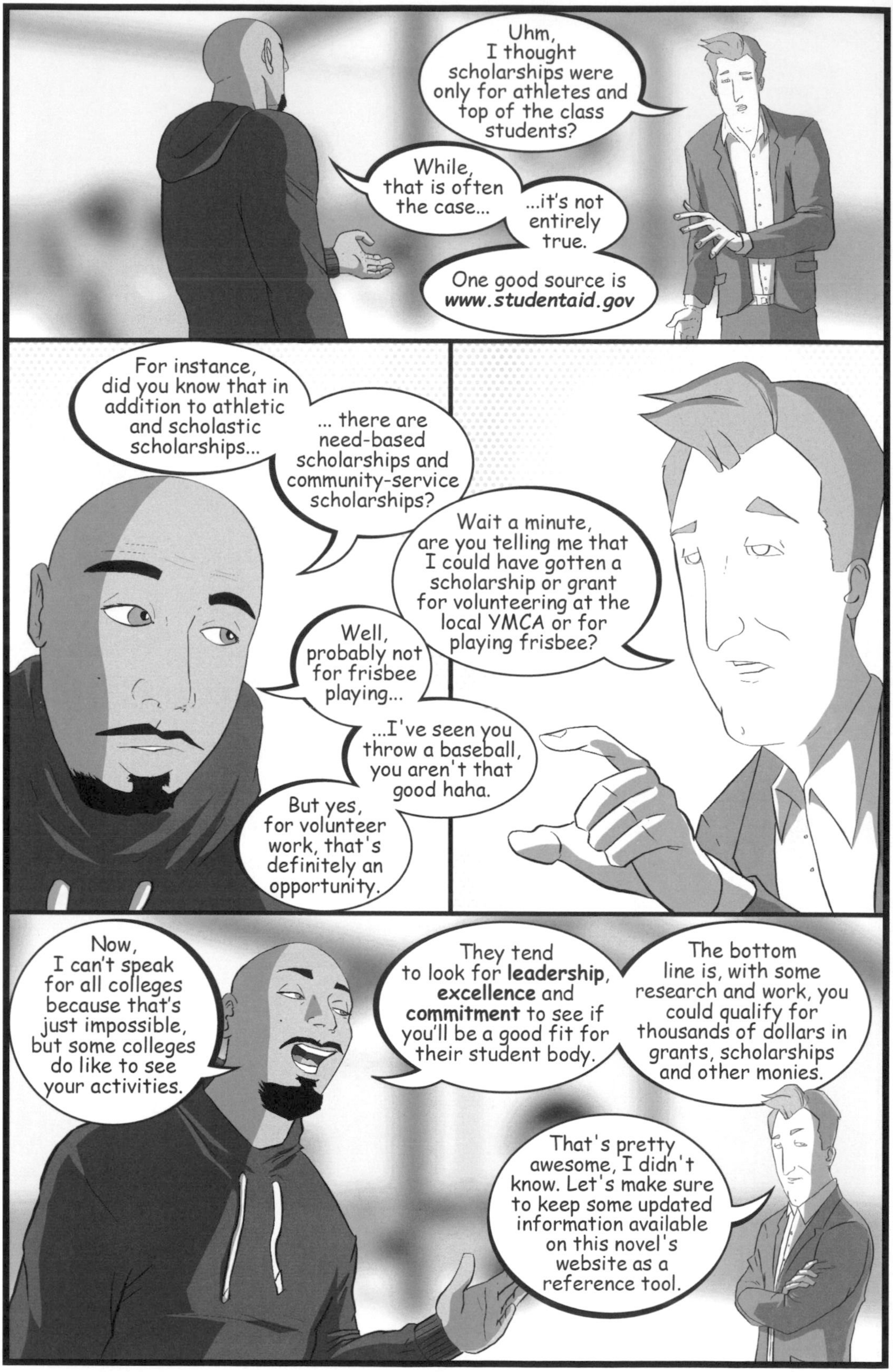
Uhm, I thought scholarships were only for athletes and top of the class students?
While, that is often the case...
...it's not entirely true.
One good source is **www.studentaid.gov**
For instance, did you know that in addition to athletic and scholastic scholarships...
... there are need-based scholarships and community-service scholarships?
Wait a minute, are you telling me that I could have gotten a scholarship or grant for volunteering at the local YMCA or for playing frisbee?
Well, probably not for frisbee playing...
...I've seen you throw a baseball, you aren't that good haha.
But yes, for volunteer work, that's definitely an opportunity.
Now, I can't speak for all colleges because that's just impossible, but some colleges do like to see your activities.
They tend to look for **leadership**, **excellence** and **commitment** to see if you'll be a good fit for their student body.
The bottom line is, with some research and work, you could qualify for thousands of dollars in grants, scholarships and other monies.
That's pretty awesome, I didn't know. Let's make sure to keep some updated information available on this novel's website as a reference tool.

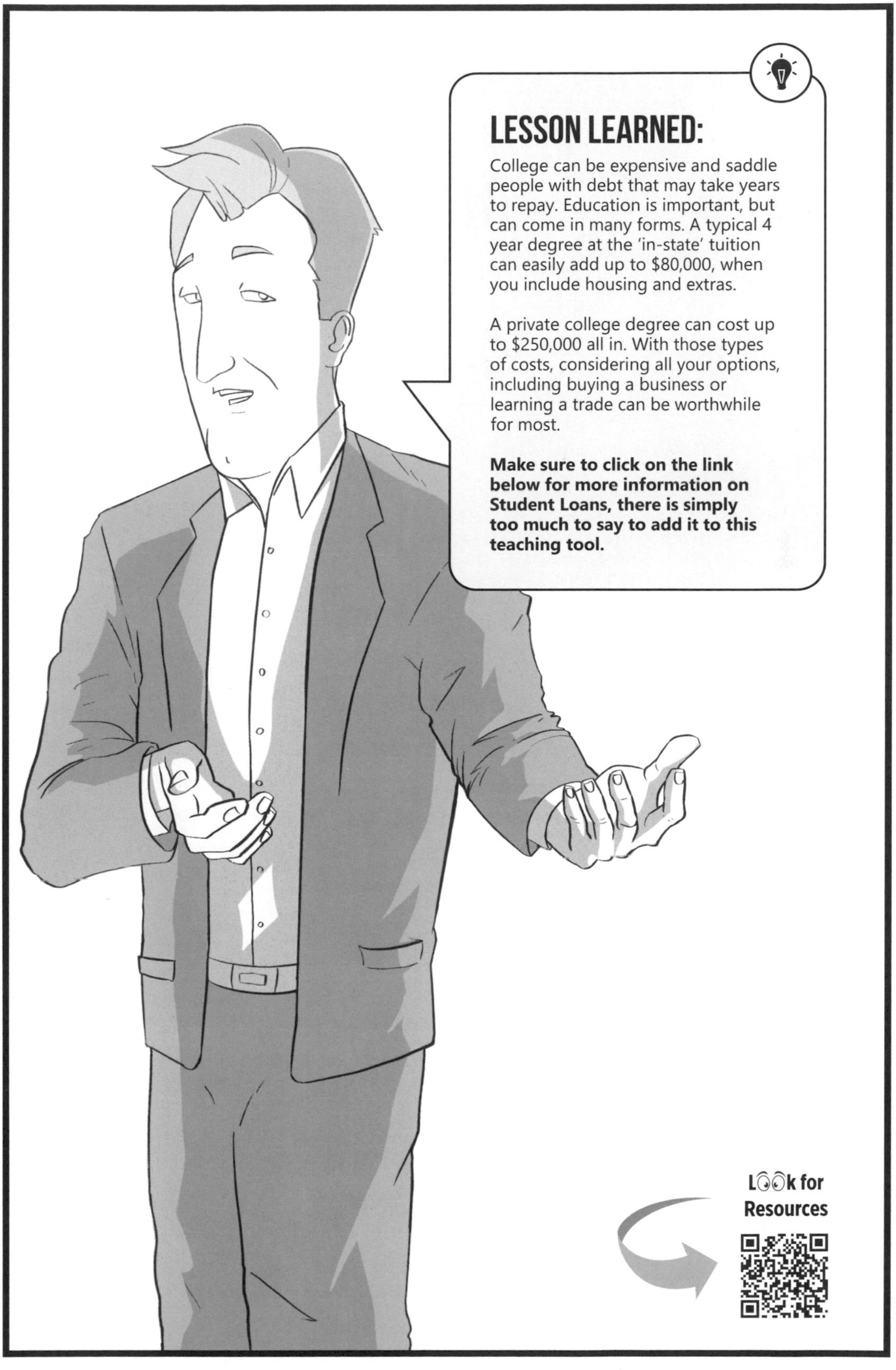
LESSON LEARNED:
College can be expensive and saddle people with debt that may take years to repay. Education is important, but can come in many forms. A typical 4 year degree at the 'in-state' tuition can easily add up to $80,000, when you include housing and extras.
A private college degree can cost up to $250,000 all in. With those types of costs, considering all your options, including buying a business or learning a trade can be worthwhile for most.
Make sure to click on the link below for more information on Student Loans, there is simply too much to say to add it to this teaching tool.
Look for
Resources

Chapter 8

Reloading

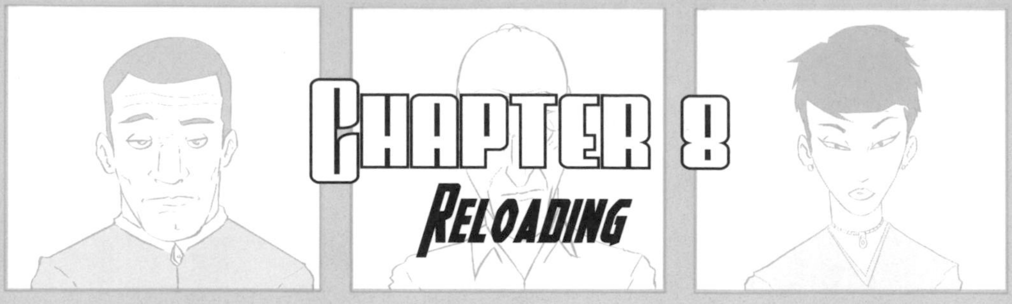

Meet Logan

Logan

Logan is obsessed with gaming and has his own Twitch and YouTube channel. He makes a living by streaming his video games and movie reviews, as well as his unboxing reviews. With roughly 110,000 subscribers, Logan isn't a popular YouTuber personality but he is working towards reaching his goal of 1 million subscribers. His office consists of headsets, microphones, multi-monitors and of course the gold YouTube plaque button that hangs in his office.

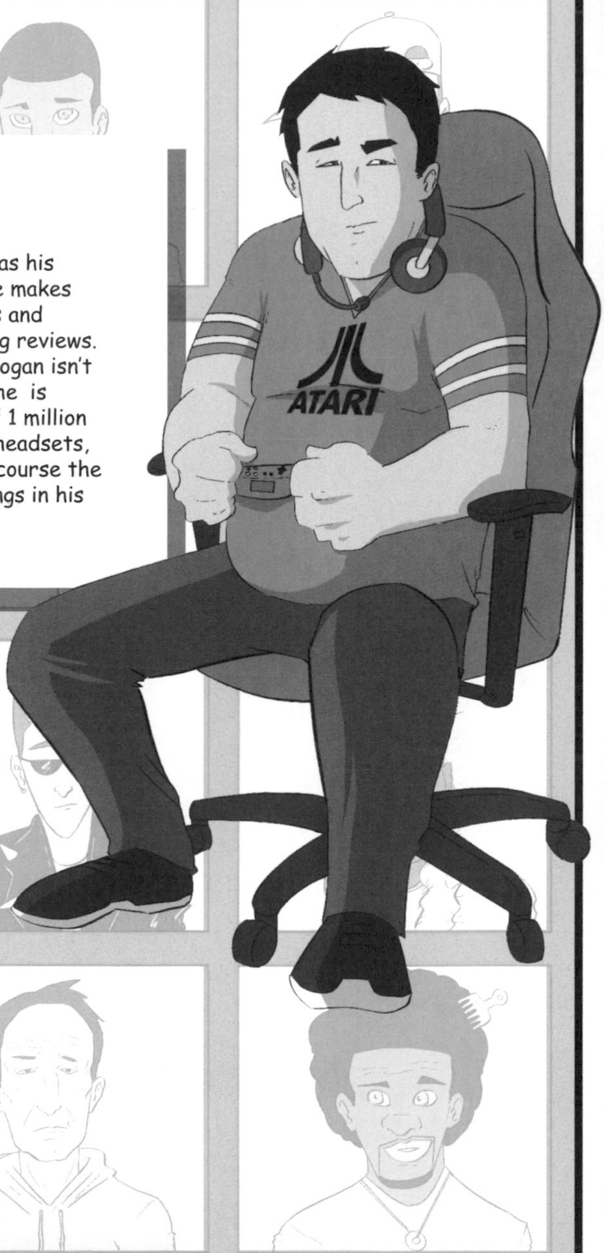
ATARI

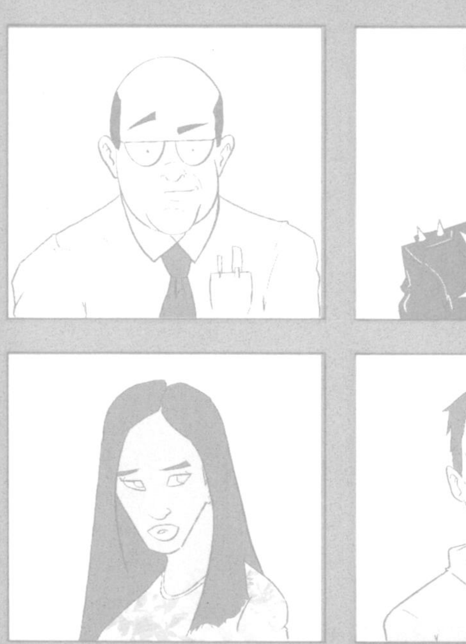

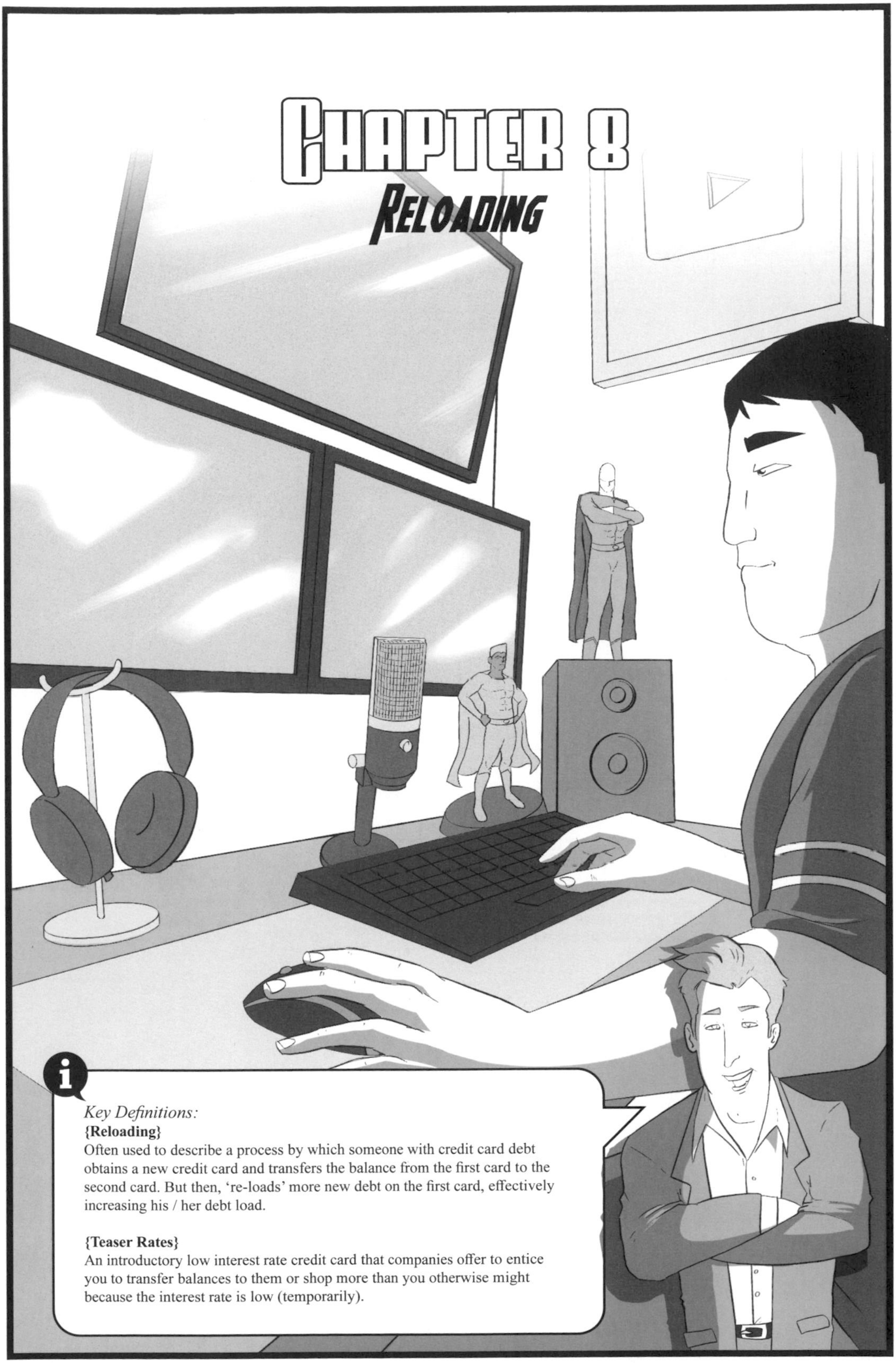
CHAPTER 8
RELOADING
Key Definitions:
{Reloading}
Often used to describe a process by which someone with credit card debt obtains a new credit card and transfers the balance from the first card to the second card. But then, 're-loads' more new debt on the first card, effectively increasing his / her debt load.
{Teaser Rates}
An introductory low interest rate credit card that companies offer to entice you to transfer balances to them or shop more than you otherwise might because the interest rate is low (temporarily).

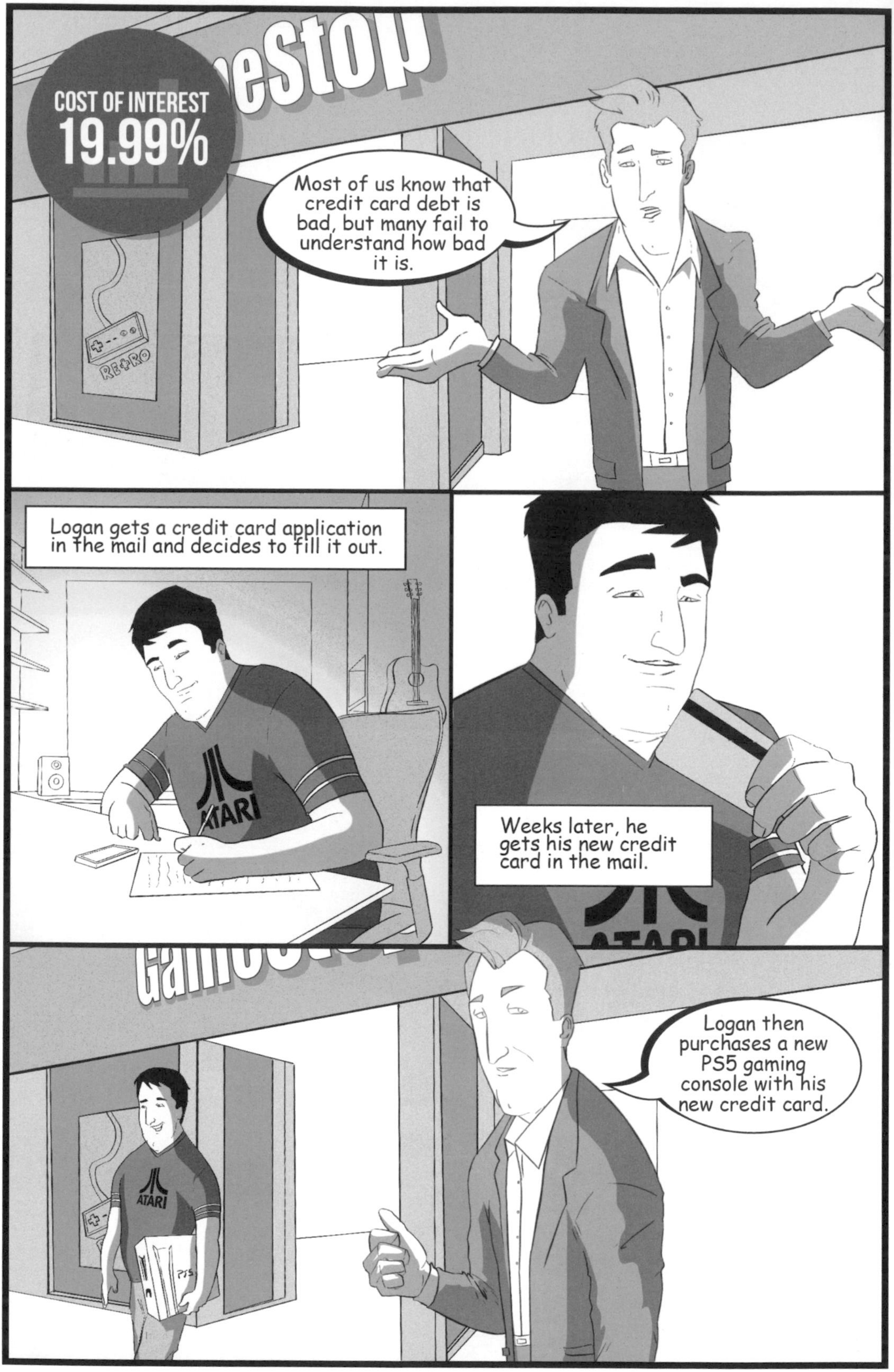
COST OF INTEREST
19.99%
RETRO
Most of us know that credit card debt is bad, but many fail to understand how bad it is.
Logan gets a credit card application in the mail and decides to fill it out.
ATARI
Weeks later, he gets his new credit card in the mail.
Logan then purchases a new PS5 gaming console with his new credit card.

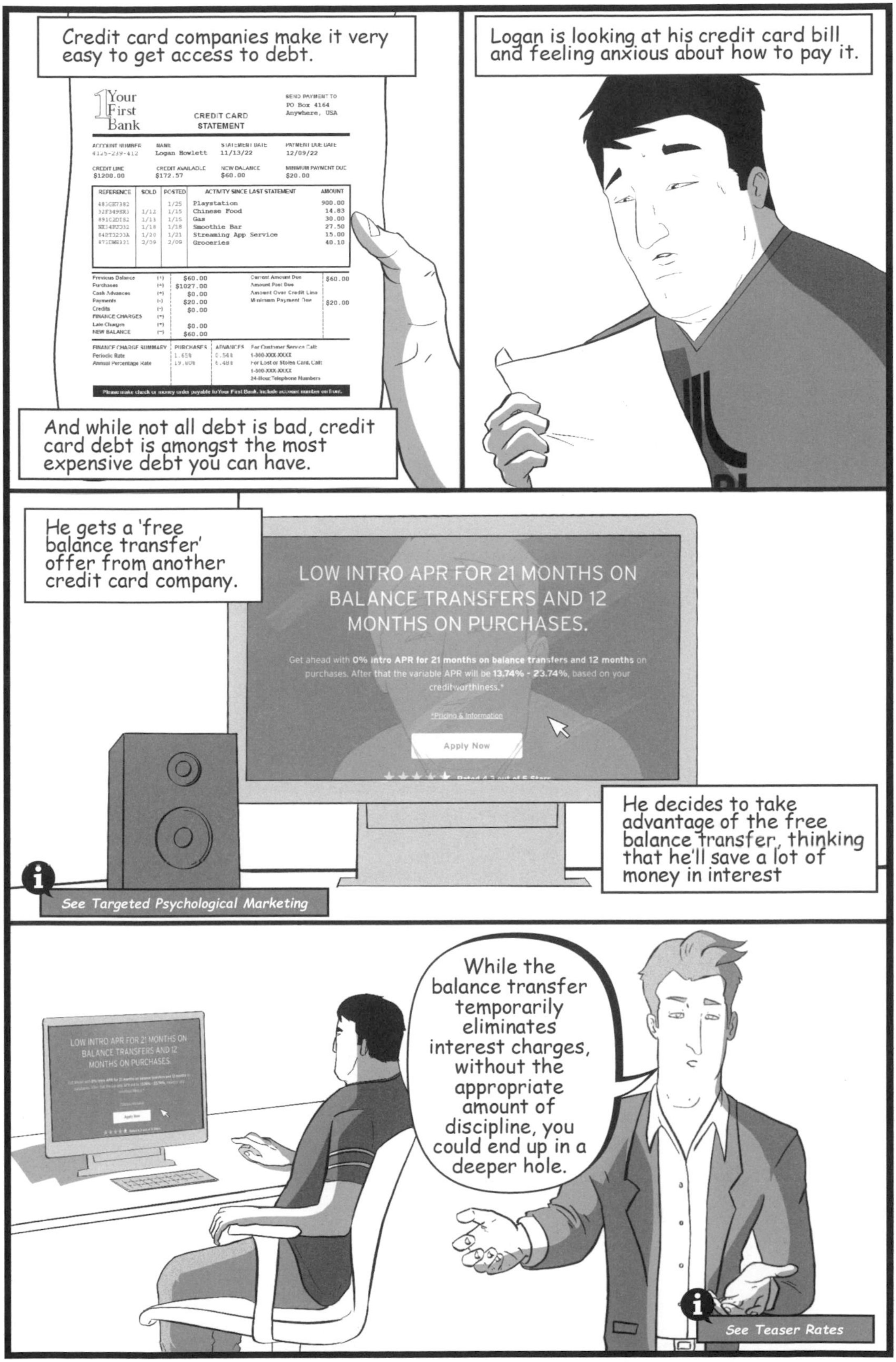
Credit card companies make it very easy to get access to debt.
Your First Bank
CREDIT CARD STATEMENT
SEND PAYMENT TO PO Box 4164 Anywhere, USA
ACCOUNT NUMBER 4125-239-412
NAME Logan Howlett
STATEMENT DATE 11/13/22
PAYMENT DUE DATE 12/09/22
CREDIT LINE $1200.00
CREDIT AVAILABLE $172.57
NEW BALANCE $60.00
MINIMUM PAYMENT DUE $20.00
REFERENCE SOLD POSTED ACTIVITY SINCE LAST STATEMENT AMOUNT
1/25 Playstation 900.00
1/12 1/15 Chinese Food 14.83
1/13 1/15 Gas 30.00
1/18 1/18 Smoothie Bar 27.50
1/20 1/21 Streaming App Service 15.00
2/09 2/09 Groceries 40.10
Previous Balance $60.00
Purchases $1027.00
Cash Advances $0.00
Payments $20.00
Credits $0.00
FINANCE CHARGES
Late Charges $0.00
NEW BALANCE $60.00
Current Amount Due $60.00
Amount Past Due
Amount Over Credit Line
Minimum Payment Due $20.00
FINANCE CHARGE SUMMARY PURCHASES ADVANCES
Periodic Rate 1.65% 0.54%
Annual Percentage Rate 19.80% 6.48%
For Customer Service Call: 1-800-XXX-XXXX
For Lost or Stolen Card, Call: 1-800-XXX-XXXX
24-Hour Telephone Numbers
Please make check or money order payable to Your First Bank. Include account number on front.
And while not all debt is bad, credit card debt is amongst the most expensive debt you can have.
Logan is looking at his credit card bill and feeling anxious about how to pay it.
He gets a 'free balance transfer' offer from another credit card company.
LOW INTRO APR FOR 21 MONTHS ON BALANCE TRANSFERS AND 12 MONTHS ON PURCHASES.
Get ahead with 0% intro APR for 21 months on balance transfers and 12 months on purchases. After that the variable APR will be 13.74% - 23.74%, based on your creditworthiness.*
*Pricing & Information
Apply Now
See Targeted Psychological Marketing
He decides to take advantage of the free balance transfer, thinking that he'll save a lot of money in interest
LOW INTRO APR FOR 21 MONTHS ON BALANCE TRANSFERS AND 12 MONTHS ON PURCHASES.
While the balance transfer temporarily eliminates interest charges, without the appropriate amount of discipline, you could end up in a deeper hole.
See Teaser Rates

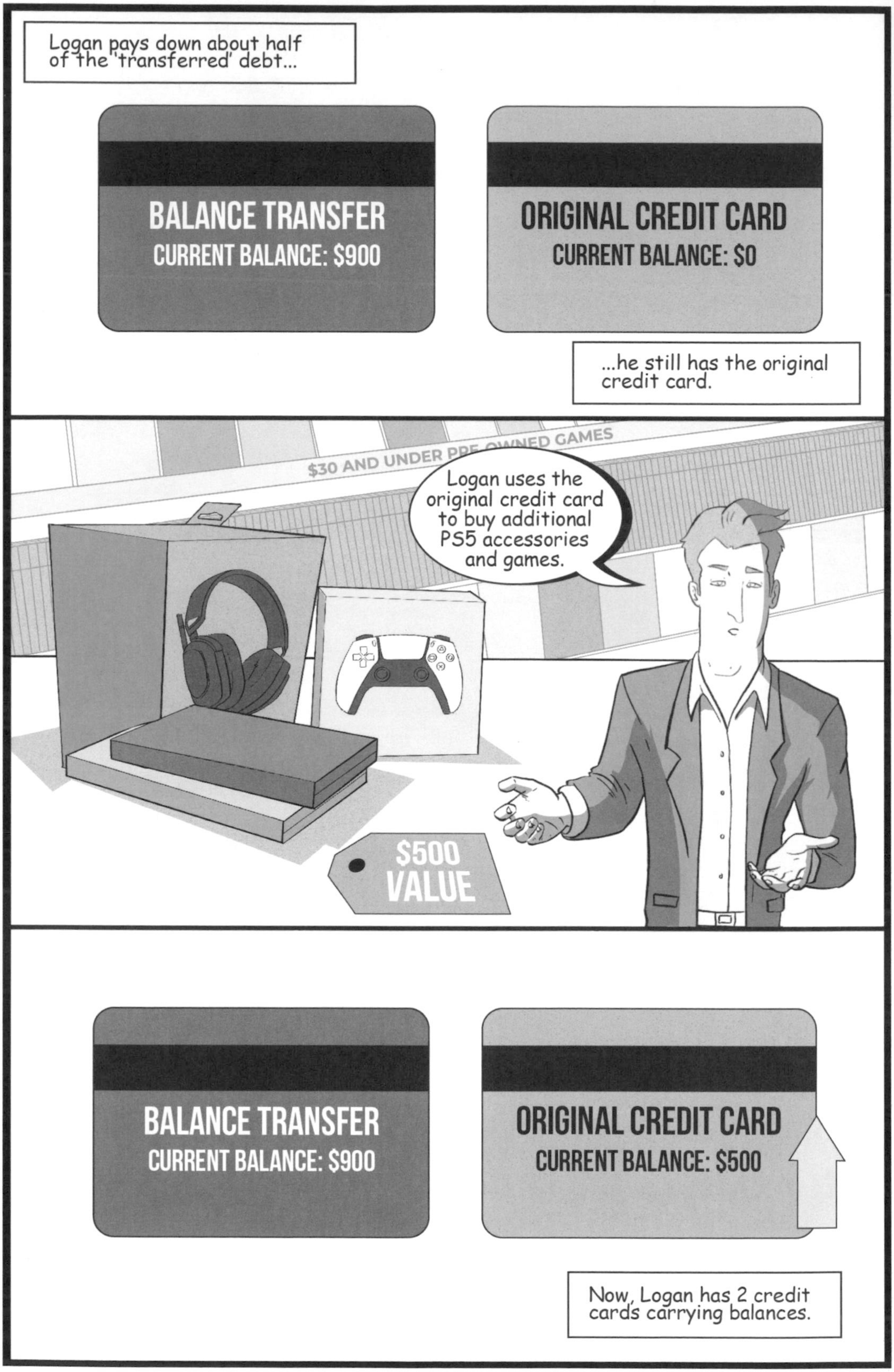
Logan pays down about half of the 'transferred' debt...
BALANCE TRANSFER
CURRENT BALANCE: $900
ORIGINAL CREDIT CARD
CURRENT BALANCE: $0
...he still has the original credit card.
$30 AND UNDER PRE-OWNED GAMES
Logan uses the original credit card to buy additional PS5 accessories and games.
$500 VALUE
BALANCE TRANSFER
CURRENT BALANCE: $900
ORIGINAL CREDIT CARD
CURRENT BALANCE: $500
Now, Logan has 2 credit cards carrying balances.

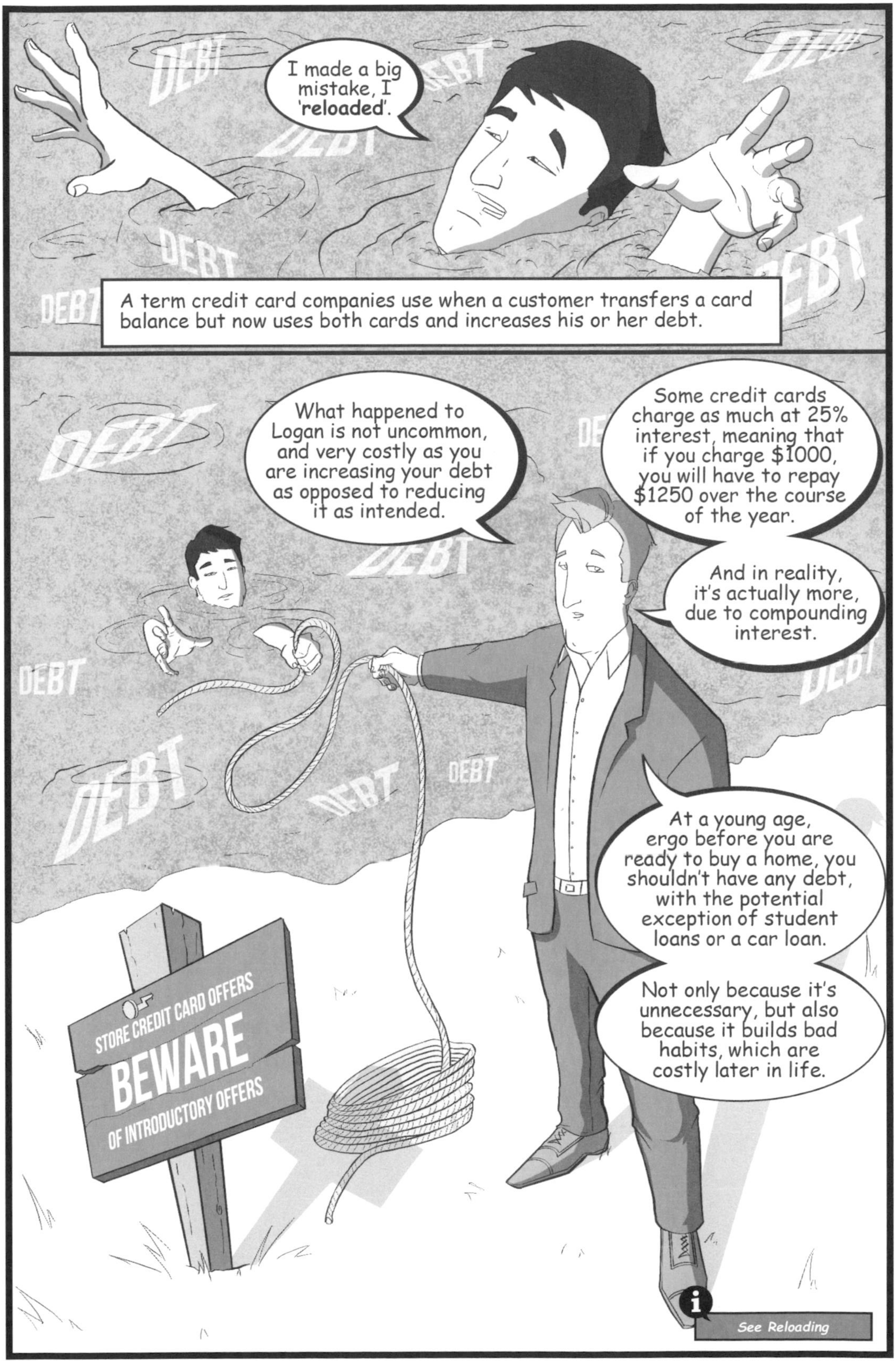

DEBT
I made a big mistake, I '**reloaded**'.
A term credit card companies use when a customer transfers a card balance but now uses both cards and increases his or her debt.
What happened to Logan is not uncommon, and very costly as you are increasing your debt as opposed to reducing it as intended.
Some credit cards charge as much at 25% interest, meaning that if you charge $1000, you will have to repay $1250 over the course of the year.
And in reality, it's actually more, due to compounding interest.
At a young age, ergo before you are ready to buy a home, you shouldn't have any debt, with the potential exception of student loans or a car loan.
Not only because it's unnecessary, but also because it builds bad habits, which are costly later in life.
STORE CREDIT CARD OFFERS
BEWARE
OF INTRODUCTORY OFFERS
See Reloading

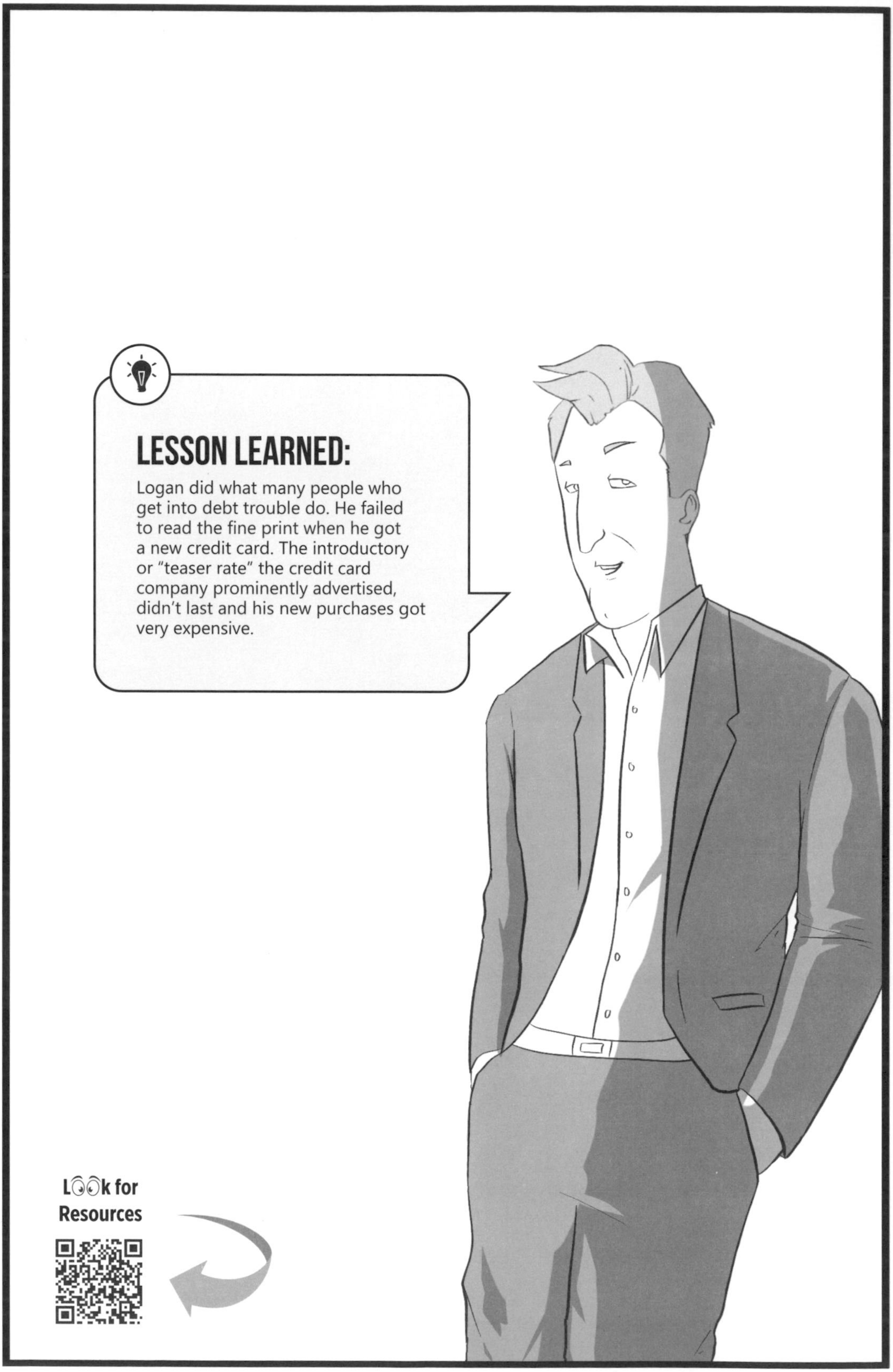
LESSON LEARNED:
Logan did what many people who get into debt trouble do. He failed to read the fine print when he got a new credit card. The introductory or "teaser rate" the credit card company prominently advertised, didn't last and his new purchases got very expensive.
Look for Resources

Chapter 9

Not all debt is bad debt

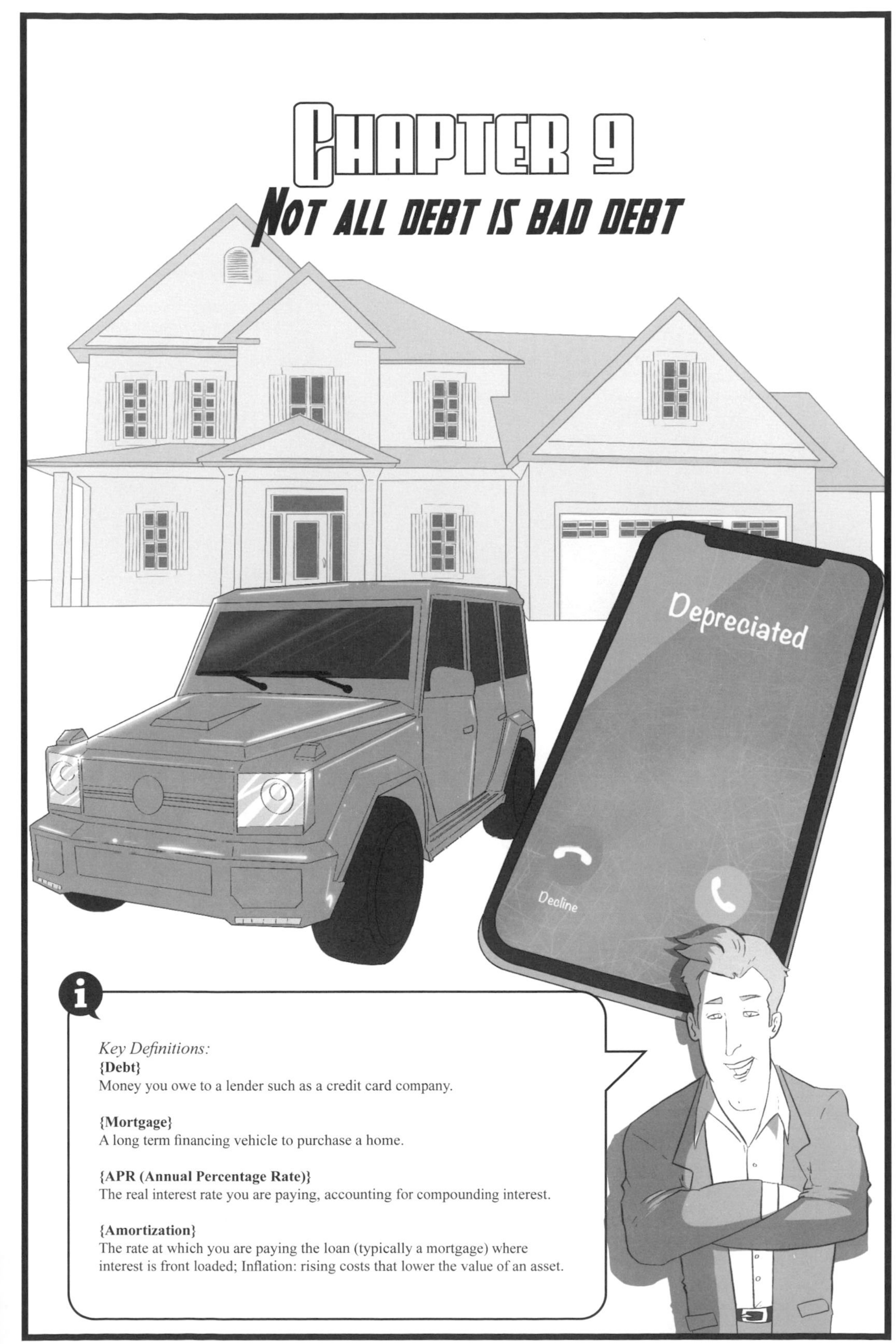
Depreciated
Decline

Key Definitions:

{Debt}
Money you owe to a lender such as a credit card company.

{Mortgage}
A long term financing vehicle to purchase a home.

{APR (Annual Percentage Rate)}
The real interest rate you are paying, accounting for compounding interest.

{Amortization}
The rate at which you are paying the loan (typically a mortgage) where interest is front loaded; Inflation: rising costs that lower the value of an asset.

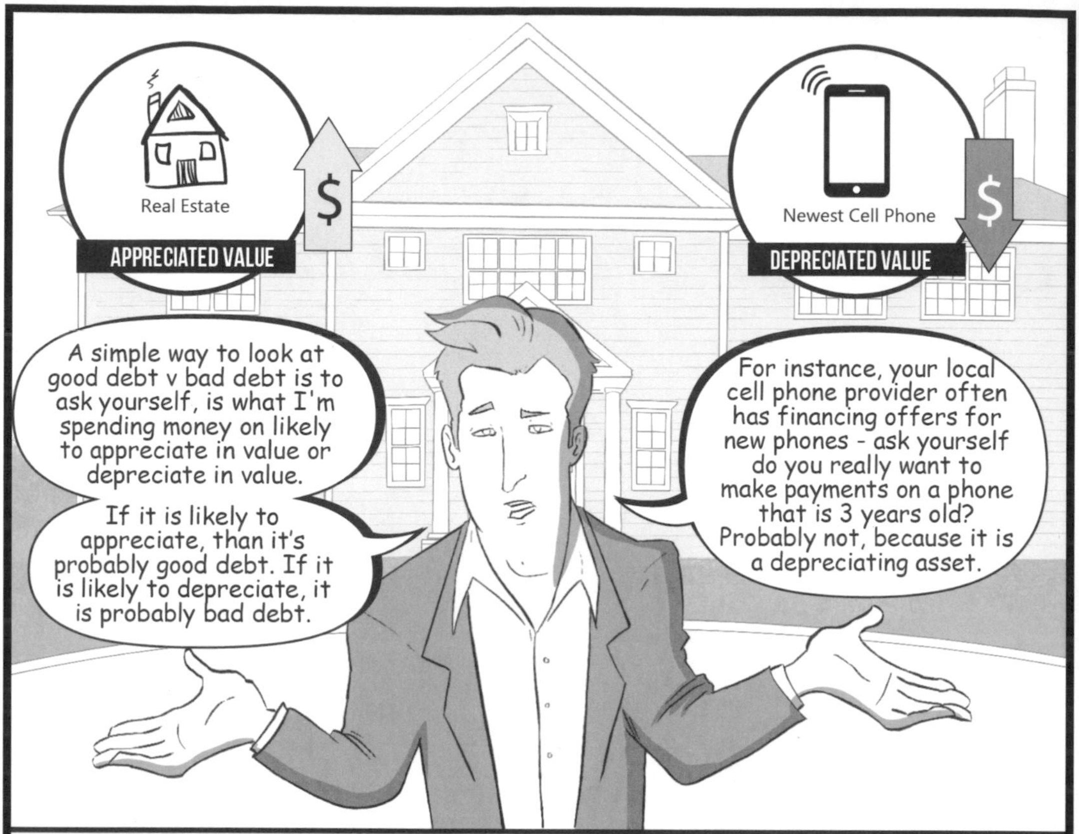
Real Estate
APPRECIATED VALUE
$
Newest Cell Phone
DEPRECIATED VALUE
$
A simple way to look at good debt v bad debt is to ask yourself, is what I'm spending money on likely to appreciate in value or depreciate in value.
If it is likely to appreciate, than it's probably good debt. If it is likely to depreciate, it is probably bad debt.
For instance, your local cell phone provider often has financing offers for new phones - ask yourself do you really want to make payments on a phone that is 3 years old? Probably not, because it is a depreciating asset.

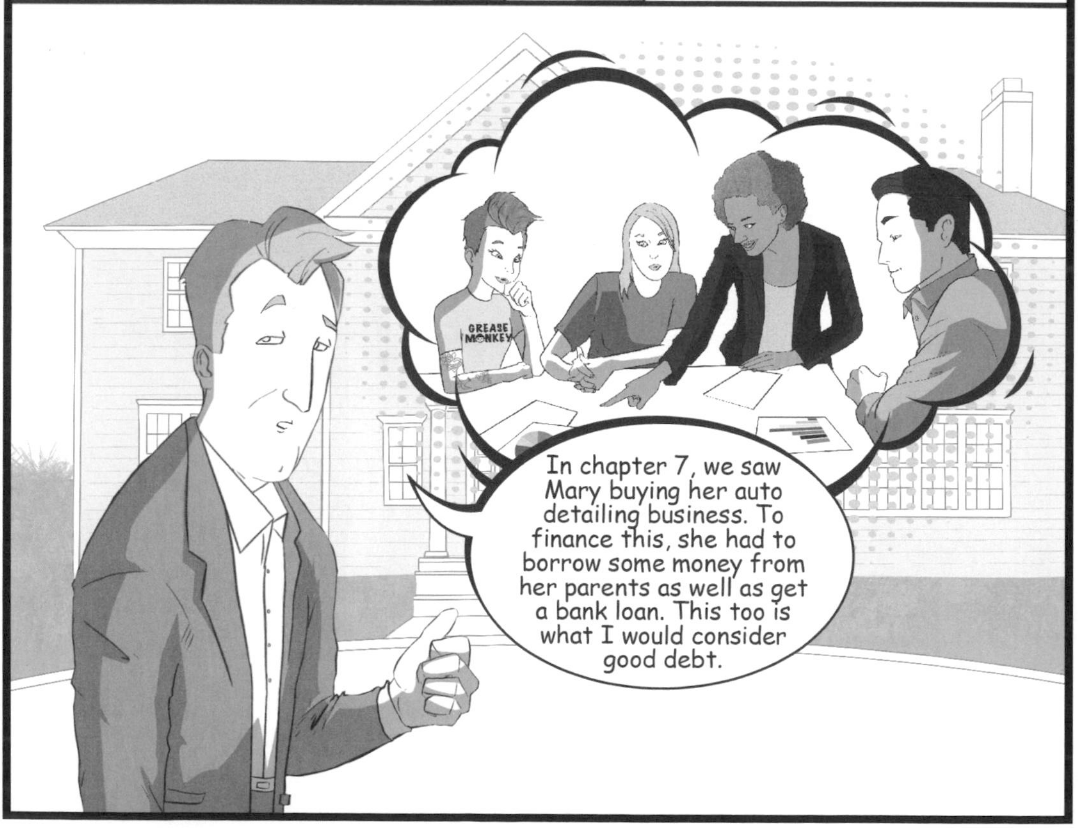
GREASE MONKEY
In chapter 7, we saw Mary buying her auto detailing business. To finance this, she had to borrow some money from her parents as well as get a bank loan. This too is what I would consider good debt.

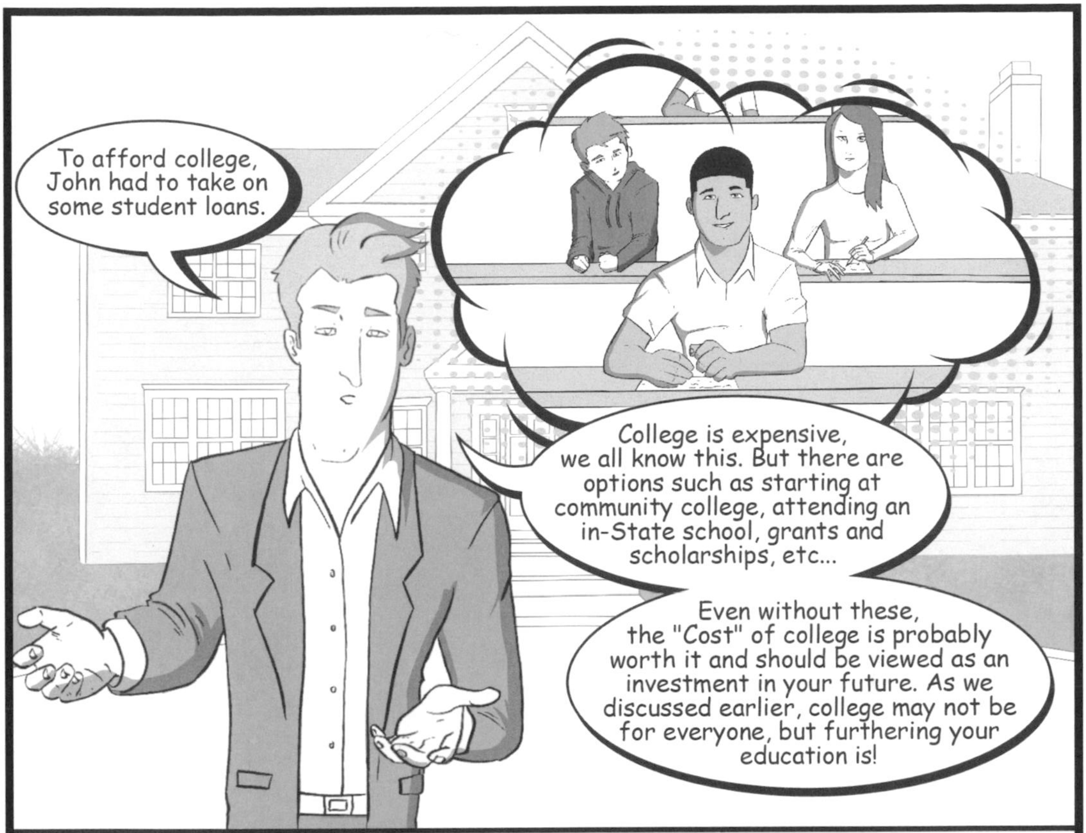

To afford college, John had to take on some student loans.
College is expensive, we all know this. But there are options such as starting at community college, attending an in-State school, grants and scholarships, etc...
Even without these, the "Cost" of college is probably worth it and should be viewed as an investment in your future. As we discussed earlier, college may not be for everyone, but furthering your education is!

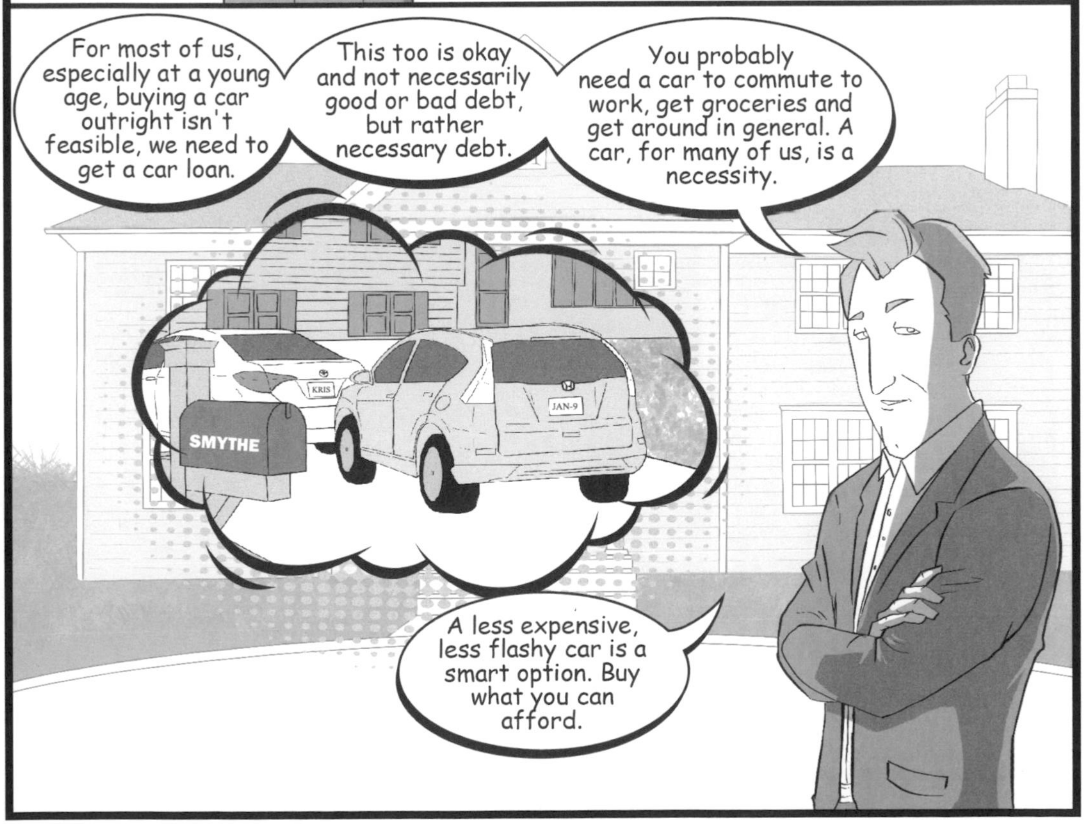

For most of us, especially at a young age, buying a car outright isn't feasible, we need to get a car loan.
This too is okay and not necessarily good or bad debt, but rather necessary debt.
You probably need a car to commute to work, get groceries and get around in general. A car, for many of us, is a necessity.
KRIS
JAN-9
SMYTHE
A less expensive, less flashy car is a smart option. Buy what you can afford.

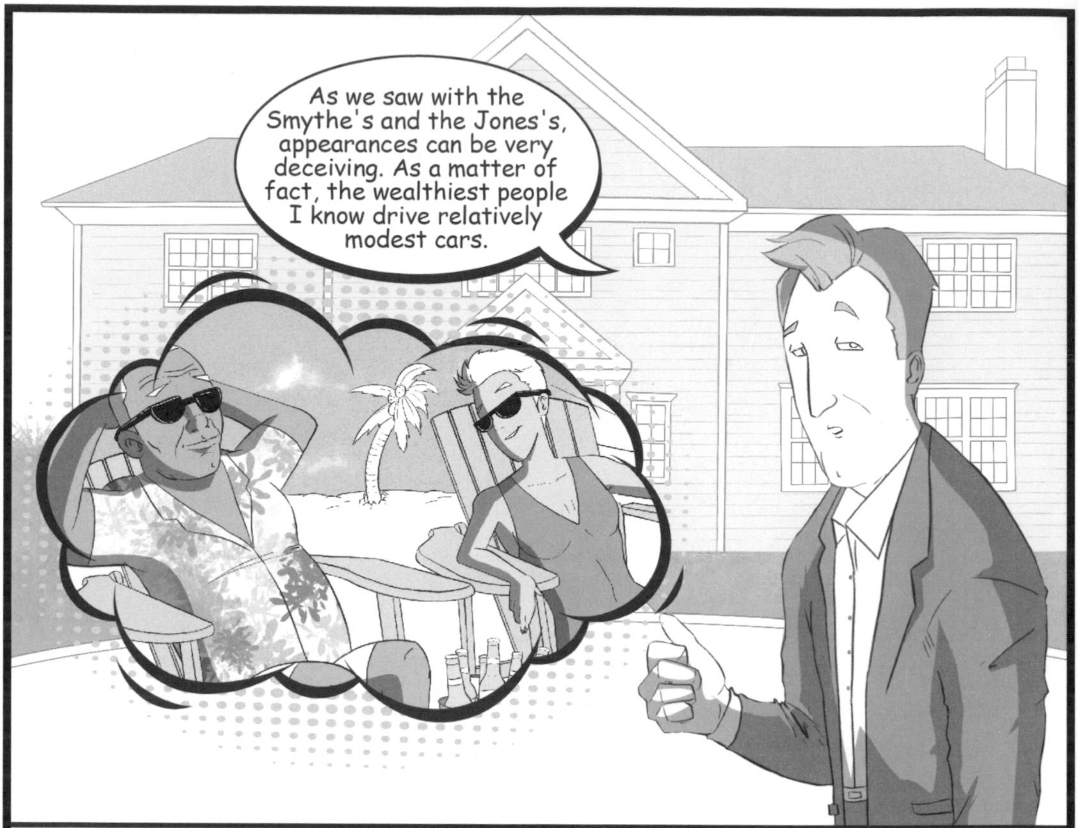
As we saw with the Smythe's and the Jones's, appearances can be very deceiving. As a matter of fact, the wealthiest people I know drive relatively modest cars.

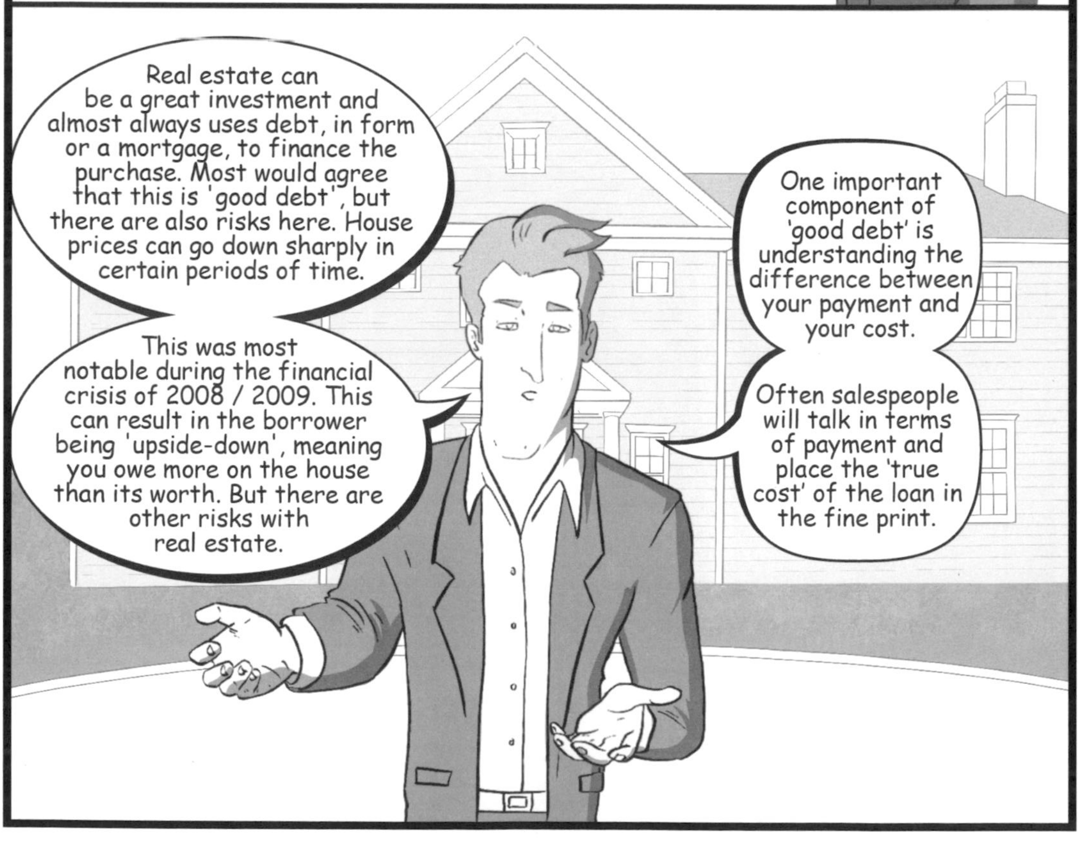
Real estate can be a great investment and almost always uses debt, in form or a mortgage, to finance the purchase. Most would agree that this is 'good debt', but there are also risks here. House prices can go down sharply in certain periods of time.
This was most notable during the financial crisis of 2008 / 2009. This can result in the borrower being 'upside-down', meaning you owe more on the house than its worth. But there are other risks with real estate.
One important component of 'good debt' is understanding the difference between your payment and your cost.
Often salespeople will talk in terms of payment and place the 'true cost' of the loan in the fine print.

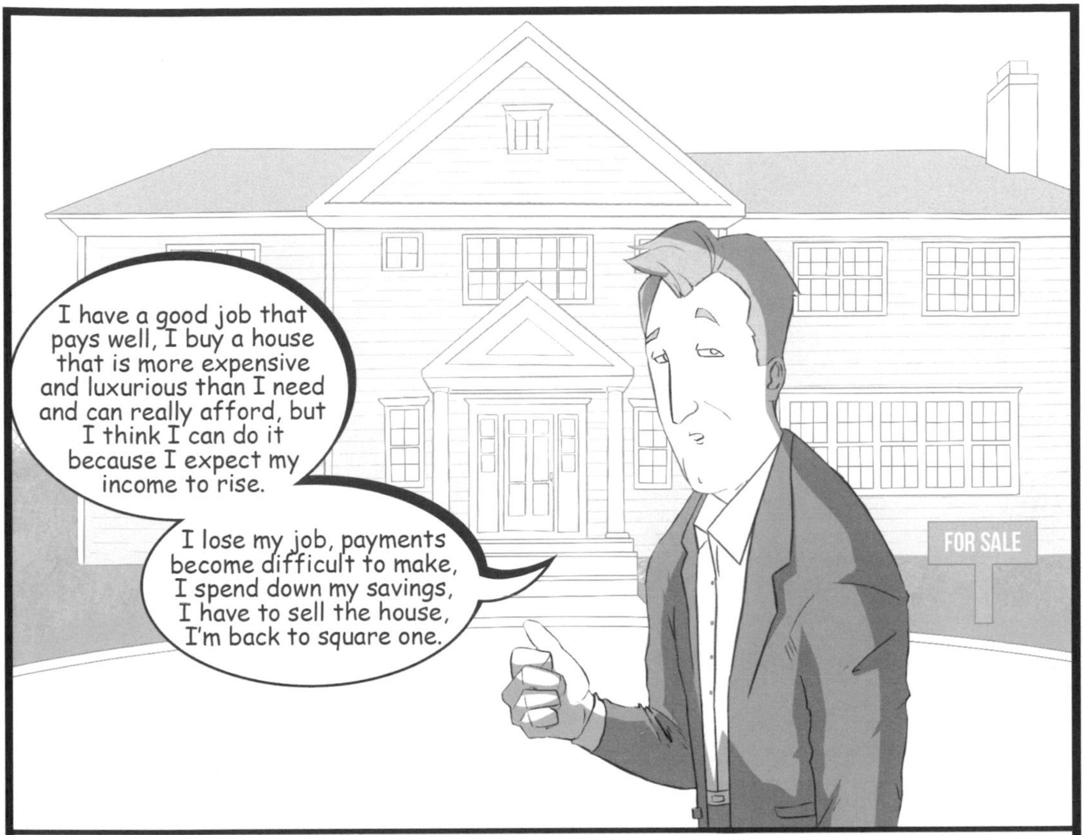
I have a good job that pays well, I buy a house that is more expensive and luxurious than I need and can really afford, but I think I can do it because I expect my income to rise.
I lose my job, payments become difficult to make, I spend down my savings, I have to sell the house, I'm back to square one.
FOR SALE

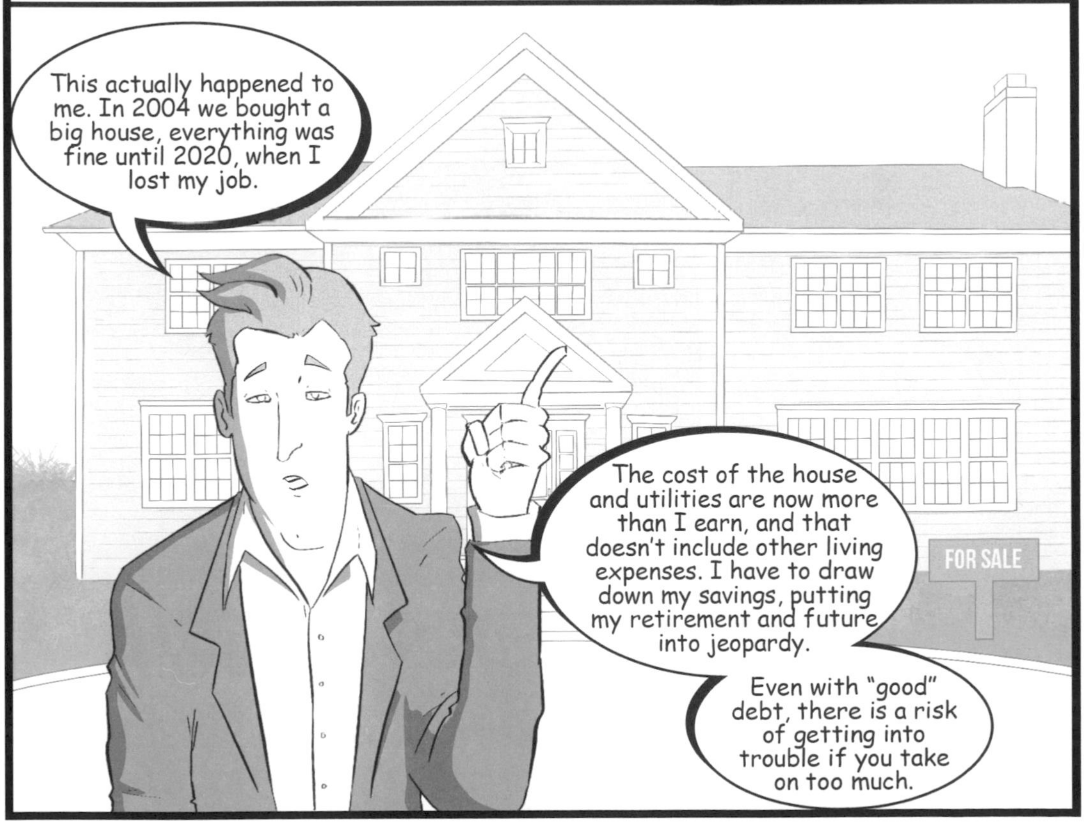
This actually happened to me. In 2004 we bought a big house, everything was fine until 2020, when I lost my job.
The cost of the house and utilities are now more than I earn, and that doesn't include other living expenses. I have to draw down my savings, putting my retirement and future into jeopardy.
Even with "good" debt, there is a risk of getting into trouble if you take on too much.
FOR SALE

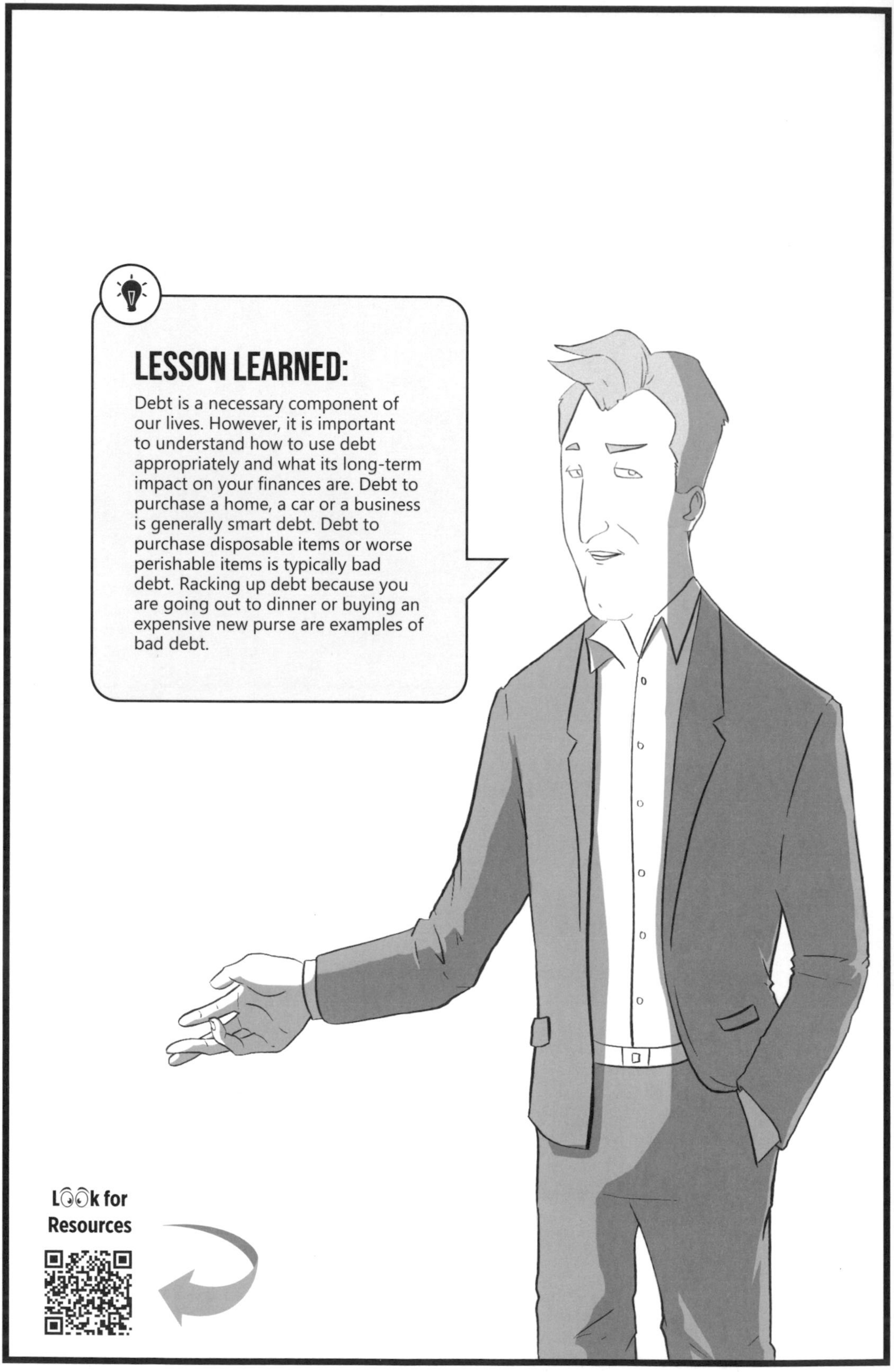
LESSON LEARNED:
Debt is a necessary component of our lives. However, it is important to understand how to use debt appropriately and what its long-term impact on your finances are. Debt to purchase a home, a car or a business is generally smart debt. Debt to purchase disposable items or worse perishable items is typically bad debt. Racking up debt because you are going out to dinner or buying an expensive new purse are examples of bad debt.
Look for Resources

CHAPTER 10
DON'T SPOIL A GOOD THING

Meet Emma

EMMA

Emma is a high school junior, attending a private school where most of her peers come from well-to-do families like she does. As a single child her parents have always spoiled her a little, but Emma has also worked hard, at times juggling school, sports and two jobs. She's a little insecure about her place in life and believes that by treating her 'friends' to dinner and other nice things, that she will fit-in better and be more popular. Her parents have given her a credit card, and as two busy professionals have largely left Emma to her own devices.

CHAPTER 10
DON'T SPOIL A GOOD THING

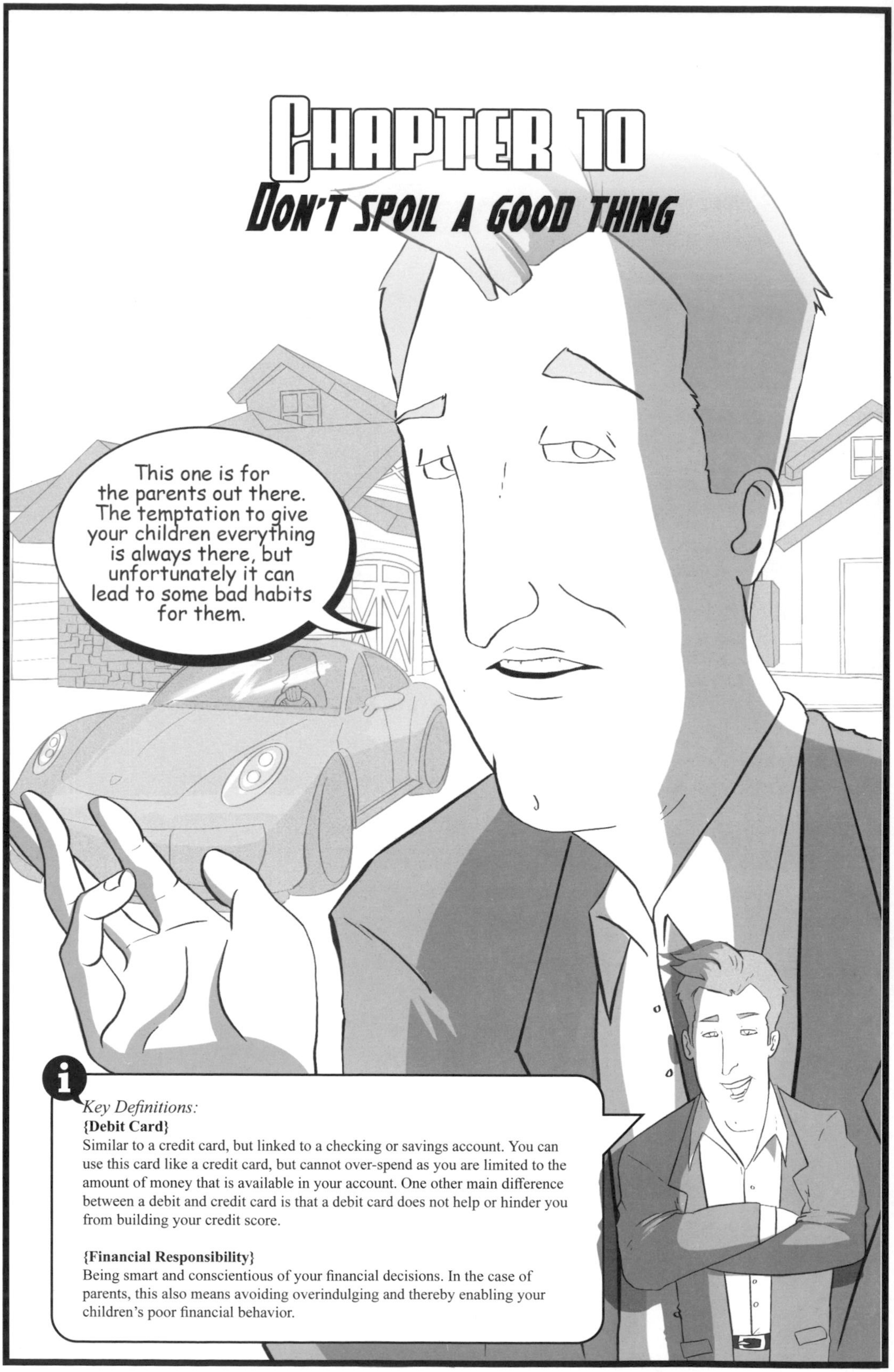
This one is for the parents out there. The temptation to give your children everything is always there, but unfortunately it can lead to some bad habits for them.

Key Definitions:

{Debit Card}
Similar to a credit card, but linked to a checking or savings account. You can use this card like a credit card, but cannot over-spend as you are limited to the amount of money that is available in your account. One other main difference between a debit and credit card is that a debit card does not help or hinder you from building your credit score.

{Financial Responsibility}
Being smart and conscientious of your financial decisions. In the case of parents, this also means avoiding overindulging and thereby enabling your children's poor financial behavior.

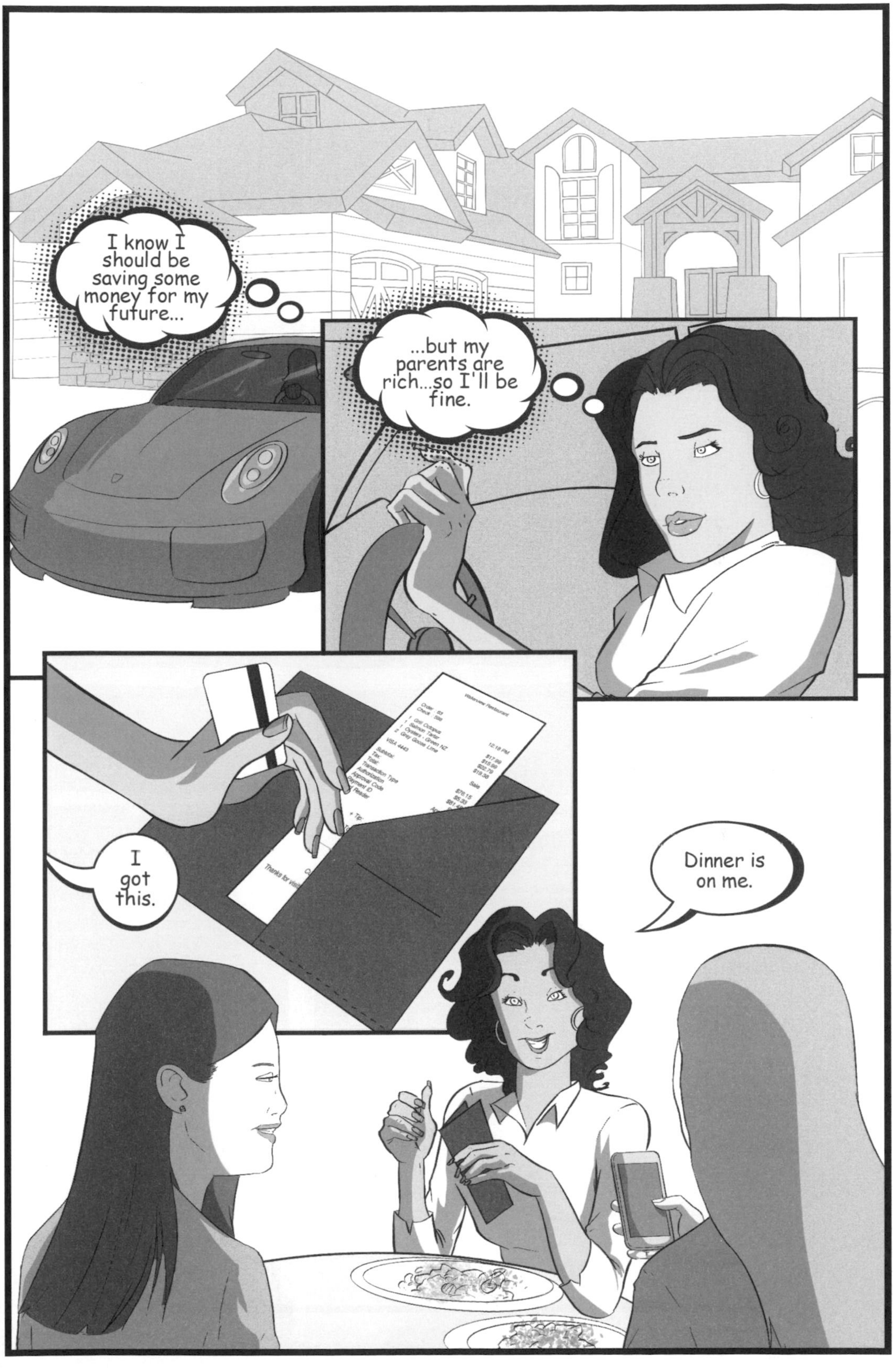
I know I should be saving some money for my future...
...but my parents are rich...so I'll be fine.
I got this.
Dinner is on me.

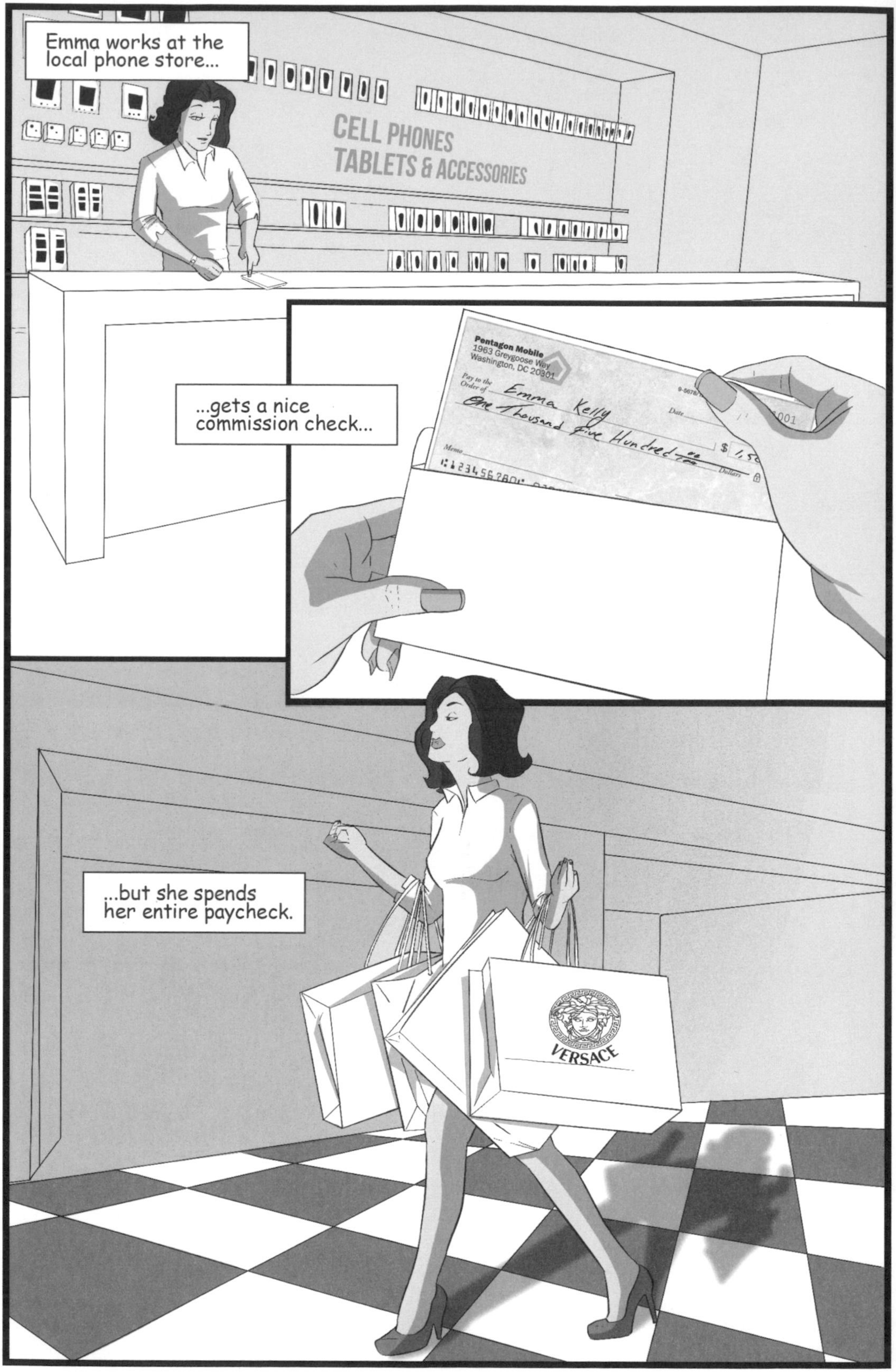
Emma works at the local phone store...
CELL PHONES
TABLETS & ACCESSORIES
...gets a nice commission check...
Pentagon Mobile
1963 Greygoose Way
Washington, DC 20301
Pay to the Order of
Emma Kelly
One Thousand Five Hundred
Date
Memo
Dollars
...but she spends her entire paycheck.
VERSACE

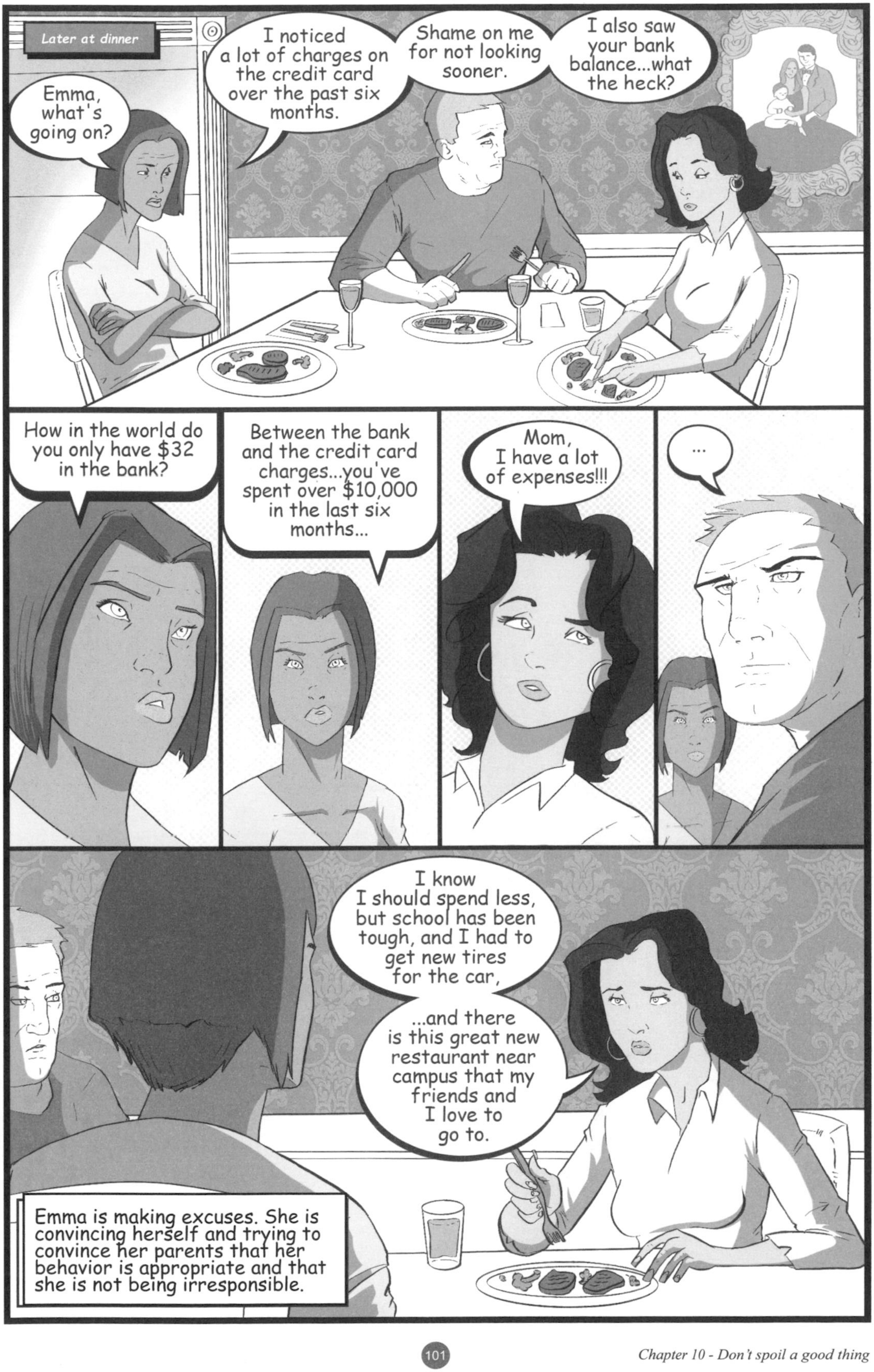

Later at dinner
Emma, what's going on?
I noticed a lot of charges on the credit card over the past six months.
Shame on me for not looking sooner.
I also saw your bank balance...what the heck?
How in the world do you only have $32 in the bank?
Between the bank and the credit card charges...you've spent over $10,000 in the last six months...
Mom, I have a lot of expenses!!!
...
I know I should spend less, but school has been tough, and I had to get new tires for the car,
...and there is this great new restaurant near campus that my friends and I love to go to.
Emma is making excuses. She is convincing herself and trying to convince her parents that her behavior is appropriate and that she is not being irresponsible.

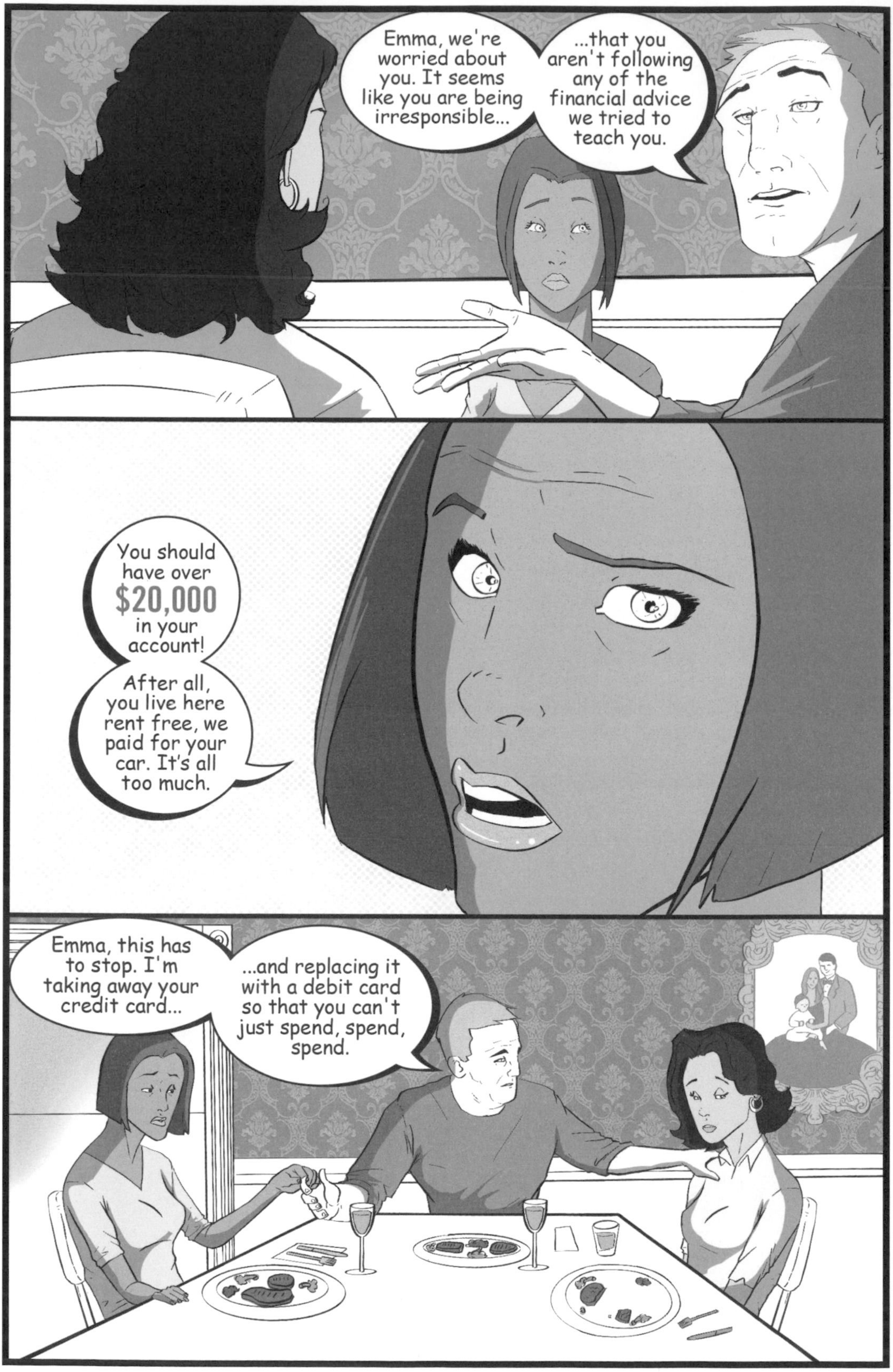
Emma, we're worried about you. It seems like you are being irresponsible...
...that you aren't following any of the financial advice we tried to teach you.
You should have over $20,000 in your account!
After all, you live here rent free, we paid for your car. It's all too much.
Emma, this has to stop. I'm taking away your credit card...
...and replacing it with a debit card so that you can't just spend, spend, spend.

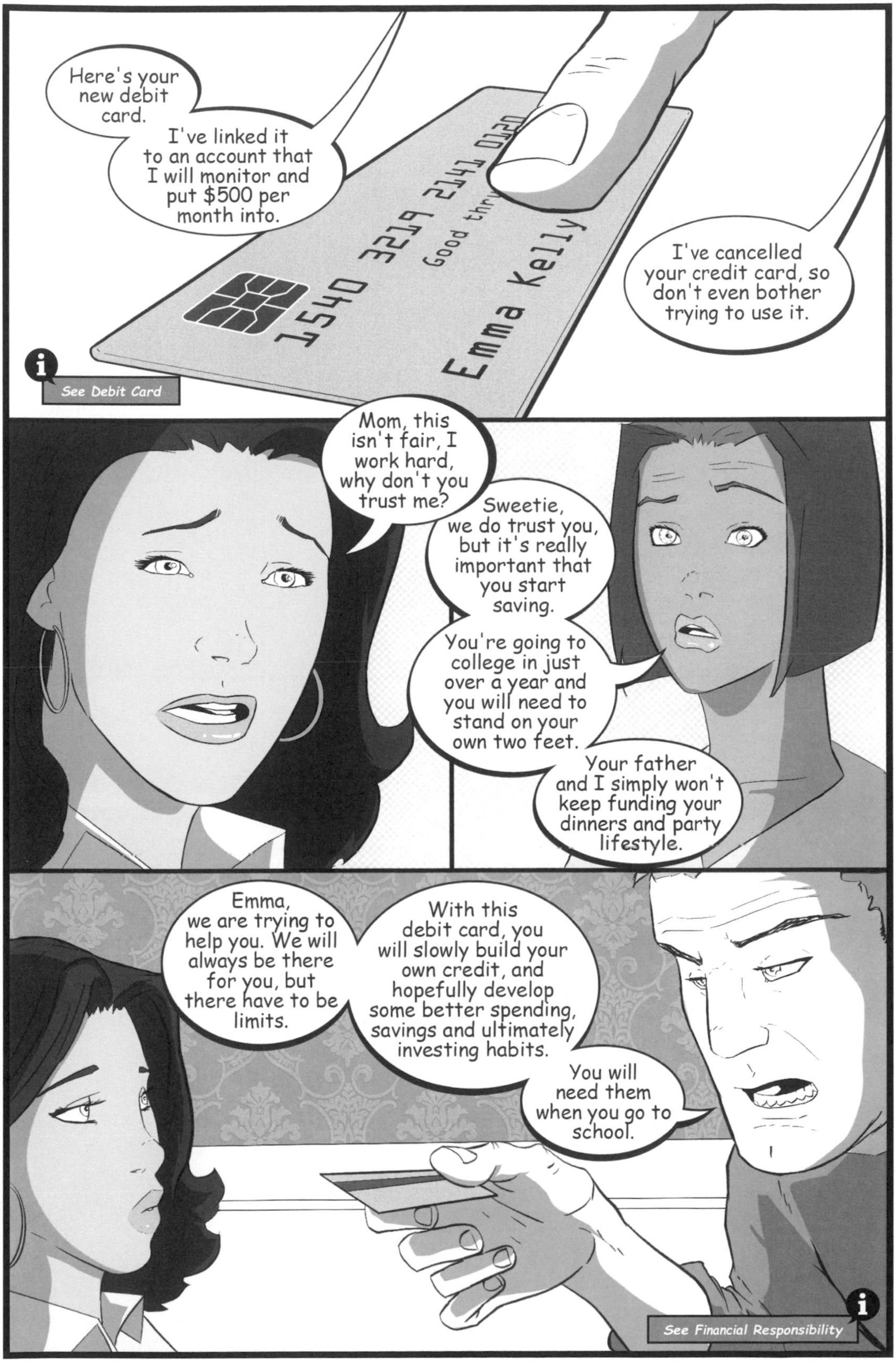
Here's your new debit card.
I've linked it to an account that I will monitor and put $500 per month into.
1540 3219 2141 0120
Good thru
Emma Kelly
I've cancelled your credit card, so don't even bother trying to use it.
See Debit Card
Mom, this isn't fair, I work hard, why don't you trust me?
Sweetie, we do trust you, but it's really important that you start saving.
You're going to college in just over a year and you will need to stand on your own two feet.
Your father and I simply won't keep funding your dinners and party lifestyle.
Emma, we are trying to help you. We will always be there for you, but there have to be limits.
With this debit card, you will slowly build your own credit, and hopefully develop some better spending, savings and ultimately investing habits.
You will need them when you go to school.
See Financial Responsibility

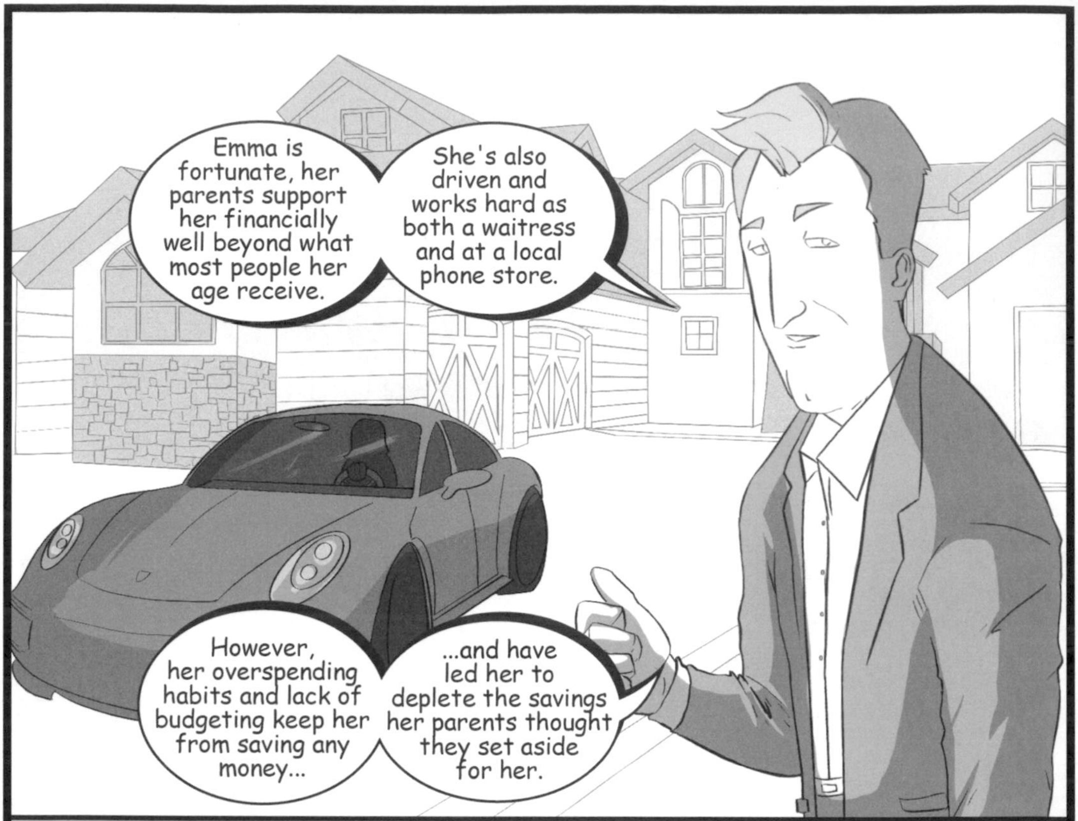
Emma is fortunate, her parents support her financially well beyond what most people her age receive.
She's also driven and works hard as both a waitress and at a local phone store.
However, her overspending habits and lack of budgeting keep her from saving any money...
...and have led her to deplete the savings her parents thought they set aside for her.

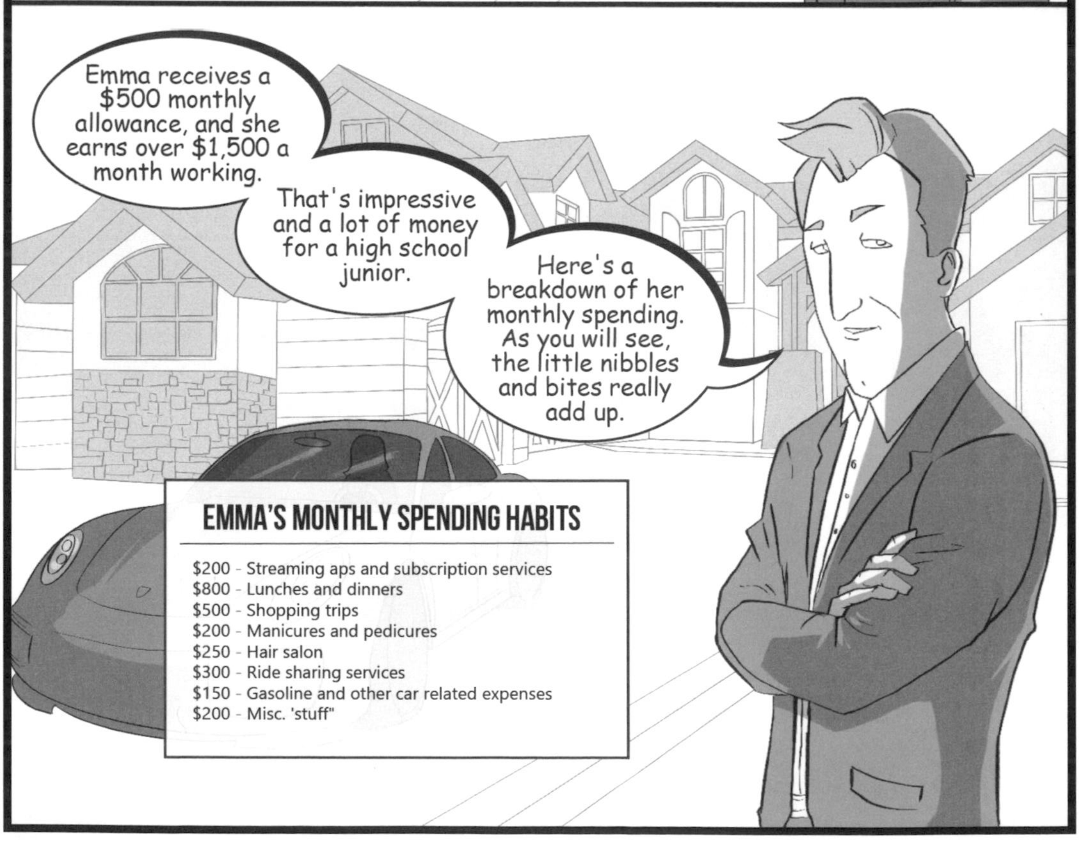
Emma receives a $500 monthly allowance, and she earns over $1,500 a month working.
That's impressive and a lot of money for a high school junior.
Here's a breakdown of her monthly spending. As you will see, the little nibbles and bites really add up.
EMMA'S MONTHLY SPENDING HABITS
$200 - Streaming aps and subscription services
$800 - Lunches and dinners
$500 - Shopping trips
$200 - Manicures and pedicures
$250 - Hair salon
$300 - Ride sharing services
$150 - Gasoline and other car related expenses
$200 - Misc. 'stuff"

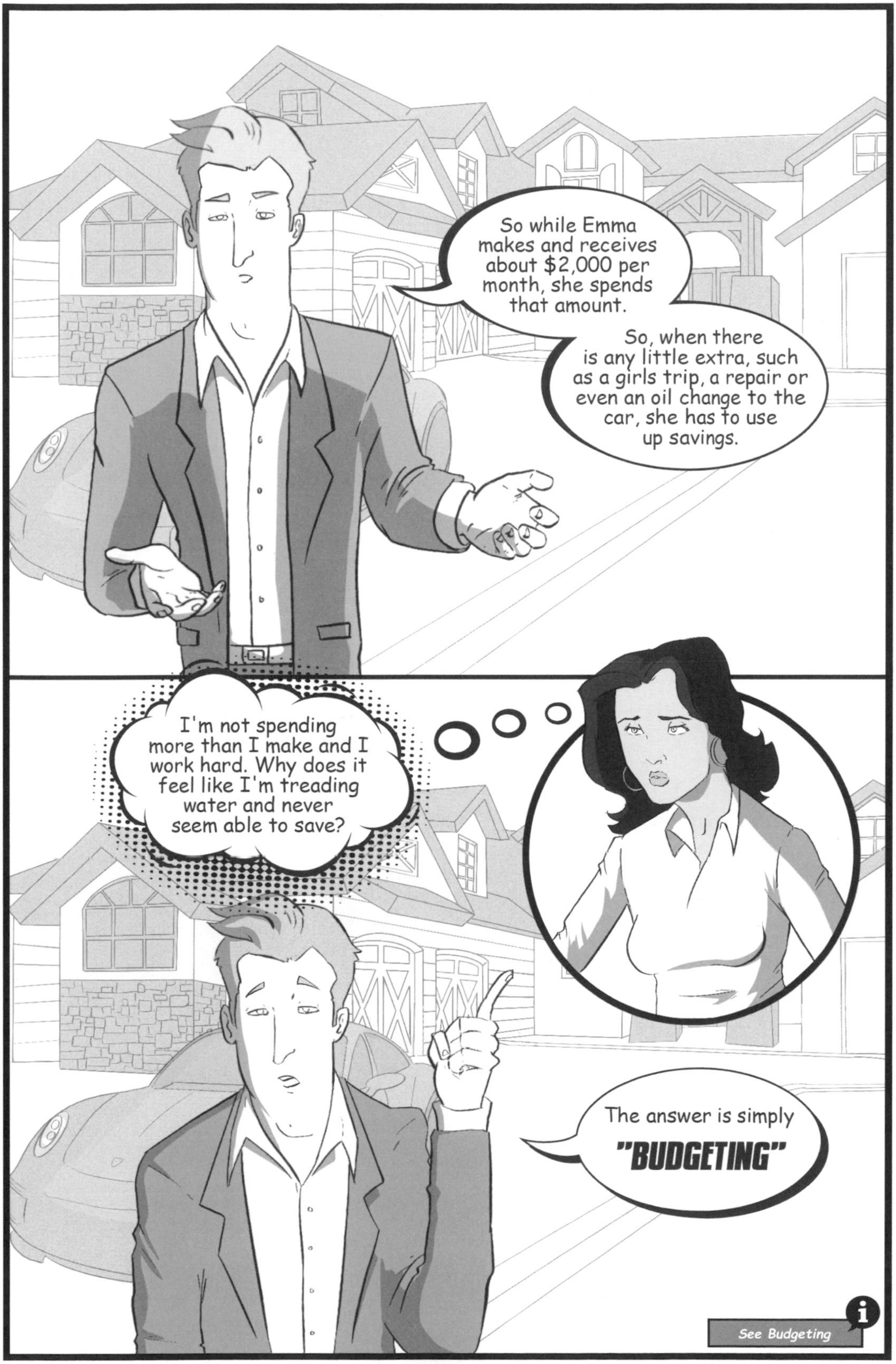
So while Emma makes and receives about $2,000 per month, she spends that amount.
So, when there is any little extra, such as a girls trip, a repair or even an oil change to the car, she has to use up savings.
I'm not spending more than I make and I work hard. Why does it feel like I'm treading water and never seem able to save?
The answer is simply "BUDGETING"
See Budgeting

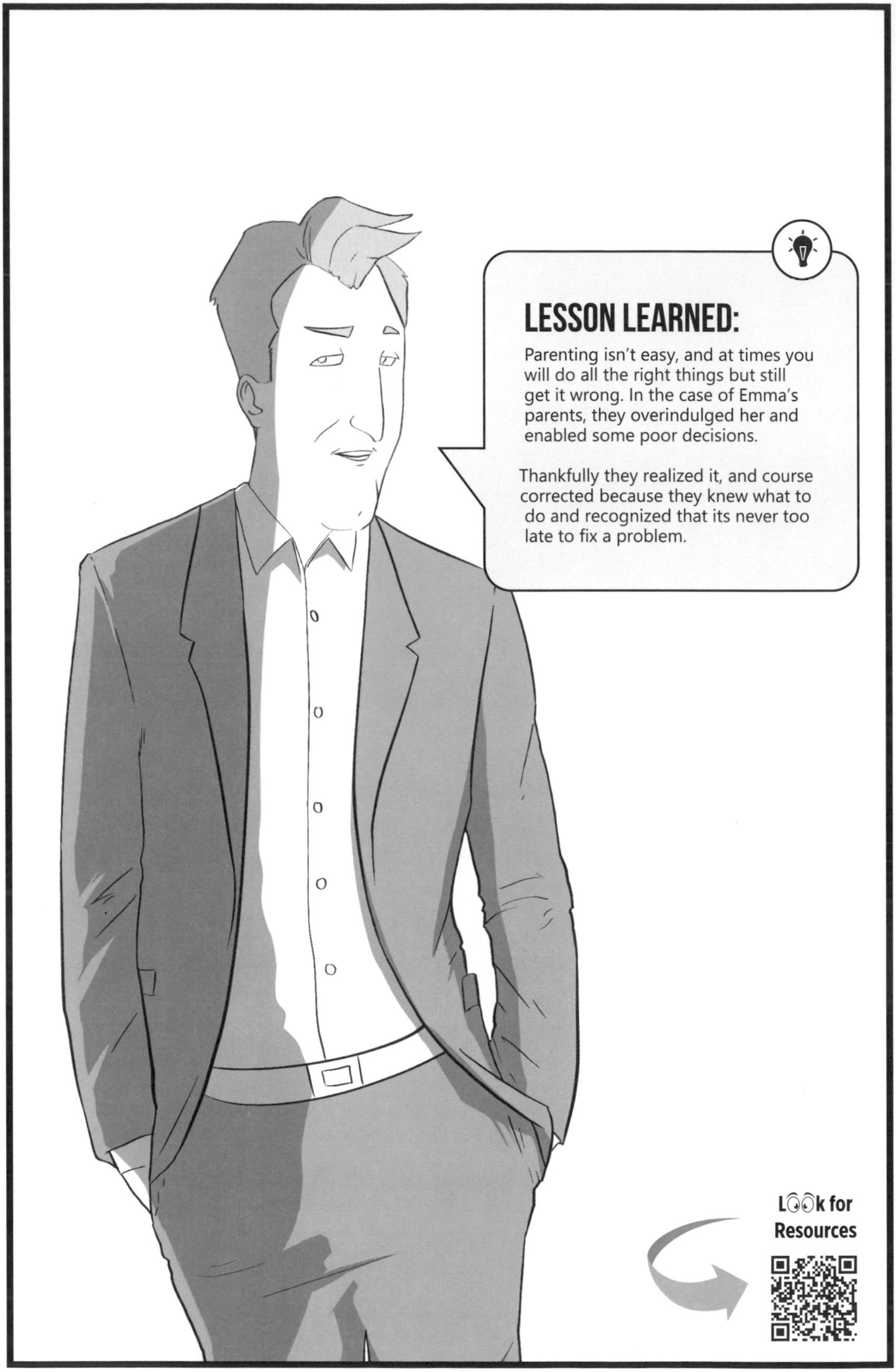
LESSON LEARNED:
Parenting isn't easy, and at times you will do all the right things but still get it wrong. In the case of Emma's parents, they overindulged her and enabled some poor decisions.
Thankfully they realized it, and course corrected because they knew what to do and recognized that its never too late to fix a problem.
L👀k for Resources

WHERE ARE THEY NOW?

JOHN

John became a true entrepreneur, owning several franchises as well as a business consulting firm. On the side, he teaches a financial literacy course at the local community college and as part of the adult continuing education curriculum in his town. He's happily married, successful and is looking forward to having children some day.

WHERE ARE THEY NOW?

ADAM

Adam is now married with two children. He got serious in his 30's and became financially responsible. Now, Adam has a great job working as the head of sales for a media company. He figured out how to have his joyous attitude and friendly personality be an asset in his life. Most importantly, he realized that he doesn't need to impress anyone and is very happy.

WHERE ARE THEY NOW?

LOGAN

Logan never learned from his financial mistakes. His YouTube and Twitch streaming career slowed down and eventually faded, sadly he didn't have a back-up plan in place. 20 years later Logan finds himself working at a cell phone kiosk in the mall, barely scraping by, living in a basement apartment. He still enjoys playing video games.

Where Are They Now?

Mary

Mary had no idea how much was involved in running a business, as opposed to working in a business. She struggled for a while, but found her footing after a few years and help from her old boss. Daren continues to mentor Mary, and has helped her expand from detailing to selling classic cars and making custom modifications. She loves owning and running her business and wakes up every morning looking forward to going to work. It is truly her passion.

Where Are They Now?

RJ

Let himself go a little as he grew older. After a football injury, he struggled and grew a little depressed. It took some time and help from his family, especially from his sister Jessica, before he landed on his feet. Thankfully his natural charm and charisma, along with his drive and will to succeed helped him overcome his struggles. Today, RJ owns an independent custom shoe shop, where many celebrities get customized art and rare sneakers. He got started in the business by selling some of his collectible sneakers to raise the funds to buy the equipment and lease the storefront he needed.

Where Are They Now?

JESSICA

Now a single mother of 2, Jessica has returned to work at another Healthcare Consulting firm and is thriving. She has to work hard to balance her home life with 2 children and work, but is managing just fine. She's in line for a promotion that would require her to move across the country, so she's reworking her budget to estimate the cost of the move and how much of a raise she should ask for in order to make the move.

Where Are They Now?

Sam

Sam is a rockstar! She was disciplined in her investment process and created her own luck with a couple of "Home-run" investments. She was smart and engaged an accountant and financial advisor early in her investment career to make sure she doesn't make any mistakes. Today, Sam owns 4 rental properties, has invested in several businesses, and works for a financial firm, where she advises wealthy families on their investments. Because she was so diligent in her investing so early, she already has more than enough money set aside for a comfortable retirement.

Where Are They Now?

Eva

With the girls out of the house and no longer needing a 3 bedroom apartment, Eva has downsized to a 2 bedroom apartment that is closer to her job. Since she didn't have much savings until she downsized, she decided to take the difference of her current and previous rent and invest it. The decision has paid off, just a few years later, along with some generous bonuses and well earned promotions at the law firm, she has saved over $100,000 for her retirement and finally feels like she is on track and that everything will be okay.

Where Are They Now?

Emma

Emma struggled for a while, but finally figured out what makes her happy and became comfortable with who she is. The 'tough love' her parents showed her by financially cutting her off, worked. It took a while, but Emma is now happily married and working as a sales and marketing consultant for a multi-national communications company. Both her personal and professional life are satisfying and make her proud of who she has become.

Closing Remarks

Years later

Thank you for joining me on this journey towards financial literacy, its been fun for me to do this and think back to some of the mistakes and good times I had over the course of my life. I hope that after reading this novel you feel more equipped to handle the financial choices you are going to have to make. It won't be easy, and at times it will feel overwhelming, and you will make mistakes - everyone does!

The most important lesson I've learned in life is don't give up, don't get discouraged, and press on!

Virtually all financial mistakes can be fixed and overcome with effort and time.

Acknowledgments

Writing this book has been a wonderful journey and learning experience. I could not have done this without the help of many, whom I'd like to thank and acknowledge.

First and foremost, I'd like to thank the book's illustrator Brian Barbosa. Brian, you've worked hard on this project, and it would not have happened without you. You helped define and refine the characters and lessons herein. Your intellectual curiosity and thirst for knowledge is only matched by your artistic talent.

I'd like to equally thank my dear friend, colleague and mentor, Jackie Kapur. Jackie, you got this thing started and more importantly were, and continue to be, the driving force behind this project. Your attention to detail and honest approach to critiquing this novel has helped shape it to what it has become, I sincerely thank you for your friendship, leadership and perseverance.

Of course, equal credit must be given to John Shableski, our editor and most certainly our friend. John your patience and guidance during the last 15 months has been reassuring and has served as a guidepost to ensure we stay on track and produce a piece of art that I am very proud of. Thank you.

Last, but certainly not least, I would like to say thank you to my parents for the lessons they have taught me (even if I didn't always listen or apply them right away). Mom and Dad, you have always supported me in the best way you could and knew how to, thank you for that, it means more than you'll ever know. To my sister, Julie, and all those who influenced my life and thereby influenced this novel, I also thank you.

And lastly, to the people who are reflected as the characters in this novel. I hope you recognize yourselves and are pleased with the way I represented you. I tried my best to stay true to the experiences and circumstances you lived through, all the while presenting the unique and wonderful person each of you are. You are my friends, colleagues, and compatriots, I cherish each and every one of you.

Oliver

GLOSSARY OF TERMS:

Amortization
Amortization is an accounting technique used to periodically lower the book value of a loan or an intangible asset over a set period of time, most frequently associated with mortgages. Concerning a loan, amortization focuses on spreading out loan payments over time. When applied to an asset, amortization is similar to depreciation. *(Pg. 91)*

APR (Annual Percentage Rate)
Annual percentage rate (APR) refers to the yearly interest generated by a sum that's charged to borrowers or paid to investors. APR is expressed as a percentage that represents the actual yearly cost of funds the term of a loan or income earned on an investment. This includes any fees or additional costs associated with the transaction but does not take compounding into account. The APR provides consumers with a bottom-line number they can compare among lenders, credit cards, or investment products. *(Pg. 91)*

Assets
An asset is anything of value or a resource of value that can be converted into cash. It is what you own. Individuals, companies, and governments own assets. *(Pg. 41)*

Asset Allocation
The percentage of your total assets that are invested in stocks, bonds, cash & equivalents (Money Market), real estate, NFTs and Crypto. Your asset allocation is the biggest long-term driver of investment returns and the commensurate risk you are taking. When thinking of how to allocate assets, the three pronged approach is advisable. 1) Your overall asset allocation - this includes everything you own, including your home or apartment. 2) Your overall assets, excluding your primary home. 3) Your marketable securities, i.e. excluding real estate. *(Pg. 55, 60)*

Balance Sheet
A balance sheet is a summary of the financial balances of an individual or organization. The balance sheet gives you a financial summary of your assets, debts and liabilities at a specific point in time. *(Pg. 41, 42)*

Budgeting
A budget is a tool to help you monitor and track your income and spending with the goal of helping you achieve your financial objectives and goals. It helps you keep your finances under control and identify specific areas that require changes. *(Pg. 20, 22, 44, 105)*

GLOSSARY OF TERMS:

Compounding Interest
Compounding interest is the addition of interest to the principal sum of a loan, deposit or investment. In other words, interest on interest. It is the result of reinvesting interest, rather than paying it out, so that interest in the next period is then earned on the principal plus the previously accumulated interest. This is overwhelmingly bad when it comes to debt, and overwhelmingly good when it comes to savings and investments. *(Pg. 12, 17)*

Compounding Returns
Similar to compounding interest, but typically refers to investment returns, which are compounding over time. Earning money on 'earned' money. For instance, if you invest $1,000 and it grows to $1,100 after a year due to a 10% return, and the following year you have a similar 10% return, not only to you earn another $100 on the initial $1,000 investment, but also $10 (10% of $100) on the previously earned $100 from the first years return. *(Pg. 55, 57, 64)*

Credit Card
A credit card is a payment card issued to users (cardholders) to enable the cardholder to pay a merchant for goods or services based on the cardholder's accrued debt (i.e., promise to the card issuer to pay them for the amounts plus the other agreed charges). [1] The card issuer (usually a bank or credit union) creates a revolving account and grants a line of credit to the cardholder, from which the cardholder can borrow money for payment to a merchant or as a cash-advance. *(Pg. 12)*

Credit Score
A credit score is a number that rates your credit risk. It can help creditors determine whether to give you credit, decide the terms they offer, or the interest rate you pay. Having a high score can benefit you in many ways. It can make it easier for you to get a loan, rent an apartment, or lower your insurance rate. *(Pg. 28, 31)*

Deal Structure
The terms of an agreement between a buyer and a seller are considered deal structure. A deal structure is a term used to describe the terms of the agreement between a buyer and seller that apply in a given business deal. *(Pg. 74)*

Debt
Debt is an obligation that requires one party, the debtor, to pay money or other agreed-upon value to another party, the creditor. Debt is a deferred payment, or series of payments, which differentiates it from an immediate purchase. *(Pg. 91)*

Glossary of Terms:

Debit Card
A debit card is a payment card that can be used in place of cash to make purchases. It is like a credit card but unlike a credit card, the money for the purchase must be in the cardholder's bank account at the time of a purchase and is immediately transferred directly from that account to the merchant's account to pay for the purchase. Some debit cards carry a Stored Value with which a payment is made (prepaid card), but most relay a message to the cardholder's bank to withdraw funds from the cardholder's designated bank account. *(Pg. 98, 103)*

Deferred Interest
Deferred interest means you can borrow money, and the interest you owe is delayed (but not absolved) for a period of time. It's only when you pay off your balance by the end of the promotional period that you can forgo paying the interest that's been accruing from the original date of purchase. *(Pg. 68)*

Discretionary Spending
Discretionary spending refers to non-essential items, such as recreation and entertainment that consumers purchase when they have enough income left over after paying the necessary expenses such as the mortgage and utilities. Discretionary spending depends, in part, on disposable income, or how much a person has left after paying for basic and essential expenses. *(Pg. 41)*

Financial Literacy
Financial literacy is the ability to understand and effectively use various financial skills, including personal financial management, budgeting, and investing. Financial literacy is the foundation of your relationship with money, and it is a lifelong journey of learning. The earlier you start, the better off you will be because education is the key to success when it comes to money. *(Pg. 20)*

Financial Responsibility
Financial responsibility is the process of managing money (and other kinds of assets) in a way that is productive and works in the best interest of an individual, his/her family or an organization. To be financially responsible means to live within a person's or company's means. For parents, this also means not overindulging and thereby enabling your children's poor financial behavior. *(Pg. 98, 103)*

Income Statement
In the case of individuals, this refers to how much you earn, less withholdings such as taxes. In the case of a corporation, the Income Statement refers to financial statements that are formal record of financial activities. The purpose of an income statement is to provide a structured view of relevant financial information in an easy to understand manner. *(Pg. 41, 42)*

Glossary of Terms:

Inflation
Inflation refers to a general increase in prices of goods and services. When things get more expensive, the value of your savings declines because you have less purchasing power. In other words, you have to pay more for the same item. *(Pg. 55, 65)*

Investing
A compliment to savings, where you take part of your saving and invest them in the hope of making your money grow. It is important to note that savings and investing are complimentary to each other, investing does not replace saving. You should consider saving while investing. *(Pg. 28)*

Leasing
A lease is a contract outlining the terms under which one party agrees to rent an asset, for instance a car or an apartment. In a lease, the leased item remains the property of the lessor. A lease typically requires lower payments than a purchase of the same item, as it takes into account the depreciation of the asset. *(Pg. 68, 70)*

Lease Servicing Cost
This is more than simply the cost of the loan (interest and principal), it typically includes any fees and monies escrowed for taxes or insurance. The Loan Servicing Cost incorporates all costs and translates a loan amount into the monthly cash-flow needed to repay the loan over its term.   *(Pg. 68, 70)*

Liabilities
A liability is something a person or company owes, usually a sum of money. Liabilities are settled over time through the transfer of economic benefits including money, goods, or services. *(Pg. 41)*

Mortgage
A mortgage is an agreement between you and a lender that allows you to borrow money to purchase or refinance a home and gives the lender the right to take your property if you fail to repay the money you've borrowed. *(Pg. 91)*

Mortgage Refinancing
Refinancing your mortgage basically means that you are trading in your old mortgage for a new one, and possibly a new balance. When you refinance your mortgage, your bank or lender pays off your old mortgage with the new one; this is the reason for the term refinancing. *(Pg. 20, 23)*

Glossary of Terms:

Mutual Fund & ETF
Mutual funds and exchange-traded funds (ETFs) have a lot in common. Both types of funds consist of a mix of many different assets and represent a popular way for investors to diversify as a result of pooling money with many other investors. While mutual funds and ETFs are similar in many respects, they also have some key differences. A major difference between the two is that ETFs can be traded intra-day like stocks, while mutual funds only can be purchased at the end of each trading day based on a calculated price known as the net asset value. *(Pg. 48)*

Non-Discretionary Spending
This is the mandatory spend you don't have a lot of control over and that you need to be a member of society, such as everyday bills, utilities and health insurance, rent, etc. *(Pg. 41)*

Reloading
Often used to describe a process by which someone with a credit card obtains a new credit card and transfers the balance from the first card to the second card; but then 're-loads' more new debt on the first card effectively increasing the overall debt and negating the potential benefit of the balance transfer. *(Pg. 85, 89)*

Return on Investment (ROI)
Return on investment (ROI) is a metric used to understand the profitability of an investment. ROI compares how much you paid for an investment to how much you earned to evaluate its success. *(Pg. 48, 63)*

Risk
Risk is defined in financial terms as the chance that an outcome or investment's actual gains will differ from an expected outcome or return. Risk includes the possibility of losing some or all of an original investment. *(Pg. 48)*

Saving
Savings refers to the money a person puts aside for future use after having spent their income on discretionary and non-discretionary items. *(Pg. 28)*

Seller Note
A seller's note is a form of financing that is often used in the purchase of a small business. The seller agrees to accept a portion of the purchase price in a series of payments that are typically generated by the business that is being sold. A seller note is designed to bridge the gap between the total purchase price and the amount the buyer is able to pay upfront for the purchase. *(Pg. 74, 79)*

GLOSSARY OF TERMS:

Targeted Psychological Marketing
Psychological targeted marketing is the powerful practice of tailoring ads to audience personality traits and is commonly based on an individual's digital footprint. Psychological targeting can be used to exploit weakness in people's characters and persuade them to take action against their own best interest.
(Pg. 12, 15, 87)

Teaser Rates
An introductory interest rate charged to a customer during the initial stages of a loan. The rate, which can be as low as 0%, is not permanent and after it expired often a higher than normal interest rate will apply. The purpose of a teaser rate is to market a loan to consumers in an attractive manner. *(Pg. 85, 87)*

The Power of Time
This is pure magic because you don't have to do anything other than wait and be patient. The Power of Time makes compound interest and returns work best. The simple fact is that WHEN you start saving and investing outweighs how much you save and invest. An investment left untouched for a period of decades can add up to a large sum, even if you never invest another dime. *(Pg. 20, 24, 58)*

https://www.oliverpursche.com/money-can-grow-on-trees

About the Author & Illustrator

Oliver Pursche is a recognized thought-leader with nearly 30 years of Financial Advisory experience. As a Sr. Vice President, Advisor working out of New York City and Westport CT, Oliver works with affluent families and business owners overseeing and helping them grow their wealth.

His opinions, views and guidance on saving and investing are frequently requested by CNBC, Bloomberg Television and Radio, Kiplinger's and Forbes Magazines as well as many other national and world-wide news outlets such as Reuters and Dow Jones.

In his role as an advisor, Oliver has been named "amongst the best of the best" by Barron's Magazine six years in a row (2008 - 2014) as part of their "Top Independent Advisor" annual ranking.

As an Author and Educator, Oliver has been a keynote speaker at both industry and private events, and has been featured in hundreds of investment seminars including events sponsored by AAII (American Association of Independent Investors), Vanguard and Fidelity.

Brian Barbosa is a freelance illustrator and graphic designer based in New York.

From an early age, Brian had a love for comic books which would fuel his creativity. Having this appreciation for the art so young sparked his curiosity to learn other art mediums such as watercolor, pastels, oil and acrylics painting as well as other art periods & movements.

Very early in his career, Brian attended the Art Institute of Philadelphia where he studied computer animation, video editing, 3D modeling, illustration, character design and more.

Now, Brian is engulfed in marketing as a full time Director of Graphic Design, broadening and focusing his skills on advertising and branding.

During his spare time, he enjoys reading graphic novels and illustrating comic book fan art. He is currently developing his own graphic novel.